COMPLETE
Folding Kayaker

Ralph Díaz

Ragged Mountain Press
Camden, Maine

Published by Ragged Mountain Press®

10 9 8 7 6 5 4 3 2 1

Copyright ©1994 Ragged Mountain Press, an imprint of TAB
Books. TAB Books is a division of McGraw-Hill, Inc.

Library of Congress Cataloging-in-Publication Data
Díaz, Ralph.
    Complete folding kayaker / Ralph Díaz.
        p.   cm.
    Includes bibliographical references and index.
    ISBN 0-07-016734-6 (alk. paper)
    I. Sea kayaking. 2. Kayaks. I. Title.
GV788.D53   1994
797.1'224—ds20
                                        94-5755
                                        CIP

Questions regarding the content of this book should be
addressed to:
    Ragged Mountain Press
    P.O. Box 220
    Camden, ME 04843

Questions regarding the ordering of this book should be
addressed to:
    TAB Books
    A Division of McGraw-Hill, Inc.
    Blue Ridge Summit, PA 17294
    1-800-233-1128

Complete Folding Kayaker is printed on recycled paper contain-
ing a minimum of 50% total recycled paper with 10% postcon-
sumer de-inked fiber. ♻

Printed by Arcata Graphics, Fairfield, PA
Design by Patrice M. Rossi
Production and page layout by Janet Robbins
Edited by James R. Babb, Patricia Miller, Tom McCarthy
Unless otherwise noted, all photographs by the author.

para mis padres,
Aurelio Díaz y
Teresa O'Halloran de Díaz,
e hijo Jason

Contents

Acknowledgments   *vii*

Foreword, by Paul Theroux   *ix*

Preface   *xi*

Introduction   *xiii*

**PART ONE
What You
Should Know**

1   Why a Foldable Kayak?   *1*

2   At the Heart of Sea-Kayaking History   *14*

3   Choosing the Folding Kayak That's Right for You   *23*

4   Evaluating the Leading Doubles and Singles   *32*

5   Equipment and Accessories that Work Well in Foldables   *49*

**PART TWO
Handling
Skills for
Foldables**

6   Paddling Techniques: The Forward Stroke and Other Essentials   *63*

7   Operating Skills: From Launch Site to Open Water and Back   *78*

8   Paddling and Operating a Double   *86*

9   Sea Savvy—A Guide to Commonsense Sea Kayaking   *93*

10   Developing Confidence, Learning Rescue Skills   *98*

**PART THREE
Using and
Enjoying**

11   Traveling with a Foldable   *108*

12   Sailing   *116*

13   Camping   *125*

14   More Fun with Foldables   *133*

15   Modifying Your Foldable   *138*

16   Repair and Maintenance   *148*

Appendix   *155*

Index   *160*

Acknowledgments

This book is the result of an ongoing voyage of discovery. The journey began a half dozen years ago when Dieter and Eric Stiller initiated me in the ways of this special breed of vessel at the old Klepper shop on Union Square in the heart of New York City. I've never tired of listening to their tales of the epic deeds of folding-kayak adventurers. Nor will I ever be able to repay their generous hand-holding as I broadened my understanding of folding kayaks.

Others have helped along the way. Doug Simpson and the crew at Feathercraft in Vancouver let me poke around the factory on Granville Island and suffered my many questions with good cheer. Over the years, Doug has shared his insights on how folding kayaks interact with their watery element and made me aware of just how much folding kayaking is a lifestyle, not merely a sport.

I'm thankful to other makers of folding kayaks who also see it as more than a business. To Carl Walther, owner of Klepper, and his father, Herman Walther, who willingly shared with me their pride in the long tradition behind these versatile skin-and-frame crafts as well as their visions for the future. Peter Schwierzke, the West Coast distributor for Klepper and the U.S. importer for Pouch, also has been generous with his time and energies.

I also feel indebted to Phil Cotton of Folbot in Charleston, South Carolina, and to Philippe Guyot of Nautiraid in Vaiges, France, for their help over the last few years. Others who have been most supportive include Bill and Janice Lozano of Atlantic Kayak Tours and Mark Balogh and Ms. Sam Carveth of Balogh Sail Designs.

Most of all, I give a special thanks to the readers of *Folding Kayaker*, the newsletter I started in 1991. Their unflagging support has encouraged me to pursue the potential of folding kayaks in the pages of that publication. They have fed me dozens of ideas for modifications and ways to use these vessels. And their many questions—in letters, on the phone, in person, and in cyberspace—are what I'm attempting to answer with the writing of this book.

Finally, I thank Donna Deeprose, my wife. She read first drafts of the book and prodded me toward better writing and clarity of thought. Readers will no doubt appreciate her persistence as much as do I.

Foreword by *Paul Theroux*

Just the other workday morning I looked out the window and saw a clear sunny day, with only a slight wind, pleasant sea conditions; and without hesitating I turned my back on my work and put my kayak on the roof rack. At Ala Wai Harbor—this was in Honolulu—another kayaker was setting up his boat. He said to me, "I look out the window this morning, see the sun, see the ocean, and I say to myself, *ono* [perfect], no work for me, I'm paddling today." So I felt vindicated, even happier, knowing that someone else was of exactly the same mind.

All over the world there are people who know the pleasures of paddling, who would rather be kayaking than doing practically anything else. And a kayaker does not need perfect weather—doesn't even need good weather. I bought my first boat ten years ago because I was sick of drydocking my boats in the winter and exercising from October until May indoors on a rowing machine. A kayak is the answer. Of course, a headwind more than 15 or 20 knots can be tiresome, and heavy surf can be dangerous; but those are the only limits. A kayak, the most adaptable (and I think among the safest) craft, can be paddled in almost any weather. Kayaks evolved in regions noted for heavy weather; they were designed for extreme conditions. Severe cold is not much of a problem.

My first kayak was a hardshell, and I remember how that first winter, paddling home through a marsh in the late afternoon, I turned back to look at the setting sun and saw that the water I had splashed had frozen in great pale casts to the stern deck. But I was warm enough (overheating is a greater danger than frostbite in winter paddling) and I was convinced that I had found the right recreation. Paddling to me is the healthiest, most liberating, and adaptable outdoor activity on earth.

It took me a while to find the right boat. But of course there is no all-purpose kayak; each style has its specific use. I have owned five different kayaks. I own three at the moment, and two of them are foldables—a Klepper Expedition single and a Feathercraft K-1. Hardshells bristle with adaptations, but the foldable is pretty close in basic shape to the old hull shape that was paddled in the Northern Hemisphere 10,000 years ago. An Inuit paddler might be bemused by my Kevlar Nordkapp (a light, fast, low-volume boat) but would easily recognize any one of my foldables.

As a restless soul, not a practitioner of horizontal or sedentary vacations, I realized that one of the annoyances of traveling in remote places was the absence of reliable transportation. Many times, on the Scottish coast, in the Mediterranean, in Southeast Asia, or in the Pacific, I found myself standing on a beach and looking at an offshore island I wished to visit. There used to be a boat that took people out, I would be told. Nowadays no one goes there. But I wanted to go there. And maybe I wanted to stay there; carry enough food and equipment to last me a week or more. Perhaps I did not want to be pinned down by a hired boatman who would have said, "Mister, what time do you want to go back?" I might never want to go back.

I began to travel with a folding kayak (I always think of them as collapsibles) and my life changed. I learned what all kayakers eventually find out: You head for the offshore island, and when you get there you see another, more distant island—invisible from the mainland shore; and so you are led onward, self-contained and self-reliant, island-hopping and utterly uplifted. That is the greatest experience in travel, the discovery of something new and unexpected. It can happen anywhere. Paddling off Cape Cod in the winter I often see seals. Many people on Cape Cod are fair-weather beachgoers, unaware that these seals exist. Paddling in Hawaii in the winter, it is not unusual to see whales. But only the paddler is able to leap into the water and hear the whales singing; everyone else is subjected to the chugging of an outboard motor.

It is almost impossible to exaggerate the usefulness of a folding kayak. Even the hackneyed phrase "flying carpet" is appropriate to this ingeniously conceived craft. When I traveled around China by train in aid of getting material for a book, I kept wishing I had my boat with me, to go from city to city the most revealing way, by river. It was not accidental that my next travel book was the series of paddling journeys I recounted in *The Happy Isles of Oceania*, and the book would have been impossible without a folding kayak. Many Pacific islanders are still people of the sea. They watched me setting up my kayak on the beach; they always recognized the uniqueness of the craft and never failed to ask where they could get one.

There is an immense amount to be known about this deceptively simple boat. I suspect the reason for the folding kayak's complexity is inherent in the boat's design. All other sailing craft have conventional similarities—a little plastic motorboat has many features in common with the *QE II*, but these have nothing in common with a folding kayak. Consider the shape and construction of the folding kayak, or any skin boat, and you have to reach the conclusion that its nearest equivalent is an animal's body, not a fish but a mammal, a vertebrate. It has an interior skeleton, ribs, joints, a spine; it has a head and a tail, it has a hide, it flexes. To this animal shape the paddler brings a brain, and energy, and guts.

Ralph Díaz is a solitary but resourceful evangelist. I was impressed when he started the first folding kayak newsletter. I am delighted that he has written the first complete guide to these boats. It is valuable, plain-spoken, and best of all, exhaustive. I am happy to help launch this book.

God bless it and all who paddle the seas.

Preface

This book explores the many wonders of this special breed of seagoing vessel. It is based in part on my work as publisher of *Folding Kayaker*, a bimonthly newsletter about using and enjoying foldable kayaks. Over the last few years of producing the newsletter, I've been in contact with nearly 1,000 folding-kayak users who have shared with me what they've learned about their boats. I've lived closely enough with all of the major models to know how best to use them and to overcome any shortcomings an individual model may have. I've learned from the manufacturers all the intricacies of how their various models are constructed and how they should be taken care of. And I've visited with voyagers who embarked on epic journeys with foldable boats. They shared how their boats performed under extreme stress, what they might have wished changed, and the techniques that worked for their survival. The book is organized in three parts:

Part One, What You Should Know, gives you an appreciation of the use of a folding kayak and helps you narrow your buying choices. It explains: the advantages folding kayaks offer over rigid boats and their link to the skin-and-frame kayaks used by Northern peoples for thousands of years; the fascinating history of folding kayaks from the beginning of the century, when they launched a revolution in recreational small boating; what to look for when choosing the right one for you; the leading single and double folding kayaks in concise review; and tips about buying basic equipment and accessories that make for pleasurable paddling.

Part Two, Handling Skills for Foldables, offers practical advice on paddling and operating this unique breed of vessel. This part covers: paddling and maneuvering techniques that work well in a foldable; landing and launching from docks, through surf, and under other conditions; confidence drills to get comfortable with the boats, and rescue exercises to practice just in case; and commonsense tips toward becoming a competent sea kayaker.

Part Three, Using and Enjoying, opens the door to this exciting world through its valuable, how-to advice: packing a folding kayak for airline travel and other public conveyances to avoid in-transit damage; speeding the assembly time once you arrive; using a folding kayak for sailing, fishing, and camping; customizing your folding kayak with modifications and add-on products; and repairing and maintaining the various types of folding kayaks.

As you read this book about folding kayaks, bear in mind that they have a long, rich tradition of seafaring. For nearly a century, hundreds of thousands of folding kayaks have been leaving their wakes on every waterway from the Arctic to Antarctica. They have crossed oceans and other major bodies of water, in frozen climes and in balmy tropics. Family groups and rugged individualists have paddled these forgiving vessels under all kinds of conditions on the way to exploration and personal discovery.

The concept of the folding kayak is not just mystique, it has its practical payoff as well: If the day ever dawns when you and your foldable get into conditions that are over your head, you can remind yourself that boats just like yours have delivered many other adventurers out of harm's way.

Introduction

A touring kayak is the ideal boat to put you close to the water and the many wonders along shore. The participation sport of kayak touring, more commonly known as sea or coastal kayaking, is rapidly growing in popularity, gaining converts every day. And well it should. Unlike whitewater kayaking with which it sometimes is confused, sea kayaking offers its pleasures in profound adventure rather than quick thrill. You can enjoy this pursuit for a few hours on a lake, slow-moving river, or nearby bay. Or you can stretch the experience into days and weeks along some interesting coastline far from home. Such kayaking is the true antidote to civilization.

Young people don't have the corner on this market. You can be any age to start kayaking. Many people first put hand to paddle when they are over 50. And for those who obey its summons, sea kayaking quickly becomes a lifelong calling.

Sea kayaking is gender blind; nearly half the newcomers to sea kayaking are women. There's nothing macho about sea kayaking; it relies more on brains than brawn. It places a premium on judgment and stamina rather than muscles and reflexes. Under certain conditions sea kayaking can be hair-raising, but generally it doesn't attract daredevils and thrill-seekers. You don't have to be on a razor's edge to enjoy it. Sea kayaking's rewards are contemplative, to be drawn out and savored throughout the hours or days of exploration and discovery.

With the growing interest in sea kayaking, a number of new books introduce the curious to the sport and help polish the skills of those already bitten by the bug. Among these sea kayaking manuals are several fine pieces of work; these are informative, enjoyable to read, and often inspiring. But they all have a serious flaw—their world largely ignores folding kayaks.

These manuals focus on the hardshell kayaks, which are made of fiberglass layups or molded plastic, or on developing the skills to use such rigid boats. If ever they do mention folding kayaks, they compress them into a paragraph or two, dismissing them as curiosity items. They advise that the only reason not to get a rigid boat is that you require the foldaway features of a folding sea kayak for storage or travel.

It is a myopic piece of advice—and dead wrong. Yes, folding kayaks have the unique advantage of disassembly into bags that can be stashed in the corner of a closet, and that can emerge like so many genies when called upon to do your bidding. And, in their bags, folding kayaks can be checked through airline ticket counters as ordinary luggage on a business trip or a flight to some exotic destination, where they'll spring to life in just 15 minutes to open new horizons for you.

But foldability is just frosting on the cake, only part of their broader advantages and appeal.

Contrary to the advice given in other sea kayak manuals, you should consider having a folding kayak primarily for its superior seaworthiness and reliability. Folding kayaks are inherently more seaworthy than their rigid counterparts. A folding sea kayak's underlying design features—flexible skin and frame construction, air tubes along each side—help keep you upright when conditions turn tricky. Under such circumstances in a rigid kayak, you would be calling on all your practiced skills to avoid going over. Folding kayaks flex with the action of the sea rather than fight it, as do rigid kayaks. Folding kayaks have more road feel; they hug the road, so to speak. They have proved time and time again that they are the quintessential open-water boat.

Stability and safety are their strong suits. You can rest inside your folding sea kayak, even take a needed snooze without fear of going belly up. A rigid kayak requires you to be alert to combat its fundamental instability. Folding kayaks are extremely difficult to capsize, and, if you ever do tip over, you can reenter easily, without the self-rescue aids needed to get back into a rigid kayak.

For basic versatility, folding kayaks have it all over their rigid brethren. To begin with, you can leave them assembled for long periods if you wish. Treat them as you would a hardshell kayak, i.e., store them already assembled in your backyard or on your car's rooftop, ready to head to a favorite paddling spot. Just because they can fold down doesn't mean you have to assemble and disassemble them for each outing.

You can easily sail a foldable kayak with a full upwind sail rig without the need for outriggers, which would be the only way you could sail a tippy hardshell. You can fish from a folding kayak with more stability for reeling in that big one than you would ever have in a rigid sea kayak. A folding kayak is voluminous, offering almost as much room for camping gear as you'd find in a comparable-sized canoe. If faced with a portage on a river or between lakes, you have the option of knocking it down into smaller components to ease the carrying weight.

While folding kayaks are soft-sided, i.e., they have decks and hulls made of fabric and coated materials, it would be wrong to think of them as delicate creatures. They tend to be long-lived. Skins can give 30 years of service before needing replacement, and frames last many decades more.

Folding kayaks can take plenty of punishment, a fact attested to by the military special operations forces of several dozen nations. Such forces have deployed them for over half a century for training, reconnaissance, interdiction, and softening up enemy shoreline defenses. Because of their strength and stealth, folding kayaks are at this very moment patrolling northern fjords and southern river deltas. These traits, imperative for military forces, make folding kayaks ideal vessels for close-up wildlife photography and observation in remote areas.

- *Why Own a Folding Kayak?*
- *What a Foldable Offers That a Rigid Kayak Can't*
- *How to Buy the One That's Right for You*

PART ONE

What You Should Know

Folding kayaks have more going for them than their ability to travel with you on a plane or store away in small spaces. They're superb vessels to trust with your life. Foldables forgive those mistakes that most paddlers make at some point on the water. Stability and seaworthiness are inherent in their materials and underlying design features, which closely resemble the skin and frame construction of the kayaks used by Nordic peoples for thousands of years. Foldables have built on that heritage to establish a tradition of their own in rugged use by noted explorers, the military, and everyday individual and family adventurers.

Picking the folding kayak that's right for you requires some thinking about how you want to use one. This section will help you decide what features are important to you. It also presents you with concise evaluations of the leading models by looking at the key factors that are likely to matter the most to you. You also get some pointers about gear and accessories that will enhance the performance of your folding kayak and ensure your safety and comfort.

1

Why a Foldable Kayak?

The sea-kayaking world is divided into two schools of thought: either the *hardshell* kayaks made of fiberglass or plastic, or the *folding* kayaks. If your choice were based solely on the number of models available in each type, the figures are skewed toward rigid boats. One paddling magazine's recent annual buyer's guide showed nearly 200 models of rigid sea kayaks being sold by some 50 producers. By comparison, folding sea kayaks are made by fewer than a half dozen major manufacturers, and they offer fewer than 20 models of double and single foldables.

Comparing the cornucopia of rigid boats with the relatively small bouquet of foldables, why in heaven's name should you consider a type of boat that has limited choices? The many solid reasons for picking a foldable sea kayak are covered in this chapter.

Going with the folding kayak crowd puts you in some pretty good company. These boats have been the choice of thousands of discerning individuals and families who have taken stock of their lifestyles and decided that folding kayaks provide the best all-around fit. Folding kayaks are the choice of the rich and famous, too. You might be surprised to learn how many rock stars, jet setters, politicians, authors, and professional people in the public eye have a folding kayak or two in their possession and use them to alleviate the stress of their celebrated lives. Among their ranks are the Kennedys, David Lee Roth, Calvin Klein, and Regis Philbin to name a few. One author, Paul Theroux, has written some of his work from the

Getting close to wildlife.
(Michael Skott)

2

seat of a foldable. He paddled a single folding kayak to gain his insights and observations for his *The Happy Isles of Oceania.* Theroux also has written several magazine articles on his reflections while solo paddling a single foldable in the Cape Cod area.

If you look extra closely at articles in paddling magazines, you'll note that many of the long-range adventures described by contributors have been accomplished in folding kayaks. The magazines don't always identify this, except perhaps with a quick passing reference, but the photos don't lie. They show mainly foldables with mountains of the gear that manages to get stored under their decks.

Just because there are more rigid models available than foldable ones doesn't mean that rigid kayaks are used more often than are foldables. Plenty of rigid boats are being advertised, displayed, and sold, but this is a fairly recent phenomenon. Rigid sea kayaks didn't begin to surface in any numbers until the late 1970s and early 1980s. Before then, foldables dominated the market, and tens of thousands were sold each year. Because folding kayaks tend to last and last, many of the pre–1975 boats are still being paddled. You may not see them, because folding kayakers don't tend to run in regular sea-kayaking circles; they do their thing in splendid solitude, surfacing every decade or so to pick up a replacement part or repair item, then they paddle on again in their very much alive boats. No reliable statistics exist, but it would be fair to say that because of the phenomenally long lives of folding kayaks, there are as many of them in active use as there are rigid boats.

What a Foldable Gives You That a Rigid Won't

If you ask around about sea kayaks or read some of the introductory manuals, you're likely to run up against some strange ideas about foldables. The boats are supposed to lack performance and are considered vulnerable, constantly in need of maintenance. Some kayak dealers and several so-called experts even deny that foldables are sea kayaks at all. Before you rush to judgment and heed what these individuals have to say, please consider the following six points that distinguish foldables from their rigid counterparts.

1. Truer Descendants of the Eskimo Kayak

Look up the word "kayak" in *Webster's Ninth Collegiate Dictionary* and you'll find the following definition:

kayak \'ki-,ak\ n [Esk qajaq] (1662) **1**: an Eskimo canoe made of a frame covered with skins except for a small opening in the center and propelled by a double-bladed paddle **2**: a portable boat styled like an Eskimo kayak

By that definition, folding kayaks are truer descendants of the Eskimo kayak than are rigid kayaks. Foldables can make that claim, because they adhere more closely to the design and materials principles of the kayaks developed by Northern peoples some 10,000 years ago. This association is far more meaningful than mere nostalgia; the underlying structures that Northern and folding kayaks have in common translate into some unique performance characteristics for both, characteristics that rigid kayaks cannot share.

If a Northern seal hunter of 2,000 years ago were suddenly to come to life and wander into the current sea-kayak scene, he would feel more kinship with the foldable kayaks he found than with the rigid ones. To the touch, the hulls of today's folding kayaks would be like those of the kayaks he hunted from. Their frame construction would be much more familiar to him than that of the rigid boats. The Northern hunter would be at home with how the folding kayak reacted

Paddling The Big Apple.

to the water around it. He wouldn't get that same sense of the water when he tried out the rigid kayaks, despite hardshell designers' attempts to mimic the narrow beam and tight cockpit of his seaworthy kayak.

How our Northern time-traveler would relate to the differences in boat shapes is anyone's guess. Upswept bows and sterns or flatter ends, narrow beams or broader ones, short or very long; they were all used by Northern people. There was a wide spectrum of hull shapes and sizes in those Northern kayaks, a spectrum as wide as the 5,000-mile arc of inhabited land and sea along the Arctic Circle, from Greenland to the Aleutians.

All Northern kayaks had three common features, three principles of construction that made them such splendid seafaring vessels. Two of these principles are readily apparent to the viewer, but the third is not. Folding kayaks enjoy the same excellent performance traits as the Northern kayaks because they inherited their three common design elements:

1. The hull is made of pliable, fabric-type material.

2. The structure uses internal frames, which consist of cross ribs and longitudinal long pieces.

3. The boat flexes, because its frame members and pliable skin have a combined "give" to them.

The materials now used in folding kayaks differ from those of the earlier Northern kayak, but they perform identically. The kayak's skin once was made of actual animal hides, and animal fat was used for waterproofing seams and coating the hull itself. Now we rely on materials such as rubber, Hypalon, or urethane or vinyl-coated nylon, and the decks are made of cotton canvas or a synthetic fabric, usually nylon or polyester. The Northern frames were bones and pieces of driftwood lashed together at crossing points with sinew and hide strips. The modern folding kayak has aluminum or wooden long pieces, and its crossribs are made of aluminum, polycarbonate, polyethylene, or wood.

Because folding kayaks are meant to disassemble, their joining points have fittings that have some flex to them. The amount of movement varies from one manufacturer to the next, but like the Northern kayaks, they allow twist and adjustment to the action of the surrounding water along the entire framework. In contrast, hardshell kayaks don't give with the action of the sea; they are rigid and inflexible.

The leaders of the revival movement of skin boats

How many people can fit on a Klepper double? (Walther/Klepper)

of original Northern designs recognize the link between foldables and the aesthetics they are trying to resurrect. George Dyson, author of *Baidarka*, readily accepts the lineage, although he would not applaud the shapes currently used for foldables. John Heath, noted scholar on Greenland kayaks and paddling techniques, feels strongly about the liveliness and flex of the skin-and-frame design. "Paddling a hardshell kayak is like dancing with a department-store mannequin, while paddling a folding kayak or skin boat is like having a real-life dancing partner."

2. Inherently More Seaworthy

John Heath's comment about foldables and skin boats points to a critical difference between them and rigid boats—the flex that underwrites the performance of folding kayaks and their Northern ancestors. The flexibility built into folding kayaks, along with several other features, makes foldables inherently seaworthy and more stable than rigid kayaks.

Folding kayaks flex in several ways. First, they flex along their length. As they ride through swells or over the wake of close-passing ferries or tugboats, folding kayaks partly hug or shape themselves to the curvature of the water. Obviously, shorter folding kayaks have less of this flexing movement, and longer ones have more.

Second, they flex or twist laterally, or sideways. In confused waters, a folding kayak will twist slightly to absorb the collision force of waves coming from different directions. When the passing tug's wake hits you at the same time you're dealing with heavy swell, or when the tug's wake bounces back off a seawall and strikes you from an additional angle, that's when you'll appreciate this second type of flex. In addition, the soft sides of a folding kayak dampen some of the impact of these water forces.

Because a folding kayak blends with the actions of the sea, it isn't tossed around as much as a rigid boat would be, and neither is its paddler. Flexibility enhances seaworthiness.

Other characteristics also contribute to the folding kayak's seaworthiness and stability. If you watch a cross-section of a folding kayak as it moves through the open water, you would notice an interesting phenomenon. Water pressure from beneath pushes the hull in slightly between the longitudinal frame pieces. This causes shallow channels or indentations between the long pieces running the length of the boat. These elongated pockets help the folding kayak resist sliding or rolling sideways due to the action of lateral waves and wakes. Some folding kayaks have more pronounced water-pressure pockets than do others, but they all have them and benefit from the phenomenon.

Width also adds to the stability of folding kayaks. As a genre, they tend to be a few inches wider than their rigid counterparts. For example, the average beam of a single rigid kayak runs about 22 inches. The narrow, so-called Greenland-styled single kayaks are about 20 inches in beam, and Northwest kayaks run about 24 inches. Foldable singles average around 27 inches in beam. An average foldable double measures about 34 inches in its beam, while a rigid counterpart would be around 29 inches.

Wider beam on foldables adds to stability not only because of these extra inches but also because of the one particular feature that creates the extra width—air tubes along the sides. Almost all folding

Nautiraid Raid 1 and its bags. *(Nautiraid)*

kayaks today have air tubes, called air sponsons, that run the length of each side. Air sponsons were introduced about 40 years ago to help speed and ease assembly. The frame halves go into a loose skin structure that is then tightened when the air tubes are inflated by mouth. But the air sponsons have the beneficial side effect of increasing stability. If a folding kayak is tipped onto its side while underway, the compressed air tubes resist being submerged, as would a balloon, and thus help keep the foldable upright.

The seaworthiness of folding kayaks has been proved countless times on the high seas. They have crossed the Atlantic and Caribbean and been paddled over long stretches of Australia's coastline and the Pacific coast of South America. They have even seen their paddlers through hurricanes during long crossings between islands and continents.

During our more common trips of less epic proportions, the folding kayak's inherent seaworthiness pays off in several ways. Let's consider what its good sea manners give you:

Faster learning curve.

When venturing out in any sea kayak, you need skills and an ability to read sea conditions. Make no bones about that. But folding sea kayaks allow you to

Hiking out! Single Klepper with S-4 rig. (Michael Skott)

progress faster in paddling; you can concentrate on developing an efficient forward paddling stroke without the need to be in a constant semi-brace to keep your boat upright if seas are acting up. Folding kayaks are not tender; you can lean them more aggressively while making turns, and you can remain calm even when hit by beam waves and wind.

To get good at paddling a rigid sea kayak, you need to have lots of time in the saddle. Some of the narrow ones require constant honing of technique to get the most out of them. Folding kayaks deliver the goods earlier and require less time to acquire the skills needed to paddle them safely under varying conditions.

Better water feel.

While some folding kayaks look clunky, they are sleek when it comes to unifying you with your surroundings. The flexible skins and frames provide a harmony with the sea that is both gratifying and inherently safer than having your boat fight the forces at play.

More forgiving of mistakes.

When you combine the boat's stability with its flexible behavior on the water, you have a kayak that doesn't require you to always be at your best or most skillful. If you goof in going out through a surf, for example, you have greater prospects of the boat seeing you through despite your mistakes.

3. As Tough and More Enduring

Contrary to what you might hear, folding kayaks are not delicate. Overall, their vulnerability is about par with that of fiberglass rigid kayaks, but they will hold up longer and, like a cat, have several extra lives. Let's take each component, one at a time.

The hull.

Basically, you treat a folding kayak hull as you would the hull on a fiberglass hardshell. Owners of fiberglass boats would never dream of dragging their vessels over barnacle-encrusted rocks or along sharp gravel beaches. Such folly would quickly destroy the thin gelcoat layer that protects their bottom, and would expose the fiberglass layer to damage. You exercise the same cautions with the hull of a foldable.

The hull on plastic hardshells can withstand being dragged over such surfaces better than can either foldables or fiberglass hardshells. Indeed, you see plastic boat owners treating their boats in that way, but they do pay a price; the scratches leave loose plastic hairs and grooves that reduce speed on the water and ultimately shorten the life of the plastic hull.

Having said this about the hull of folding kayaks, it is surprising how much the skins can take. Punctures are very rare even in urban areas where "beaches" are mainly made of broken glass and jagged metal parts. Howard Rice, who circumnavigated Cape Horn in 1989 in a folding kayak, found himself at one point hemmed in on an island by a huge surf through which he had barely managed to land. The surf continued to build, stranding him. After exploring the island, Rice found a beach on the other side with surf that was less imposing. The trouble was, this second beach was nearly a mile away, and he had to climb a high bluff to get off the first beach. He knocked down his folding kayak, carried everything up the bluff in several trips, *then using the skin of his foldable as a toboggan*, he dragged his gear to the other side in several trips. All this caused no damage to Rice's hull.

One folding-kayak dealer loves to drag his boats on the kayak try-out beach at sea-kayaking symposiums. He demonstrates like this even when an outgoing tide has exposed scallop beds and sharp rocks, when his hardshell competitors are being very dainty about their demo boats.

The frame.

The skin-over-frame construction of a folding kayak is quite strong and able to absorb plenty of punishment. It takes a lot to break a frame member. The conditions that would break some frame pieces, such as a huge dumping wave crashing a sea kayak onto a beach, are also likely to crack the hull of a rigid fiberglass kayak or create serious stress fractures that would compromise water integrity. Such force could also dent or crimp a plastic boat.

The frames have proved their toughness for the military. One standard operating procedure for military special forces calls for dropping fully-loaded folding kayaks from helicopters. The distance of the fall is often between 10 and 15 feet to keep the hovering helicopter above waves and swells. No damage is sustained by the boats despite the considerable stress created by the cargo and the distance dropped.

Folding kayaks have impressively long lives. Frames last and last. Wooden frames have been around

the longest, having first been used around 1907 by the Klepper company for its folding kayaks. Some frames sitting around the Klepper factory in Rosenheim, Germany are 80 years old and still capable of being used safely, if you were to put a new skin on them. Aluminum frames have been used for folding kayaks only for the last 15 years or so, but they show every sign of holding up well.

Hulls give long service as well. Hypalon, which is used for most folding kayak hulls, is good for about 30 years. Older natural rubber hulls lasted about 20 years. By comparison, plastic rigid boats get brittle with age, like Clorox bottles. Their hulls become suspect after around 8 to 10 years of service, and at that point they can't easily be patched. Fiberglass holds up well when used in power and sail boats, but the fiberglass layups in hardshell kayaks are relatively thin, especially compared with those on the larger boats. The trend in fiberglass kayak construction is toward ever thinner layups to keep their weight down. Such light layups make fiberglass kayak hulls vulnerable to stress fractures, so they won't last as long as folding kayak hulls.

4. Greater Versatility of Use

Folding kayaks are much more versatile than rigid ones. The fact that you can fold them into bags raises all kinds of possibilities. A rigid boat is rigid in how you can use it, because it's limited by that large bulk and size. To show just how versatile a folding kayak can be, take a look at the question of assembly.

Some people think foldable kayaks must be assembled and disassembled each time they're used. But, if you wish, you can leave your boat assembled, treating it just as you would a rigid boat. This means you can store a folding kayak, already made up, on a rack in your garage. Many folding kayak owners leave their boats assembled in storage buildings and garages, rarely knocking them down except for air travel. Ordinarily, they cartop their assembled folding kayaks to a put-in spot. Cartopping and storing assembled will do no harm to a folding kayak.

Rigid boats, on the other hand, don't usually break down into conveniently carried pieces. You can find some "take-apart" rigid boats on the market, i.e., fiberglass kayaks that have intentionally been cut into three or four sections that can be bolted together when needed, but these take-aparts have limitations. You

Folbot Aleut arrives UPS, New York City.

Looking it over at home.

Genie out of the bag, West Point, New York.

Laying out the parts.

Assembling a frame half.

Finishing touches.

Maiden voyage.

have to be extremely careful not to strip the bolts or get sand into their threads, which would make joining difficult. The seals at the joining points are vulnerable to dents that will affect watertightness. Also, you can assemble and disassemble one only so many times before you have trouble with the bolts. Folding kayaks, in contrast, can be taken apart and assembled tens of thousands of times; that's the intention of their design.

If you plan to use the take-apart feature of a sectional fiberglass boat only a few times a year, you'll probably have little problem with it. However, if you intend to knock it down more often than that, you could run into difficulty.

Foldability works to your advantage in many ways. Storing a disassembled kayak is easy, because it takes up far less room than a rigid boat. When it's stored in its bags, a folding kayak is safe from the elements, especially from ultraviolet sunlight, which damages any boat, rigid or folding. Even when you're moving a boat by car, foldability plays one of its strongest suits. When it's inside your trunk or in the back of your mini-van, any kayak is much safer from thieves than it would be on your car's roof. Increasingly, kayaks are being stolen from roof racks, because people often don't take the time and trouble to cable and lock them securely.

You can take one-way trips almost anywhere in the world using public transportation. In the New York area, for example, the train that runs along the Hudson River has many stations within easy walking distance of the river. Board a train with your foldable packed away, get out at your favorite launching site, assemble and launch your boat, paddle along the river for a distance, take out near another station, knock down your boat, and ride the train back home. In places like the Pacific Northwest, you can paddle to any of a dozen picturesque islands and then take a ferry back.

Sometimes one-way trips are unplanned but prudent. Many folding kayakers report being hit by bad weather that prevented them from finishing a paddling trip to a specified destination. Knocking down the foldable boat and taking a ferry, train, or taxi back home proved to be the safer alternative to slugging it out on rough water.

Air travel is the advantage most people think of first. The ability to fly with your boat to a faraway destination opens up the possibility for all sorts of good paddling. On most major airline routes, the folded-up boat can be checked in as ordinary luggage at no added charge. And it's easy to pack it well enough to prevent breakage. When you switch to smaller planes that drop you off in harder-to-reach spots, in Alaska for example, you'll pay extra to carry your foldable with you. But you'd be charged much more for a rigid boat, if it could be carried at all.

Versatility doesn't end with foldability. Because folding kayaks are much more stable than rigid boats, you can do more with them. Superb stability means that foldables make good sailing boats. Almost all of them come with fixtures that will accept the manufacturer's mast-and-sail rig or one that you find in the aftermarket. Sailing rigs run the gamut—from downwind rigs to full-range sails capable of pointing into the wind.

Fishing is also possible from a foldable without too much worry about capsizing. Some foldables have cockpits large enough for you to easily cut up bait, handle fishing tackle, and land those tasty fish.

Foldables work well for scuba diving and snorkeling, too, because reentering is so easy. Even with air tanks, getting from the boat to the water and back again is no problem. This is one of the reasons why the military relies so much on these boats.

Camping with a foldable adds a whole new dimension. Camping gear packs away in the underdeck space in front and back, and you still have the space around your body for carrying gear you want to keep especially handy. The payload of the doubles runs between 700 and 800 pounds including the paddlers, and between 350 and 550 pounds in single folding kayaks.

5. Easier to Repair

Into every paddler's life there comes the day when something goes wrong with the kayak. When that day comes, you'll find that your folding kayak is easy to repair, whether you're at home or in the field.

First of all, duct tape, the universal fixer-upper, adheres tenaciously to the hulls of folding kayaks, more so than it does to plastic hulls. A piece of good duct tape will stay on a folding kayak for months and months without working loose. You can even temporarily repair broken ribs or long pieces on a folding kayak with the handy stuff.

Folding kayaks really excel when you need to make permanent repairs under field conditions that are far from ideal. In temperatures below freezing, a Hypalon hull will accept a permanent patch, but not so with a plastic or fiberglass hull, because their repair material just won't function below about 45°F.

Because a folding kayak is made up of its various components, replacing one or two pieces is easy. Getting an older kayak back to almost-new state is also easy. You have the option to replace pieces, not repair, which becomes increasingly important as your kayak ages.

Rigid kayaks aren't made of components, so you don't have the replace-not-repair option. Plastic boats don't willingly accept repair patches after they reach a certain age. Plastic hulls grow brittle and inflexible with time, so the pliable patch material has difficulty adhering properly. How well a plastic kayak has been stored and treated determines the age at which it becomes too old to patch. Some experts advise that beyond about five or six years, a plastic hull cannot take a reliable patch. If you have to repair a five- or six-year-old plastic hull, they advise for safety's sake that you relegate the boat to light use from then on. On the other hand, fiberglass, like the hull materials on folding kayaks, should remain safely repairable as long as there is some surface for a patch to adhere to.

6. Safer at Sea

Safety is the most outstanding benefit paddlers gain from folding kayaks. In just about every aspect, folding kayaks are safer boats than rigid kayaks.

The risk of capsizing and getting dunked is far greater with a rigid boat than it is with a folding kayak, which is much more stable. Even under severe conditions, the average paddler with only moderate ability to *paddle brace* can keep a foldable kayak upright. In a rigid kayak, that same paddler would need greater bracing ability and other much more advanced stabilizing techniques such as *sculling*. (These techniques are explained in detail in Chapter 6.) Your ability to *Eskimo roll* is considered your first line of defense when using a rigid kayak. It's quite difficult to perform an Eskimo roll in a folding kayak, but then again, it's very hard to capsize one in the first place.

In the unlikely event that you find yourself overboard, foldables are far easier to reenter, whether they're singles or doubles. A double can be reentered when both paddlers are in the water without the need for outrigging a paddle float, which is invariably required of a rigid boat. Under most circumstances, reentering a single foldable doesn't require a paddle float either. Even under the worst circumstances, a single foldable offers a far more stable platform for reentry than would any comparable rigid kayak.

Safety benefits reach beyond the getting-back-in issue. During a storm at sea, you can hunker down into the relative comfort of the cockpit of your folding kayak, while you ride out the turbulence. Try doing that in a rigid boat, and you'll capsize for sure, because the rigid kayak requires you to keep paddling or sculling to stay upright under such severe conditions. If you wrench your shoulder and can't paddle, a folding kayak will continue to float along nicely. If food poisoning suddenly incapacitates you and you must lean over the side, perhaps vomiting, your foldable will remain stable beneath you. In a rigid boat, you'd probably capsize without some helping hands alongside.

Misconceptions Unmasked

Like Rodney Dangerfield, folding kayaks "get no respect." Several bad images and misconceptions about foldables still float in and out of the kayaking world, but most of them have very little basis in truth. Let's examine the most common doubts people have about foldables, and let's allow the track record to respond to these notions and prove them true or false.

"They Lack the Performance and Efficiency of Rigid Kayaks."

That exact phrase has been used in several sea-kayaking manuals, so it requires some discussion. Exactly what the writers meant by "performance" was never spelled out, but in the context in which the statement was made it seems to refer to the ability of the paddler to perform his or her skills.

Indeed, given their stability, it is difficult to perform an Eskimo roll in a foldable kayak, and you'll find that your ability to scull is limited by your relative position in the boat. But Eskimo rolling and extreme sculling are less necessary in a foldable kayak to begin with.

"Efficiency" appears to have something to do with speed. Folding kayaks are considered slower than rigid boats and less efficient. That is partly true but not to the degree that the statement implies. Folding kayaks are wider, which ordinarily tends to slow a boat, but the width differences between the two kinds of kayaks are not so great where it counts—at the waterline. Most folding kayaks taper down sharply from their decks to the bottom of their hulls, so although the average single foldable may be five inches more beamy than its rigid counterpart, the difference between them at the waterline is more likely to be about two inches.

At cruising speeds—where most people do the majority of their paddling—folding kayaks move just fine. Folding singles are as fast if not faster than at least 80% of the rigid singles. In mixed recreational class races, foldables don't normally dominate first place honors, but they come in ahead of many rigid kayaks. For example, in the Angel Island 8-mile Race in open water off San Francisco, a Klepper Aerius single has come in as high as third in a field of 70 kayaks made up almost exclusively of hardshells. In a special recreational class race that was part of the last leg of the 1993 Finlandia Challenge, one folding kayak beat out some 20 rigid boats on a 12.5-mile course off New York City, a course that headed into current and wind.

When sea conditions get rough, folding kayaks really enter their element. The folding-kayak paddler can put all his or her energy into moving forward, without having to devote some of that time and effort to semi-bracing and other strokes required for maintaining stability in a rigid boat.

"Foldables Are Not Really Sea Kayaks."

If seaworthiness is any measure of what makes a sea kayak, then foldables have rigid hulls beat hands down. Earlier, we discussed the many unique characteristics of foldables that contribute to their seaworthiness. Thousands of offshore and open-water trips have been successfully completed all over the globe in folding kayaks. Try telling those explorers and adventurers that their boats weren't sea kayaks.

Folding kayaks have weathered dangerous storms on the open sea, including hurricanes and tropical disturbances. Consider all the surf landings and launches made without upset in these boats.

When all these factors are tallied, folding kayaks must be recognized as sea kayaks. If not, then what are they?

"One Might Accidentally Fold up on the Water."

This imaginary vision arises from a misunderstanding of the term "folding." The misconception is: "If it's a folding boat, might it not fold up on me when I'm on the water?"

No, it won't. It's not as if one single fastener or device acts like a linchpin, holding the whole boat together. A folding kayak's rigidity relies on a series of such fasteners in a progression of overlapping layers, thus making them fail-safe, and all folding kayaks are structured with built-in redundancy. If one fastener fails, others are sufficient to keep the boat together. Even if several fasteners were to give up the ghost, the frame would maintain its integrity. A storm won't break the frame apart, nor will it come apart on its own.

"Folding Kayaks Require Lots of Maintenance."

Not true. According to the instructions for folding kayaks with wooden frames, they should be varnished annually, but few owners do. Most never varnish their frames at all, and they have no problems. At worst, it means that their frames, instead of lasting 80 years, might survive for only 30 to 40 years.

Folding kayaks that have aluminum frames need occasional attention with some lubrication at joining points to make certain these don't stick. But it's a minor inconvenience and takes only minutes each year.

"They Are Costly to Purchase."

True. Generally speaking, folding kayaks do cost more than rigid boats, especially plastic ones. However, the price difference is not so great when comparing them with fiberglass kayaks, especially top-of-the-line models. The price range of foldables is wide, and their depreciation is far less than that of rigid kayaks, due partly to the foldable's longer life and utility.

A top-of-the-line fiberglass double costs from about $2,500 to $3,000, and a similar folding double will run from about $3,200 to $4,200; altogether about a 30 percent price difference. In five years, you could sell that double foldable for anywhere from $2,800 to $3,500. The fiberglass double would be lucky to fetch $1,500, more likely around $1,200. The rigid model would have depreciated some 50 percent, but the foldable only about 12 to 15 percent.

When pricing new single kayaks, you'll find that the differences are much narrower, especially since the recent advent of smaller foldables. A top-quality mini-single foldable runs from $1,500 to $2,000, which places it just a bit higher than comparable small fiberglass singles that cost from around $1,200 to $1,600.

Don't overlook the several less expensive folding doubles and singles on the scene. You can get a single for around $1,000 and two of the doubles for just under $1,700. In this price bracket, these foldables are very close to the prices of the least expensive comparable plastic hardshell kayaks. Though these foldables are relatively inexpensive, they are not shoddily made and have proved popular with many satisfied folding kayakers.

"Foldables Are Heavier Than Hardshells."

People who say this, or write it in manuals, are comparing apples and oranges. They look at a sleek fiberglass single that weighs about 50 pounds and hold it up against a double foldable that may tip the

The Boat that Goes by Mail

Shipping a folding kayak is inexpensive, and it's the only sea kayak you can order by phone and have delivered to your door by mail or private parcel carriers. For example, UPS charges less than $60 for surface transport of a double foldable from one coast to the other. Shorter distances and smaller foldables travel via UPS or U.S. Postal Service for about $30. Folding kayaks that are packed in shipping boxes at the factory or distributor have a clean record in the breakage department.

Because rigid kayaks are much more bulky, shipping them is more costly and more of a hassle. Rigid-boat manufacturers have to find a bulk carrier traveling from the vicinity of the factory or distributor to somewhere in your area, and your wait can be up to six weeks or more. Unless your rigid kayak is handled very carefully, it is subject to breakage, especially if it's fiberglass. One large mail-order house in Maine stopped fulfilling orders for fiberglass sea kayaks listed in its catalog because of the breakage problem—too many boats were arriving with small cracks. TIP: Be sure to save your folding kayak's original packing box. Whenever you go on vacation, you can use that box to ship your boat on ahead. This eliminates checking your kayak through as airline baggage, and it lets you use up your whole baggage allowance with all kinds of extra gear.

---

scales at 75 pounds. The "heaviness" charge falls apart when like type boats are considered.

If you compare single kayaks, you'll find that most foldables are in the same mid-50-pound range where fiberglass and plastic boats generally reside. One single foldable does weigh in at 62 pounds but several plastic singles are 65 pounds in heft! Doubles, both folding and rigid, generally weigh between 72 and 85 pounds. In contrast, the mini-foldables tend to be lighter than their rigid counterparts. The lightest mini-foldable, which can do sea duty, is just 29 pounds; it is the lightest paddling craft around that can claim to be a sea kayak.

"Assembly and Disassembly Take Forever."

Nonsense. Most models can be assembled in about 15 minutes. Of course, the process takes a little prac-tice. And, when you've just received your new folding kayak via mail or parcel post, plan to spend quite a while putting it together for the very first time. You'll be reading the instructions carefully, and no doubt you'll be a little apprehensive about the process.

You can even improve on the normal 15-minute assembly time, if you choose. In folding kayak races, non-factory teams (i.e., ordinary people) have speeded assembly times to about seven minutes, including rudder and spraydeck. The fastest assembly for a double folding kayak is around four minutes.

Still, even 15 minutes is not a lot of time. Considering the time required to tie a rigid boat securely onto a car roof, handling a foldable doesn't take all that much longer. And, if you had to drive to a storage area to pick up your rigid boat, owning a foldable might actually save you time.

CHAPTER 2

At the Heart of Sea-Kayaking History

Modern sea kayaking began nearly 90 years ago with the commercial development of the folding kayak. When present-day paddlers venture out in today's sea kayaks, they hardly comprehend the vast history of the sport, because, like the tip of the iceberg, so much lies out of sight.

Today, if 15 or 20 sea kayaks are on the water at the same time (other than at a symposium), it's a big event, a signal that sea kayaking is really taking off. But in the 1920s and 1930s, 20 kayaks would have been considered a small gathering, not uncommon. Then, hundreds, if not thousands, of kayaks, all foldable, dotted the immediate horizon on any weekend afternoon. Most of this kayaking boom occurred in Europe, but North America was also caught up in it. Folding kayaking was a small-boating revolution that, in a world torn by unrelenting political and economic tension, let people escape the madness for awhile.

Sea kayaks are now made by about 60 manufacturers, but during the 1930s, more than 80 manufacturers thrived in Germany alone, and dozens more did business elsewhere. In that era, they were all folding-kayak companies. Today, sea-kayaking circles are buzzing whenever some daring voyage is made here or there in a hardshell. But, between the world wars, major bodies of water were crossed as frequently as calendar pages were flipped; every one of the landfalls was made in a foldable sea kayak. Land masses everywhere were being circumnavigated, all ends of the earth explored, in the ubiquitous folding kayak.

It's a rich heritage and legacy. Even as sea kayaking grows sharply in the 1990s, it isn't likely to approach the numbers and impact of that earlier period.

How the Kayaking Revolution Began

Some people mistakenly believe that the kayak-touring movement started when Johann Klepper first began producing folding kayaks in Bavaria, in Southern Germany in 1907. Not quite. It's true that the Klepper company did touch off the commercial development of the boat. But for nearly half a century before, the basic designs for such a folding kayak—constructed of canvas skin over a wooden frame—were kicking around both Europe and North America.

There's evidence of such a design in the U.S. as early as 1850. And, during the latter half of the 19th century, England was in the midst of a budding love affair with the Rob Roy "canoe" made of canvas and wood lath; some of these home-crafted skin boats could be taken apart for transportation and storage. The first known patent was taken out in 1887 in Germany for a "faltboote," or folding boat, but the boat was never produced and the holder lost the patent due to nondevelopment.

Not until 1905 was a workable folding kayak first built by Alfred Heurich, a German architectural student. He paddled his creation on the Isar River near Munich and took out a patent on the design the following year. Heurich's folding kayak model, the Delphin, or dolphin, had a bamboo frame that, in a symbiotic relationship with its sailcloth hull, stretched out the skin and, in turn, was held in tension by it. This is the same principle underlying every folding kayak made since that date. Heurich's foldable went into three bags, each of which weighed less than 10 pounds. The rod bag was cleverly sized to fit in the overhead luggage racks of passenger trains.

Alfred Heurich with first foldable, 1907. (Walther/Klepper)

Heurich's concept was revolutionary and practical. The Delphin was portable enough for one person to carry. By fitting in bags that could easily go on a train, his folding kayak opened up all sorts of possibilities for ordinary Germans—who were then getting their first symptoms of "wanderlust fever."

Heurich had no real notion of how to produce the folding kayak on a commercial basis. He was having trouble with the materials for the hull and didn't have a clue how to set up a sewing shop, so he contacted Johann Klepper, an established tailor in nearby Rosenheim. Klepper had dreams of cashing in on the wanderlust that had fellow Germans passing through this Bavarian town in great numbers on their way to fabled Alpine lakes and mountains. Recognizing a golden opportunity, Klepper got a license from Heurich in 1907 to produce the boat commercially.

Immediately, Klepper began making improvements on Heurich's foldable. He changed the frame material to ash wood to achieve better strength and bend properties and to eliminate splintering. He increased the number of frame members to make the assembled boat less floppy, and he raised the cockpit coaming to keep water out. Klepper also improved the hull material, making it more waterproof. One thing he did not fiddle with was the packed size; Klepper knew that portability would sell the boat.

The Wanderlust Years

Klepper's production-model folding kayak was the right product for that time, the perfect getaway vehicle for a restless society. It hit Germany and the rest of the Continent in big and small ways.

Rugged individuals immediately began to embark on voyages that tested the toughness of the underlying design, first using foldables exclusively from Klepper and later from other producers as well. The English Channel was crossed in 1909 in one of those first Kleppers. In 1923, Karl Schott, paddling a double Klepper solo, went first from Germany to Cairo, and two years later he pushed on all the way to the Persian Gulf. Roald Amundsen took some folding kayaks on his North Pole exploration in 1926, and Admiral Richard Byrd did the same when he went to the South Pole in 1928. In 1929, Carl Borro Schweria used a single Klepper foldable to run the Frazer and Columbia rivers, as well as the Colorado River through the Grand Canyon. A pair of intrepid folding kayakers hopscotched from Germany to Hong Kong, taking more than six years to complete the journey. In 1933, Fridel Meyer paddled her Klepper halfway

Folding kayakers on the
Hudson River, New York City,
circa 1936. *(John Walther)*

around the British Isles to win a long-distance contest.

These globetrotters were traveling billboards for folding kayaks. Accounts of their adventures stirred the imagination of newspaper and magazine readers back home. This led to more wanderlust, and, of course, more purchases of Kleppers, Pioneers, and scores of other folding-kayak brands.

The voyager who most deeply moved the public was Captain Franz Romer, when he crossed the Atlantic in 1928 in a custom-made 19-foot Klepper. He managed to get to Puerto Rico despite being hit twice by hurricanes. Romer's transatlantic passage was the ultimate test of seaworthiness for a folding kayak, and his boat was only slightly different from the production models anyone could buy off the shelf. Romer's exploit made banner headlines on both sides of the ocean. In a poignant ending to his tale, Romer disappeared without a trace in another hurricane while crossing from Puerto Rico to the U.S. mainland. Pundits point out that he had added a motor to his foldable for that last leg of his journey, and it probably compromised the sea trim of his boat.

While these folding-kayak voyagers were almost bumping into each other as they crisscrossed the globe, ordinary people were creating folding-kayak traffic jams closer to home as they sought their own more modest adventures. Thousands upon thousands of wandering kayakers packed their folding kayaks for weekends and vacations, and they paddled every inch of water on the rivers, lakes, and coastlines of Europe.

Trains traveling south into the Alpine lake country would arrive in small villages to release an avalanche of folding kayakers from every passenger-car door. Kayakers by the hundreds would load boat bags and gear on local carts and roll down country lanes to the lakesides or riverbanks where their adventures would unfold. It was an impressive summer weekend sight that dwarfs anything we see today, even the sea kayak symposium at Port Townsend, Washington, that draws 800 participants annually.

It was not all touring. Folding kayaks quickly took to the whitewater during that period. Photographs of the day show narrow folding kayaks deep in the white foam of fast moving rivers, their paddlers expertly negotiating around rocks and bends, through chutes and over falls.

Folding-kayak racing events even became part of the Olympics. They were the only kayaks used in

Pope John Paul II, Kleppering in his student days. *(Walther/Klepper)*

whitewater events until the late 1950s, when rigid boats were introduced. The ancient Eskimo roll was rediscovered by Edi Hans Pawlata in a folding kayak; one classic method of kayak rolling now bears his name.

The Post-War Era

World War II brought a hiatus to kayak wanderlust. Folding-kayak touring turned to folding-kayak warfare, and the boats participated in action on both sides of the conflict. They accounted for heavy toll in "enemy tonnage sunk" that is almost unbelievable considering the relative tininess of the kayaks doing the attacking. (See "Folding Kayak As Dreadnought" later in this chapter.)

Most folding-kayak companies in Germany didn't survive the war's devastation, but Klepper and a handful of others literally rose from the ashes. Klepper's factory had been severely bombed, not because folding kayaks were a strategic target (they should have been), but because the building abutted the main marshaling yards for trains that crossed the Alps to support the German war effort in Italy.

Elsewhere in Europe, the industry thinned out. The UK, for example, lost its respected folding-kayak industry that had provided boats for the military during the war. Even with fewer makes to choose from, Europeans began hitting the waters again in folding kayaks. But because their need for economic recovery outweighed their need for recreation, the golden age of kayaking began to dwindle.

Meanwhile, the American scene turned dynamic. The manufacturer Folbot had moved to the U.S. from England just prior to the war, so by the post-war era, it was producing an inexpensive foldable that brought the sport within reach of most people. Thousands of Folbots were sold each year. In the Northeast, the railroads ran what were billed as "Foldboat Trains," weekend specials that took hundreds of paddlers to the region's popular lakes and rivers.

Kleppers also began to sell vigorously in the U.S. market. A weak Deutschmark, in relation to the strong post-war U.S. dollar, allowed Klepper to export thousands of its sea kayaks to the U.S. at prices considered affordable by just about everyone. Several other developments helped sales.

In 1953, the company introduced its new Klepper Aerius model that for the first time incorporated air sponsons on a production folding kayak. This feature greatly helped assembly and disassembly of foldables. The skin fit could be designed to be looser, thus allowing easier insertion of frame halves; you then tightened the hull fit by blowing up the air tubes. Prior to this innovation, the fit had to be more taut, making assembly or disassembly a tricky chore.

Another boost to Klepper's post-war success, especially in the U.S., came from another epic seafaring voyage that made news—Dr. Hannes Lindemann's 1956 crossing of the Atlantic, totally unassisted, in a stock Klepper Aerius double folding kayak. Dr. Lindemann was so unassisted that he bought his Klepper out of his own pocket from a dealer in

The Folding Kayak as Dreadnought

Folding kayaks have a long military history that, by necessity, is shrouded in secrecy. Enough information has leaked out, however, to testify that these tiny vessels are capable of taking punishment and providing a stable platform for transporting soldiers and ordnance over vast distances through rough sea conditions.

Although they may have been deployed by German forces earlier, folding kayaks first surfaced publicly as a British weapon of war in 1940. The British Navy's elite special operations unit started life in July 1940 as the Folbot Section. Its assignment: employ folding kayaks for raiding and reconnaissance. The original name was quickly changed to the Special Boat Section (SBS), because it gave away too much about what the unit might be up to. The founder of the section was Roger Courtney, one of those many folding-kayak wanderers from the 1930s, who had once paddled 3,400 miles down the Nile.

Throughout the war, SBS units and similar folding-kayak warriors from other British services menaced enemy shipping and shore installations, and they scouted beach defenses for amphibious landings. The most famous SBS raid was Operation Frankton in 1942. Five double-kayak teams set out with magnetic mines to destroy vital enemy cargo aboard ships in Bordeaux, 62 miles up the Gironde Estuary. Folding kayaks provided the only means to crack the port's defenses unseen and to attack the shipping with pin-

point accuracy. The following year, the SBS's Australian counterparts used three folding kayaks to sink a half dozen enemy ships in Singapore; the Japanese defenders never suspected the raiders had come from the sea. As in Bordeaux, the folding kayaks had allowed their crews to approach targets undetected, so they could place their mines.

Folding kayaks remain a military "asset" for several dozen nations. For example, several Scandinavian countries continue to patrol long stretches of sensitive coastlines with folding kayaks. The boats can cover long distances and, unlike motor patrol boats, are hard to spot. This keeps would-be intruders guessing about where a patrol may be at any moment and whether they are being observed. Similar patrols are deployed by both Iraq and Iran in the vast Tigris-Euphrates Delta, all the better to infiltrate and interdict each other. There is good reason to believe that, during Desert Storm, U.S. and British forces used foldables to run long-range reconnaissance missions on these same rivers as far north as Baghdad.

Earlier, Great Britain used folding kayaks extensively in retaking the Falkland Islands from an Argentine occupying force. Foldables first transported reconnaissance teams to study defenses. Then, as the British fleet and troop carriers lay offshore, teams went in again to cut communications and clean out mines and shore installations.

The military continues to buy many Klepper and Nautiraid kayaks for its training and operations. The boats are often treated roughly, loaded beyond their intended capacities, manhandled from submarines and small vessels, dropped fully loaded from helicopters, and later winched back into the air with their crews and all their gear. Special operation forces drag their boats over rocks, use them for prolonged periods in freezing and tropical conditions, and generally put more wear on them in one year than civilians would in 20. Because these folding kayaks survive the torture, military procurement officers keep coming back for more.

SBS crew, training exercise, 1992. *(Walther)*

Germany. He had the boat mailed to him in the Canary Islands, then set out for the Caribbean with some modified sails, a primitive outrigger, and 154 lbs. of canned food, garlic, beer, and water. Seventy-two days and 3,000 miles later he emerged from a Caribbean rain squall to startle some onlookers on a beach in St. Martin.

He made the cover of *Life* magazine in 1957 and wrote a very popular book, *Alone At Sea*. He became a modern-day icon of sea kayaking, someone to point to whenever anyone doubts the seaworthiness of these small, vulnerable-looking craft. In the wake of all the publicity, the rush to buy Kleppers, Folbots, and other foldables created a boomlet for sea kayaking.

To the Present

But lifestyles were changing. A society caught up in modern conveniences, television, and the automobile turned its back on the outdoor life. Camping, canoeing, bicycling, and exercise were not the way society wanted to spend its leisure time in the late 1950s and most of the 1960s. If people boated at all, it was in motor-powered craft, not muscle-driven ones. Reduced interest in physical pursuits prevented any resurgence to the level of sea kayaking seen earlier.

In the 1970s, commercial production of rigid kayaks began in earnest, forcing foldables to yield their exclusive hold on the world of sea kayaking. Fiberglass kayaks were relatively easy to make. The cost of starting up an operation was low, and production could begin in a barn or garage. Plastic sea kayaks, which came on the market during the late 1970s and early 1980s, required a sizable initial investment in equipment, but they could then be mass-produced inexpensively at a large mark-up.

Fiberglass and plastic boats both took advantage of new materials, a move that projected their image as modern and sleek. Foldables, because they were made of canvas and wood, were considered relatively old-fashioned and vulnerable.

One new maker of folding kayaks bridged the gap between these perceptions of modern and traditional. In 1980, Feathercraft began operations out of Vancouver, British Columbia, with a one-person folding kayak that offered an aluminum frame and synthetic deck. It even had a small cockpit opening similar to those on hardshell kayaks. These innovations helped Feathercraft buck the trend and draw customers.

Meanwhile, the Klepper conglomerate that produced folding kayaks had also taken on tents, clothing, sailboats, and car trailers. So far overextended, it went bankrupt and closed its folding-kayak production in 1978. Herman Walther, a retired international businessman from Germany, paid a chance visit to the dormant factory to get spare parts, and his

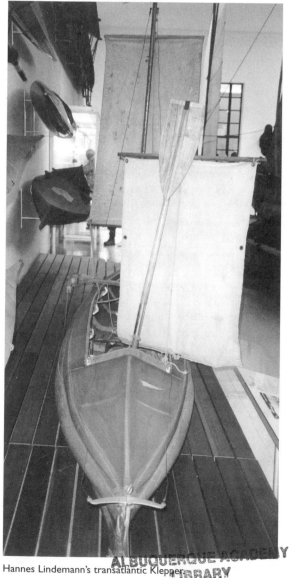

Hannes Lindemann's transatlantic Klepper.

A Visit to a Factory

Have you ever been curious about how a typical folding kayak like a Klepper is made? Forget those images of Bavarian craftsmen whittling out ribs, apprentices forging fittings, seamstresses with spectacles perched low on their noses sewing away by hand. It isn't like that, never was, even in Hans Klepper's days. The process does include a great deal of skilled hand labor, but it all revolves around industrial machinery, templates, and jigs. Here's a glimpse of how the pieces are made and put together at the factory in Rosenheim in Germany's Bavaria.

The Rosenheim operation at one time did all its woodworking on the premises. Now all wooden parts are made at a lumber subcontractor's factory about a half hour away. The wood factory has an exclusive contract with Rosenheim, an arrangement that assures a steady supply of quality to Klepper and steady income for the wood factory.

The process begins with careful selection of the wood: mountain ash for the long pieces that need to be flexible, and Finnish birch for the nine-layer plywood laminations used for ribs. The ash is aged three years, and the birch is cut and glued into marine-quality plywood.

The long mountain ash pieces are milled in fairly large automated machines that spit out the stringers and the rails used to form gunwales and keelboards. These are then cut to size, sanded, etc. The birch plywood is cut into ribs by a skilled worker using an industrial saw stand and template in which the centers are cut out and the outer lines formed. A similar process is used to form the bow and stern endpieces. Then the edges are beveled and sanded.

The gunwales and keelboards are put together at the lumber factory. The reinforcement plates for the gunwales are glued to the rails using jigs to assure precision in placement. The keelboards are glued together in a similar fashion on jigs to get just the right angles.

The wooden parts travel to Rosenheim every Monday. The pickup is a rush process because of concern that differences in humidity and temperatures can affect the dimensions of the wood, even minutely, and throw off exact placement of fitting, and the precise alignment of the frame.

By late Monday, Rosenheim workers have drilled any holes needed for later placement of fittings and started the varnishing process. The machinery and jigs used for drilling represent some of the most costly equipment used in Rosenheim. The jigs are made of metal and allow up to a half dozen parts, let's say Aerius II No. 3 ribs, to be drilled at once. Worn jig parts have to be replaced often to assure continued precision. The costs are so prohibitive that Klepper is not quick to rush into new models with different ribs, gunwales, or other parts.

Varnishing is done in huge vats placed in the concrete ground floor. The parts are held on overhead racks, just so many parts to each rack. They are dipped in three baths of high-grade marine varnish, first one of a thin viscosity to assure deep penetration of the wood, then two more baths of a thicker viscosity to provide the needed protective layers. The dipping process is done at a rate of so many feet per minute to get the right amount of varnish on the wood. The varnished parts are then left to dry for at least 24 hours before going upstairs to receive fittings.

Fittings are made of a corrosion-proof aluminum alloy. If you've ever looked carefully at a Klepper frame, you know there are a lot of fittings, and each fitting is made of a number of parts—rivets, plates, springs—that all require precision fabrication.

All fittings are made by subcontractors, most of which are run by former Klepper employees. The main fittings are made in one factory very close to Rosenheim. It would amaze you to see how much equipment is needed to do all the work. One whole machine just forms the bend in the tongue fittings.

Klepper uses just-in-time inventory, which leaves it with only two weeks' worth of parts. It can do so because all the subcontractors are nearby, and there are ways of backing up anyone that may run into a problem.

When the frame pieces get to the main factory floor, they go into a time-consuming process of fitting placement. It's done by hand. Several skilled workers place the fittings by hammering rivets into the precision holes made earlier. The plastic holders for stringers are also hammered in with rivets at this point, and caps are placed on the stringers.

The next step is to test it all. Before a frame is readied for shipment, it is fully assembled from the parts bins. This assures Klepper that everything fits together. Because of the elaborate processes that proceeded this step, very few rejects or parts ever need to go back for fixing. In this test-assembly phase, the frames are also placed into boat skins to make certain they fit well within desired tolerances.

Klepper boat skins are made of cotton canvas joined to Hypalon hulls. All work on these is done in-house. Hypalon and canvas arrive from their sources in large rolls. Decks and hulls are cut on one huge table that is also used for cutting sails, spray decks and skirts. Working with patterns, the sewing staff cuts as many as four decks at a time. But hulls are usually done one or two at a time.

Several seamstresses work first on the decks. They sew on paddle pockets, deck D-rings and other such fittings, and the pockets that hold air sponsons. The air sponsons themselves come from a subcontractor, and to be sure they hold air, they're blown up and tested for a few days.

The seamstresses usually work on specific orders rather than just make decks for stock. The same sewing machines used for making the deck fittings sew the spraydecks, spray skirts, sails, and the bags used to store and carry the boats.

Klepper has a special proprietary process for attaching decks to hulls. First, using the heavy-duty sewing machines mentioned above, the seamstresses sew a ribbon binding to the perimeter of the deck. This ribbon binding, unique to Klepper, is about an inch wide and made of a specially blended material. Then the seamstresses haul the hulls and decks over to a very different sewing machine, one unlike any other in the Klepper factory. Here the hulls and decks are sewn together. The company's seam-binding process results in a seam that is absolutely watertight.

subsequent involvement led to the revival of operations by 1981. Walther got a license to build boats from the thousands of warehoused spare parts and eventually bought the machinery and plant. He introduced new cost-cutting methods of management, such as farming out many operations, and, to assure continuing quality control, much of this subcontracting went to former Klepper employees.

Folbot also had spread itself in too many directions, and production quality suffered when it offered dozens of models including kits and hardshells. Then Jack Kissner, the man who had founded the company in London in the 1930s, died. Again, only happenstance brought Phil Cotton into the picture. An engineer working in the same industrial park where Folbot was located, Cotton bought the plant from Kissner's estate in the early 1980s. Cotton then streamlined

production methods, got rid of most of its models, and concentrated on a new design, the Greenland series, which had synthetic decks and aluminum frames á la Feathercraft.

What Now?

The good news for anyone thinking of buying a folding kayak is that both of these two major manufacturers are strengthening, and Feathercraft, the relative newcomer, is now a major player. Moreover, Nautiraid, the French folding kayak manufacturer, is improving its presence in North America with a full-service distributor and lineup of dealers.

The industry is positioning itself to meet what it sees as emerging customer needs. For example, all four have introduced smaller, lighter-weight single foldables.

In weight, they harken back to the early days of fold-ing kayaks, i.e., in the 29- to 42-pound range, which makes them lighter than most rigid sea kayaks. And they fit in a single bag. These new foldables are well suited for smaller people, particularly women, who make up more than 40 percent of new sea-kayak buy-ers. People who aren't using sea kayaks for long expe-ditions don't need heftier boats. These lighter folding kayaks suit paddlers who mainly do day trips or out-ings of less than a week.

The companies also feel that the pendulum is swinging in their favor in other ways. There are so many look-alike rigid sea kayaks on the market that would-be buyers get confused about all the choices. Lifestyles are changing, and home sizes are shrinking. More peo-ple are living in condos instead of houses with yards and garages. Apartments are smaller. The problem of where to store a 17-foot hardshell looms ever larger. With a kayak that can fold, the problem is solved.

Paddlers are being drawn to other benefits of fold-ables. The faster learning curve for safely using folding kayaks appeals to individuals who want to get out on the water fast, as opposed to spending months honing the skills required in hardshells. Conspicuous con-sumerism is giving way to greater appreciation of nature and the environment, a trend that's particularly favorable to foldables. They allow a wider range of travel for exploring great expanses of fresh and salt water. Paddlers can hop on a plane, bus, or train and get to new waters quickly. And, when they get there, they enjoy a greater degree of seaworthiness and safety that are required for exploring unknown areas.

CHAPTER 3

*C*hoosing the Folding Kayak That's Right for You

Here are three important points to remember when shopping for a folding kayak:

1. You have a surprising number of real choices. The differences between the leading models are fundamental divergences in designs, materials, and approaches. You're not dealing with dozens of look-alikes, as you are with rigid boats in which differences are often cosmetic.

2. You get what you pay for. This market doesn't support designer labels. Some folding kayaks cost more because they are better boats, not merely because they are imported or constructed of space-age materials. On the other hand, lower-priced models are not shoddily built and are proving satisfactory for many paddlers.

3. You'll never regret buying one. Owners of folding kayaks tend to hang onto their boats for decades, as witnessed by the scarcity of foldables on the used-kayak market. The boat you buy will give you long service and see you safely through your adventures, just as such boats have done for many thousands of paddlers.

As with any purchase, there are many factors to consider when selecting the exact folding kayak you'll be happy with. For one, you bring certain personal elements to the decision process: your size, interests, and skills. For another, the often radical differences between individual folding-kayak models require that you really do think through how you'll be using your foldable. You'll see these difference in the next chapter, when we'll evaluate more than a dozen models.

Sizing Up Your Needs

Sea kayaking is a very personal sport. Needs differ. You should be wary of people recommending a particular model unless they have asked you some basic questions and then listed salient features that match your responses. The XYZ Walrus Hunter may be a great boat for one individual and be a lousy one for another. The easiest way to lose a friend is to praise some model highly and insist that your friend get one—without sizing up whether it will fulfill your friend's needs.

When making a decision about a folding kayak, you have more questions to answer than you do with rigid kayaks. The questions posed below are intended to raise the key issues, but they are not necessarily the only considerations. Use them to get your thought juices flowing, so you'll find the best boat for you.

Do You Need a Single or a Double?

This question comes up for couples and for any individual who may be paddling at some point with a companion. If you're a couple, think through how you're likely to paddle. Will you want to be in the same boat for conversation, sharing the paddling load and the experience more intimately? Or will you want to move at different paces, one crossing from point to point, the other exploring the shoreline. Many couples start with a double and later pick up at least one single for the times one may want to go alone. This opens the option of bringing along another person, perhaps someone new to the sport. The novice can

23

Solo paddling a double.
(Michael Skott)

paddle in the double with one of the couple, while the other goes in the single.

For a couple, costs may complicate this decision of buying one double or two singles. Two singles are almost always more expensive than a double of the same quality.

Some individuals buy doubles with the thought that they might want to have a friend along. They feel that they can paddle the double alone the rest of the time. Don't do that to yourself unless you are very certain you'll have company enough of the time to warrant the less-than-optimum paddling you'll experience alone in a double.

Solo paddling is best done in single boats. All doubles paddled solo are a compromise. However, if you plan to sail a good amount of the time, a double will have the advantage of greater stability and no particular disadvantage for the person going off alone, since the boat will be mainly wind-powered. Also, if you are planning to paddle in remote areas for weeks, possibly months at a time, a double will carry all the gear you're likely to require.

If you're absolutely determined to buy a double that you'll be paddling alone most of the time, get the best solo-paddling model you can. Some models are not too bad when paddled solo, but others are dogs. Look into how conveniently the boat can be set up for solo paddling, which usually involves moving one seat into a better trim position. Solo seats for some models can be costly. You may also want to have a solo spraydeck, which costs more money. You could save the extra expense by making your own solo seating arrangement and deck. On a temporary basis, you could also put some weight in the front seat to improve the kayak's trim a bit and keep the nose from being pushed around by the wind.

Certain paddlers can manage solo paddling a double quite well, and it doesn't necessarily correlate to muscle mass. Some of these paddlers stand about 5 feet 8 inches tall and don't appear exceptionally strong.

Will You Need to Assemble It Regularly?

Remember, we are talking about *foldable* boats. So, if you won't be leaving it set up most of the time, consider how fast and easily a particular model assembles and takes apart. Some foldables can normally be assembled in 10 to 15 minutes. Others take closer to 20. Still others require 30 to 40 minutes even after you become totally familiar with the assembly process. Notice the assembly times in the evaluations of different models in the next chapter.

If you plan to use the boat mainly for camping weekends and week-long trips, longer assembly times are not critical. If you'll be paddling for a few days before knocking the boat down to go home, what difference is an extra 15 or 20 minutes? But if you only have time for day trips or just an afternoon, then the long assembly time will probably discourage you from going paddling at all.

Where Do You Intend to Paddle?

Be realistic. If you plan to remain on calm lakes and sheltered coastlines, if you'll never venture out in anything but clear weather, give serious consideration to a lighter-duty model that will save you money and weight.

Author assembling Nautiraid Mini-Raid, 10:00 AM.

10:02 AM.

10:06 AM.

10:09 AM.

10:14 AM.

It's similar to buying a tent. A Eureka three-person dome tent will cost you less than $200. By comparison, a North Face VE-25 runs more than $500. Of course, the North Face expedition tent will handle heavier winds and weather than the Eureka, but the Eureka is probably all you need. It's the same with foldables.

But if you'll definitely be paddling under severe conditions, then you would be better off with a more substantial foldable. In fact, your life may depend on it. Similarly, if you're pretty sure of encountering sharp obstacles or having to make many rough landings, the same rule holds true. A more substantial boat, one with thicker skin and keelstripping, will resist punctures and stand up to excessive wear.

This durability is even more important if you're buying a single. If you paddle alone, you'll have to drag your kayak a few boat lengths to clear the surf or crashing waves. In a double, there would normally be two paddlers who would carry—not drag—the kayak to a more secure spot.

How Will You Use It?

Folding kayaks offer plenty of versatility, but be careful not to choose one just because it offers more possibilities. If you're definitely planning to sail, you'll need a model that can handle a full-range sailing rig, and some models are better natural sailing vessels than others. But, if sailing is something you just *think* you may want to do some day, don't buy a particular foldable just to have this sailing potential.

The same goes for fishing. The best fishing boats are extremely stable, enabling you to cast or pull fish confidently, and they have wide open cockpits that let you get at all your fishing gear.

If you plan to do many extended camping trips, bear in mind how all your cargo will fit.

What Are Your Skill Levels?

All folding kayaks are more stable than their rigid-boat counterparts, but some foldables are more tippy than others. If you think you'll be uncomfortable in one of the more tippy models, then opt for a foldable that feels more stable.

Some single foldables have lots of rocker in their hulls, which makes them easier to turn. But rockered boats also tend to turn into the wind and waves more easily, a trait that makes them difficult to keep going in the right direction. If you don't have the paddling skills to keep a rockered boat going straight, you'll need a rudder. Most double-boat owners consider a rudder crucial, but single paddlers often find them a nuisance. Assembling the rudder adds to your set up time, and it increases the boat's drag, slowing you down.

How Strong Are You?

If you're looking for a single, your strength should be your first consideration. If the single boat you're eyeing is too big or heavy for you, you'll never enjoy carrying its bags or hefting the assembled boat down to a dock or beach. Sea kayaking is supposed to be fun and liberating, not a chore.

Some of the singles are heavy, make no mistake about it. One model weighs around 62 pounds, which puts it in a weight class with the heaviest plastic boats around. That's a lot for a small person to deal

Folding kayak in the Arctic. *(Walther/Klepper)*

with. This particular foldable may be a terrific boat, but do you really need it? Instead, go for one of the mini-foldables that will make you a lot happier in the long run.

If you don't have the necessary upper-body strength but are absolutely determined to get a heavy-duty, sea-crashing boat, be prepared to use a boat cart. And when your boat's being hit by wake or surf, you'll need to work out a way to get it away from the water's edge.

If you're buying a double, you don't face quite as much demand on your strength. The weight of a double foldable is generally the same as a hardshell double. The lightest model weighs in at a little under 70 pounds; the heaviest is up around 85 pounds. These weights have proved manageable for just about any two people.

What Are the Best Materials?

When you start to investigate folding kayaks, you'll soon hear about comparisons of the materials that go into their frames, hulls, and decks. One manufacturer may claim its frame material is superior to that of other folding kayaks, while another company says its decks are the best.

Experience with many hundreds of folding kayaks through years of service has showed that each material has its advantages and disadvantages. Compare materials to suit your particular needs, but don't think for a moment that any particular material used for a frame or hull could be best in every way.

Wood Versus Aluminum

Two of the major manufacturers, Klepper and Nautiraid, continue to use wood for all of their frames, including long pieces and crossribs. Two other manufacturers, Folbot and Feathercraft, both use aluminum for their long pieces, and their crosspieces are made of other synthetic materials, such as polyethylene and injection-molded polycarbonate.

The wood-versus-aluminum arguments seem endless, not unlike the sleeping-bag controversy. Some people would rather give up camping than switch from their down-filled sleeping bags, while others swear their bags filled with synthetic fibers give them many extra advantages. On a cold night, either material is sure to keep a person warm, so neither is "superior" to the other.

It's really a matter of preference rather than objective analysis. Some people like the modern, up-to-date associations aluminum gives them, while others like the tradition and aesthetic sense they get with wooden frames. If the modern-versus-traditional point is important to you, follow your heart.

But beyond that, don't worry about wood-versus-aluminum arguments unless the way you plan to use your foldable will make one material work better for you than the other. For example, if you paddle frequently in cold weather, you may find that non-conductive wood is more pleasant to handle while assembling the boat than is cold aluminum. It's a minor point, but it might be critical to your enjoyment of your kayak.

Be careful about the claims that are made in the wood-versus-aluminum argument, because they don't hold up in the real world. Here are a few of the most common:

> **"Aluminum frames are no good; if they break in the field, unlike wood, they are impossible to repair, so you'll be stuck."**

Not true. Repair kits provided by the manufacturers often contain aluminum sleeves of a diameter slightly larger that regular frame members. You slip a sleeve over the two broken ends of the long piece, tape or tie the repair sleeve tightly in place, and you're free to paddle on. You can get a replacement part when you're back from your trip.

> **"Aluminum frames are better than wood, because they need no maintenance, unlike wood, which has to be varnished regularly."**

This is not true. It's amazing how little varnishing many people do and get away with it. Aluminum, on the other hand, does require attention at the points where tubes connect. These points should be lubricated several times a year and washed every so often. Wash and lubricate especially if the frame has been lying on sand or been kept assembled with saltwater sitting in the bilge. If you don't maintain the aluminum, you may find the frame very difficult to disassemble later.

> **"Wood is no good because it's fragile and breaks easily."**

It takes a lot to break a wooden frame member. Under ordinary use, it won't crack or split. There are many 40-year-old wooden frames around that have been used regularly and show no breakage. Even extraordinary abuse of wooden frames causes only minor damage. For example, the Aussie Challenge expedition that covered some 4,000 miles along Australia's east coast suffered little damage to the frame of the Klepper double it used. The foldable landed through the country's famous rough surf during some 100 days of the voyage, a tough test for any kayak.

> **"Wood is better than aluminum in the tropics because it's less susceptible to corrosion and therefore holds up better."**

Actually, both materials suffer equally under tropical conditions. Several touring services use Feathercrafts for all their Caribbean and Baja trips, and they've had no particular problem. And the boats stay assembled for long periods at a time. Kleppers and Nautiraids are used by other touring services in the same way. Both types of material need maintenance to hold up. Wooden frames should regularly be taken out of the hull and allowed to dry thoroughly to prevent rot. With aluminum, take the precautions mentioned earlier, i.e., lubricate and wash tube ends when you can.

Deck and Hulls

On decks, it's Klepper versus the rest of the pack. All Klepper decks are made of cotton canvas. The other major manufacturers use synthetic materials, albeit with differences in weights, coatings, and methods of waterproofing.

Cotton has the advantage of breathing. The environment under the closed decks of a Klepper is considerably less humid than under decks with synthetic coverings. Cotton canvas has another unique property: it doesn't require coatings to be waterproof. As in old canvas tents, the material is tightly woven. Individual threads swell when they get wet, so the openings between them close up, rendering the entire surface waterproof. When wet, the cotton deck also tightens up, giving you the benefit of a tauter skin fit when underway.

But cotton has its downside. Because cotton is less abrasion resistant than synthetics, cotton decks have to be thicker to compensate. Cotton canvas is heavier than synthetics of equal thickness; even when it's dry, you have a lot more weight to contend with. The

weight problem is compounded when a cotton deck gets wet and absorbs water as part of its natural waterproofing process. The boat gets even heavier. Finally, a wet cotton deck takes longer to dry than does a synthetic one.

Synthetics are stronger than cotton, but they do require coatings to achieve watertightness. Synthetic decks vary in the number of coatings they must carry and upon which surface the coatings go—the underside or the top. Nautiraid opts for three layers of coating on the top, but other companies choose the underside of the deck. This inside-outside question remains a quandary. An inside coating gets rubbed every time you insert or remove frame halves or stow or pull gear. On the outside, it gets rubbed by everything else in the world. Take your pick.

Then there's the question of which synthetic to use. Companies have been moving away from nylon and Cordura nylon decks in favor of polyester. Nylon is particularly susceptible to UV damage; that's why nylon decks require UV inhibitors. Nylon becomes stretchy when wet, as much as 5 percent. This forces manufacturers to compensate by making their nylon deck skins on the tight side. Polyester is somewhat more UV-resistant than nylon, but it still requires some added waterproof coatings, which it doesn't hold quite as well as nylon. Polyester has little stretch, assuring you of consistently taut skin.

UV light, by the way, harms all material used in kayaks, soft or hard. Like folding kayaks, rigid kayaks also should be kept out of direct sunlight as much as possible. UV dries out both plastic and fiberglass decks, making them brittle and more susceptible to hairline stress fractures.

The hulls on folding kayaks are now mainly made of Hypalon, a synthetic rubber-like material, bonded to a textile core material. Hypalon-covered hulls have an advantage over those covered with natural rubber, which was the main material used previously. Hypalon lasts much longer—30 years under normal use. Natural rubber tends to last about 20 years before it gets scaly.

Hypalon hulls vary in several respects, such as their thickness and the types of adhesives used to bind the Hypalon to the core material inside. For example, all of Klepper's hulls, even its non-expedition boats, are thicker than those of its competitors. But Feathercraft uses a Hypalon coating that is molecularly denser than Klepper's Hypalon. Polyester has replaced cotton as a core material, since cotton absorbed water and tended to rot from within. Adhesives are a complex subject. You'll hear esoteric arguments about which works best to bind Hypalon to its core material, but generally all you need to know is that Hypalon works well.

You'll find hulls made of materials other than Hypalon. Vinyl is used in some models because it's cheaper and lighter than Hypalon. You'll also see hulls of urethane-coated nylon, which is supposed to be more puncture-resistant than Hypalon but may not wear as well. It has the definite advantage of being lighter than Hypalon. One way to get the best of both worlds with a urethane-coated material is to opt for Hypalon keelstripping at wear points.

Strategies for Buying a New Foldable

As mentioned in Chapter 1, folding kayaks generally cost more than rigid kayaks. So it's good to have some strategy for getting the best buys if you are looking in the new-boat market.

How Much Leverage Do You Have?

You don't have a lot of play in prices because of the relatively shallow markups with which folding kayak dealers and distributors have to work. In plastic hardshells, dealers have as much as an 80 to 100 percent markup over the price they pay for their stock; fiberglass retail markups are generally about 40 to 60 percent, depending on the dealer's own leverage with his supplier. Folding kayak prices run 25 to 35 percent over what a dealer or distributor might pay for his supply, so dealers selling plastic boats can be very generous in discounting their prices. Folding-kayak sellers don't have much leeway.

But don't give up. Here are several tactics that will increase your leverage, depending on which make you're looking at.

Folbot has regular sales that bring down the prices of its boats as much as 20 percent in some instances. If this is the brand of foldable you want, and if you can wait to get it, a simple inquiry for information will get you on the company's mailing list so you'll receive notice when these sales are running. (See Appendix for all major manufacturers' addresses.)

Nautiraids are available again on the North American market because the company has finally found a suitable distributorship. To reposition itself in the U.S., Nautiraid will likely offer some good deals, so look for them. Also, some older models are still around gathering dust on dealers' shelves. If you shop around by phone, you may find a dealer who has one and wants to dump it. On this basis, some unused Nautiraids have gone for 25 to 35 percent less than their list price.

Feathercraft and Klepper don't regularly discount their prices, nor do they have any regular sales. But if you buy a Feathercraft at the factory, you may save something if you buy with Canadian dollars—not a lot, but something. Then there is the issue of Canadian provincial and federal taxes. Some rebates are available for goods bought by foreigners who take the items out with them. But, you are legally liable to pay duties on reentering your home country.

You can save some money by buying a Klepper in Germany. Your savings come in the rebate of the value-added tax when you leave Germany, minus import duties when you reenter your own country. But getting this savings is neither quick nor easy. Kleppers are made to order, so they have scheduled deliveries and waiting lists. The boats aren't sitting around on shelves at the Klepper factory or at the various dealers. If you plan to be in Germany over a summer or for a year, then you can probably sit out any delays in production and delivery. But if you're there only for a quick business trip or a two-week vacation, you may be unable to get your hands on a boat in time to bring it home. To avoid hurting its overseas distributors, the company will not sell directly to you outside Germany. And only as an exception will Klepper make a direct sale at its factory.

The Cost of Accessories

Here are a few pointers about paddles, spraydecks, and rudders that you might want to buy at the time you are purchasing your new boat:

Accessories for folding kayaks can sharply add to the total package cost because not all makes come fully equipped. Feathercraft includes the price of the spraydeck or skirt and usually a basic rudder in its quoted prices. It also has initiated a policy of including sea socks in the basic purchase price. Klepper includes a set of wooden paddles but charges steep prices for other components such as spray decks and rudders. So while the list price on a Klepper model may be within $100 of a similar Feathercraft, you could wind up paying hundreds of dollars more for the Klepper package when you add these other components.

Folbot sometimes throws in an accessory such as a paddle in the basic price, particularly during its special sales. If you already have a paddle, or plan to buy a better paddle later, you usually can get the factory to let you use the credit from the Folbot paddle toward the purchase of some other items such as a rudder or spraydeck. Nautiraid used to include several accessories in the basic price, but no longer does so. Check with your local dealer or the North American distributor for current policy,

You may be able to bargain.

The price margins on accessory components are generally much higher than on the basic boat; some of the items are marked up 50 to 100 percent. If you're buying a fully equipped package, you may get something thrown in free. Do whatever bargaining and finagling you can before you purchase the boat; you're less likely to get a break later.

Less-Expensive Alternatives

You won't find many other folding-kayak manufacturers out there. Every so often a new company gets started, albeit as a very small shop. Also, from time to time, folding kayaks from nontraditional export sources come into the market, such as foldables from the former Soviet Union and other ex-socialist countries. Generally these boats are offered at substantial savings over what is available from the Big Four (Feathercraft, Folbot, Klepper, and Nautiraid and Pouch), but you'll have to make tradeoffs.

The biggest point to consider is that the company may not be around in a year or two—after you've bought your foldable. Several companies that started up in the North American market in the last few years have stopped producing foldables. Boats coming in from the ex-Eastern Bloc countries are, with one exception (see Chapter 4), being brought in on a speculative basis with no solid distribution or service behind them. An individual gets his or her hands on, say, 10 Russian boats at some bargain price and then re-sells them for a quick profit.

If it were merely a matter of *buying* a rigid kayak

from such a source, there would be no problem, assuming you were happy with the boat to begin with. With a foldable, however, you have to contend with the possibility that down the line you may require a spare part and, much later, even a new skin to place on the frame. If the source is gone, you may be stuck.

In some cases, you don't have to shy away from purchasing from a startup company or an irregular import source. If you're considering buying one of these foldables because it seems a good fit for you and is inexpensive, take a careful look at the frame. Does it have exotic fasteners for its crossribs and long pieces? Are the pieces made of unusual material? If the answers are yes, then the boat would be difficult to deal with if anything ever were to go wrong. If the answers are no, then you may be able to remedy any later problems.

For example, with a wood frame, you can probably get a carpenter to replicate the shape of a crossrib if you ever damage one. If the part's means of fastening to the rest of the frame is fairly simple, you'll be okay. The same is true for aluminum ribs and tubing, because you can get a metalworking shop to replace a part should it break. Again, the key is how simply it attaches to the rest of the frame.

The hull is another matter. If the source of the boat has disappeared, it's highly unlikely you'll find anyone who can make a satisfactory hull for you. Even if you got one sewn up by some local source, it's not likely to hold up and will probably create assembly problems for you. Don't kid yourself. The major manufacturers are not going to do one up for you.

Winning at the Used-Boat Buying Game

Used rigid kayaks are cheap to buy. They depreciate 50 percent or more within just three to five years of the initial purchase. Folding kayaks, on the other hand, hold their value for decades. It's not unusual to see a 20-year-old foldable, one that cost its buyer $500 when new, easily resell for $1,200—more if its accessories are intact. The seller is basically pegging the selling price to what it would cost to buy a new boat. For a used foldable of more recent vintage, the owner can usually get what he or she paid for it new, minus sales taxes and a slight depreciation factor.

Still, you can do nicely on the used market if you have a strategy.

Sources for the Best Used Buys

By the time someone places a used-foldable boat into the regular sea-kayaking pipeline, the person is likely to be asking top dollar. The seller will know what he or she can get for it, based on other ads and advice from knowledgeable individuals. This means club newsletters and paddling magazines are not the places to look for bargains. Here are some better sources:

Penny Savers and other local buy-sell tabloids.

Generally people who list folding kayaks in these publications have little or no inkling of what they can ask. These sellers are more likely to look at that 20-year-old foldable that cost them or a spouse $500 (and can fetch $1,200) and ask just $100 or $200 for it. This happens often enough that such publications are a viable source.

Non-paddling friends and relatives.

You'd be surprised how many individuals bought foldables 20 or 25 years ago when they seemed fairly cheap and, after using them a few years, carefully stashed them away in an attic. Ask around and you may find one of these. A number of happy paddlers have done just that. Most were giveaways.

Outfitters.

Several dozen outfitters and touring services regularly use foldables for their trips and instruction. You won't get a terrific price, but it's generally less than what an individual seller will ask. The boats will have some wear, however, which is why they come on the market at a price that's lower than other used foldables.

Out-of-town sources.

Your immediate area may be very competitive for would-be buyers of foldables, but the situation may not be as tight in other regions. For example, a folding kayak for sale in a large coastal city is likely to bring a higher price than one being offered in a smaller town located well inland. You can arrange an out-of-town sale in various ways. For example, if you have the kayak sent to you C.O.D., you will be able to examine it before paying up. It may seem risky to buy a foldable sight unseen from a stranger thousands of miles away, but this arrangement has worked well for many buyers.

Looking Over the Used Boat

In buying a used foldable, you're buying a boat made of parts, so don't be put off if every part isn't perfect. You can repair or replace any parts that are in poor shape or that may temporarily render the boat unusable. Here are some tips on evaluating a used boat:

Find out what parts of that particular model are most likely to have suffered damage over time.

For example, on wooden frames, you sometimes find that a used boat has developed some twist in the end pieces at either the bow or stern. This can happen to a boat that has been left assembled for months with water sitting in its bilge. The twist can affect performance, so the piece should be replaced. Other parts may look bad but don't hurt the boat. For example, polyethylene ribs used in Feathercrafts can develop contortions if the boat wasn't assembled properly and was then left standing that way for a long time. If you test these crosspieces by placing them on a flat surface, they'll wobble and not lie flat. Although this may look like something is drastically wrong, it's not a problem as long as the ribs will attach to the rest of the frame.

Make certain to have the latest price and parts list for the model you're considering.

If anything seems wrong with the boat, you'll have a good idea how much it will cost to replace particular items. You can even point this out to the seller, who, generally, will lower the asking price by the cost of the needed replacement parts.

Ask a distributor to photocopy the assembly instructions for you beforehand.

This will help you determine if anything is missing. If the boat, say, is being sold by someone who inherited it and doesn't know how to assemble it, you'll be able to check it out yourself.

Don't be turned off by a less-than-perfect hull.

If the price of the entire boat is low enough and the frame is usable, you can buy a new hull. Then you'll have a boat that will serve you for another 30 years. See if a replacement is available for the model you're looking at, and find out its price. Also, you may be able to make a repair that will help you get a few extra years of life from what looks like a bad hull. Some suggestions are listed in Chapter 16.

CHAPTER 4

Evaluating the Leading Doubles and Singles

There is a folding kayak for everybody, but not all are suitable to everyone. Some are expensive; some are less costly. Some are very well made; others less so. Some use high-tech materials and design; others resort to traditional materials and proven shapes and features. Some go together very quickly; others are more tedious to assemble. Some should probably not be used under certain conditions; others can safely handle the widest range of activities.

This chapter will help you wade through the uncharted waters of the buying decision, to get you beyond the general model specifications and advertising hype. To find the boat that's best suited to your needs, you need to know the specifics about the leading single and double foldables, so we'll look at eight crucial factors of each one. (See sidebar.) These key factors are the outgrowth of questions raised in the previous chapter.

The boat evaluations avoid assigning numerical scores or rankings. You'll never come up with your "perfect" boat just by adding up columns of numbers. One factor may be so pivotal to your own needs that it outweighs most of the other factors. Other people might value different factors more highly for their needs. For that reason, you won't find an overall recommendation of any particular boat.

The best way to benefit from these boat appraisals is, first, to make certain that you've narrowed down your personal requirements by reviewing the points in Chapter 3. Then, zero in on those aspects among the eight factors that match your individual needs. Finally, look over the remaining factors to see if any create a problem for you. These remaining traits should register a "neutral" or a "no big deal" as far as you're concerned. Voilà! You've probably identified the folding kayak that you'll be most happy with.

Double Folding Kayaks

Doubles are considered the "coin of the realm" in the folding-kayak world. They account for 80 to 90 percent of sales for three of the leading manufacturers, Folbot, Klepper, and Nautiraid, although these figures are changing as the companies introduce leaner and lighter new singles. Feathercraft's double represents a sizable business, between 15 and 20 percent of its sales on the North American market.

This is in sharp contrast to plastic and fiberglass sea kayaks. Tandems are just a sliver of the rigid-boat market, accounting for 2 to 5 percent of rigid sea kayak sales. Rigid doubles are an anomaly; you don't see very many around.

Not so for foldables. Doubles are the defining element for folding kayaks, not just in the number of sales. Doubles are what most people conjure up as the image of a foldable: two people carrying some bags to the water's edge, miraculously creating a craft of integral frame and skin, throwing in mountains of gear, and taking off without too much concern about conditions, because they're confident the resulting vessel will see them through.

Now let's look at the five leading models produced by these major folding-kayak companies, as well as a sixth double that is being distributed in the U.S. from the former East Germany.

Eight Key Factors in Evaluating a Foldable

1. Assembly/Portability. How long do assembly and disassembly take? This factor is crucial if you must assemble and knock down your boat each time you paddle. If the process takes more than 15 minutes, even after you get the hang of it, the evaluation will note this. Portability becomes a factor when you have to carry the disassembled boat aboard trains or ferry boats, through airports, etc.

2. Stability/Seaworthiness. Stability tells you how much the boat will resist tipping. Seaworthiness assesses the boat's ability to deal with the conditions of open seas and high winds.

3. Tracking. How good is the boat at going straight ahead without a rudder, despite cross seas and wind? This is especially important in the single foldables. In a double, two paddlers normally need a rudder to offset the difficulty of coordinating their paddling strokes.

4. Maneuverability. How easy is it to turn the boat by using paddle turning strokes, body lean, or both?

5. Speed/Efficiency. What is the top speed of the boat? This is important when you want to cover long distances quickly. How efficiently does it move at lower speeds? How much effort is required to get up to and then sustain its cruising speed?

6. Versatility/Access. What can you do with the boat besides paddle it? Can you sail it upwind, attach a rowing seat, cut fish bait in it? Can you customize the boat to meet any particular need? If it's a double, can it easily be paddled solo? Can camping gear and belongings be loaded and unloaded easily, or is the access restricted?

7. Quality/Durability. What is the workmanship like? How long is the boat likely to last? What kind of punishment can it take? For example, can it stand up to the demanding use of expeditions or outfitters?

8. Cost/Depreciation. How much does the basic boat cost? What other items are included as standard equipment? How much do the needed accessories add to the price tag? What can you sell the boat for later?

Feathercraft K-2.

Feathercraft K-2

First introduced in the early 1980s, this model is the longest and narrowest of the folding doubles. The K-2 is unique among folding doubles, because it has individual cockpits, and it appeals to paddlers who want a foldable that seems most like a rigid boat.

The frame consists of aluminum long pieces and high-density polyethylene crossribs. Decks are Cordura nylon, and the coating is applied on the underdeck surface. You have two options on the K-2 hull: either all Hypalon, or Feathertex, which is a proprietary urethane-coated nylon with Hypalon reinforcement keelstrips.

Assembly/Portability.

The K-2 takes 35 minutes to assemble, even when you get proficient at the process. It has lots of parts and can be tricky to put together. The boat is on the heavy side, due mainly to its greater length. However, Feathercraft has an optional bag setup you'll probably want. It consists of special carrying bags with full backpack harnesses, including padded shoulder straps and hip belts, that make the K-2 comfortable to carry.

Stability/Seaworthiness.

Although it is narrower than the other folding doubles, the K-2 is quite stable largely because of the added length. Its frame is on the flexible side, because the boat lacks floorboards, so many of the joining points are meant to have give. This makes the K-2 a highly seaworthy vessel in rough conditions when the boat must shape itself to the turbulent surface of the sea. The K-2 is the only one of the doubles that includes an important safety feature, sea socks, which are devices that fit over the cockpit coamings to keep water from filling the boat. The K-2 provides a stable reentry platform, but it's slightly harder to get back into than other foldables because of its relative height and smaller cockpits.

Tracking.

The boat tracks well even in crosswinds. The assumption is that, as in any double, you'll normally use a rudder to help you go straight. The rudder is top quality; Feathercraft is a choice rudder supplier for a number of hardshell manufacturers.

Maneuverability.

The boat will turn even without a rudder, especially since you can easily and safely lean it on its side.

Speed/Efficiency.

The K-2 is fast, giving what is probably the highest potential top speed of the bunch. It has some slight inertia on the first paddling stroke or two because of its weight. But once underway, it's very efficient to paddle; its cruising speeds are easy to maintain with minimum effort.

Versatility/Access.

The K-2's individual hardshell-like cockpits limit the number of ways you can use the boat or customize it. The K-2 is meant mainly for paddling. It does not come equipped to take an upwind sail rig, just downwind sails and spinnakers. The K-2 can be fished from but doesn't have a roomy, move-around cockpit for cutting bait, as do most other doubles. You can't easily paddle a K-2 solo, because you can't get yourself into a better trim position; you're stuck paddling from the rear cockpit. Access to underdeck areas is superb. The K-2 has watertight hatches through which you can store gear or reach through to adjust loads, thus maximizing your use of underdeck space.

Quality/Durability.

Workmanship on Feathercrafts is excellent, as is the quality of the materials that go into them. The K-2 stands up to rough landings and expedition use, especially when equipped with the all-Hypalon hull. Since the model has been around only 12 years, we have no track record to help us predict how long it will last, but older K-2s are aging well.

Cost/Depreciation.

The K-2 is near the top of the price ladder, but it comes standard with rudder, spray skirts, and sea socks. Because relatively few K-2s are made, used ones are hard to find; they demand top resale dollar.

Folbot Greenland II

The Greenland II has proved to be a very popular boat since coming on the market in 1989. It is lightweight and inexpensive, and it performs well in a lot of activities. Many folding kayakers report they are happy with this model and the service they're getting from it. The Folbot company has gained a solid reputation for customer service and for standing by its products.

The Greenland II's frame is aluminum with polycarbonate cross members. Hulls are of Hypalon. Decks are now being made of polyester, coated on the underside surface.

Assembly/Portability.

The Folbot double assembles in a jiffy—no difficult moments—thanks to some subassemblies and easy-to-manage connecting points. There is only one small fitting part that you have to be careful not to lose, the turn-knob at the apex of the washboards or cockpit coaming. Although it's the lightest of the double foldables in this review, its storage bags are awkward to lug and lack padding in the carrying straps.

Stability/Seaworthiness.

The Greenland II has plenty of initial stability because of its width and air sponsons. Its seaworthi-

Folbot Greenland II.

ness, however, is affected by a tendency to wallow in heavy beam waves and winds. This makes the Greenland II a boat for lighter-duty use, although individuals have pushed the boat further.

Tracking.

The Greenland II will go quite straight on its own without a rudder in most cross seas.

Maneuverability.

The boat is a bit more difficult than others to put on its side for carving turns. As with other doubles, you'll want to use a rudder, but the rudder is awkward to attach and is troublesome.

Speed/Efficiency.

This model is slower than others at top speed. It's also somewhat less efficient, requiring a bit more effort at cruising speeds, but it will get you where you want to go.

Versatility/Access.

The Greenland II is a very versatile boat that lends itself to full-range sailing and fishing, thanks to its high stability and open cockpit. You can easily customize a Greenland II as many users do. Full deck zip-

pers are reliable, and they help when you're assembling the boat and loading gear. However, once the air sponsons are blown up, getting at that gear becomes more difficult, because you can't unzip without releasing some air. The boat is easy to paddle solo, especially when the inexpensive solo-seat setup is added.

Quality/Durability.

Workmanship is good but not like that of its pricier competitors. For example, seams are sometimes uneven and the external metal end pieces may be slightly out of line. The Greenland II will hold up to normal family and individual use, but it's not generally up to the consistent hard abuse dished out by outfitters and long-range, remote-area expeditions.

Cost/Depreciation.

The Greenland II is the least expensive of the doubles and is occasionally on sale at substantial savings. Generally, its accessories are sold separately, but they aren't costly. Depreciation won't bring down the resale value of the Greenland II as quickly as it would a comparable rigid boat. But since you can buy a new Folbot so cheaply, this model won't hold its value as well as some of the other folding boats.

Klepper Aerius II.

Klepper Aerius II

The Klepper Aerius II has seen more paddling miles—under the widest and wildest conditions—than any other model of sea kayak currently in production, rigid or foldable. Although it's undergone some 100 modifications, its underlying design has not been tampered with during the 40 years since it was first introduced. You'd be hard pressed to spot the differences between the boat you can buy today and Hannes Lindemann's 1956 transatlantic Klepper, which is on display in a Munich museum. All of the frame and hull on his boat are virtually 100 percent compatible with Aerius IIs currently being built.

The Aerius II has a cotton deck and a thick Hypalon hull. It comes in three models: the basic Classic; the California, which adds deck fittings such as paddle pockets and D-rings; and the Expedition, which adds deck fittings and has a thicker hull that includes keel-strips. (The Quattro is a separate version of Aerius II, so we'll look at it separately.)

Assembly/Portability.

The Aerius II practically assembles itself despite having no subassemblies. It's the fastest of the fold-ables to assemble on a consistent, trouble-free basis under any conditions. The boat varies in weight from around 75 pounds for the Classic to nearly 85 pounds for the Expedition model. Carrying bags have padded straps, and they allow the crew to share the load fairly comfortably, although not quite as well as does the Feathercraft K-2.

Stability/Seaworthiness.

The Aerius II is highly stable in both initial and secondary stability. It takes a lot to capsize this boat, and the Aerius II is at home on the open sea. It is impervious to side swells and flanking waves, and it rides up them as well as the best of the narrow, rigid sea kayaks of the British.

Tracking.

This model tracks well through open water without being blown or thrown off course by anything. A rudder is needed mainly to even out the different paddling styles of the two paddlers.

Maneuverability.

You can lay this boat on its side to carve turns. It responds well to its rudder, which has a large bite.

Speed/Efficiency.

The Aerius II does not have the top speed of the Feathercraft K-2, but it paddles efficiently at cruising speeds despite the drag of the large rudder. In capable hands it can cover long distances quickly and safely.

Versatility/Access.

The Aerius II is capable of handling the widest range of uses of any foldable; you can even mount an electric or gasoline motor if you wish. It performs well under sail. Solo paddling is fine but is best done with a solo seat, which is costly. To save money on this solo seat, you can make your own special seating arrangement. (For some suggestions, see Chapter 15.) Gear access is only possible through the cockpit area, and you have to push the gear over and past ribs that tend to catch it. But the Aerius II will hold a lot, and you'll have well-designed space around you in the cockpit for additional equipment.

Quality/Durability.

Quality is top-notch in every respect. The boats are extremely durable, as attested by their military use. Even the wooden frames of boats that came off the assembly line in 1953 are still going strong. The hulls have proved to be tough and long-lived.

Cost/Depreciation.

The Aerius II is generally expensive, but the Classic model is very close to the price range of top-of-line hardshell doubles, which it will outperform. Not much comes standard with the Aerius II, and accessories are pricey. Depreciation is absurdly low on all the models, reflecting the long life expectancy and utility of this craft.

Klepper Quattro

The Klepper Quattro is an extremely heavy-duty Aerius II designed to meet increasingly stringent military demands of a number of nations. It differs enough from the rest of the Aerius line in several key factors to warrant a separate evaluation.

The Klepper Quattro is based on the Aerius II Expedition, but it adds an extra set of air sponsons. This feature distinguishes the Quattro from every other kayak, double or single. It allows you to change the shape of the hull's cross-section, and it raises the boat's effective weight payload through the added buoyancy. The Quattro comes equipped with military-specified features, including many lifeline D-rings along the entire perimeter of the craft and Braille-type markings for identifying ribs and other parts in pitch darkness.

Assembly/Portability.

Except that the Quattro is a bit heavier, these factors are rated the same as the regular Aerius II Expedition.

Stability/Seaworthiness.

When the extra sponsons are inflated, the Quattro rises to a stability league all its own. It's virtually impossible to flip the Quattro except under the most extreme conditions. With all tubes fully inflated, it can be paddled even when it's filled with gear and water and being pounded by heavy waves. This is a feat any other boat would be hard-pressed to match.

Tracking.

The Quattro tracks as well as other Aerius IIs.

Maneuverability.

With *all* its tubes inflated, the Quattro is slightly less maneuverable, but you have the option of only partially filling the extra tubes or leaving them deflated.

Speed/Efficiency.

Inflating all tubes will rob you of speed and make the boat harder to paddle, unless it's very lightly loaded.

Versatility/Access.

In this factor, the Quattro is the same as the Aerius II Expedition, except that it does have a higher weight payload.

Quality/Durability.

The Quattro offers the same top-notch quality and durability as the Aerius II Expedition model.

Cost/Depreciation.

The Quattro lays claim to being the most expensive production sea kayak on the market. It will depreciate slightly more than the rest of the Aerius line because of its high initial price and competition from new boats of less costly Aerius II models.

Nautiraid Raid 2 Expedition

The Raid 2 Expedition is a jack-of-all-trades because of its size and performance features. This

Nautiraid Raid 2.

French boat is supplied to the military of a number of nations.

The frame is all wood, and the Raid 2 sports a polyester deck coated on the outer surface. Hulls are all Hypalon and come standard with keelstripping. (The company is introducing a new lighter model in 1994 called the Raid 2 Touring that we could not test before publication.)

Assembly/Portability.

The Raid 2 can take longer to assemble than might be apparent, since you'd expect its numerous subassemblies to speed up the job. However, the boat has external sponsons, which figure only minimally into the skin-tightening process. This means that fitting the frame halves into the skin is more exacting, since tolerances are tighter than on foldables that have internal air sponsons. The Raid 2 weighs less than some of the other boats. The bags are moderately easy to carry.

Stability/Seaworthiness.

The Raid 2 is extremely stable thanks to its external air sponsons, which form channels that cup the water and resist sideways sliding and tipping. Seaworthiness is good, although the relatively flat bottom tends to make the boat be a bit bouncy in heavy seas.

Tracking.

The Raid 2 will go straight and does not get sucked into beam seas or crosswind action.

Maneuverability.

The Raid 2 is very maneuverable, as befits the shortest of the foldable doubles. It has a rugged rudder that works well.

Speed/Efficiency.

The Nautiraid Raid 2 has a light, nimble feel when on the water. Its sides are relatively low compared with several other folding doubles, so you can reach the water better, which makes it easier to paddle. As far as cruising speeds, the Raid 2 is about in the middle of the pack.

Versatility/Access.

For solo paddling, the Raid 2 is arguably the best of the double folding kayaks because of its smaller size. The company provides a way to use the existing seat to achieve a good paddling trim at no extra expense. Again, arguably, the Raid 2 is one of the best

natural sailing vessels of the folding-double crowd. It can be heeled over radically while sailing with little danger of a capsize. Access is like that of Kleppers, although you must push cargo through smaller rib openings.

Quality/Durability.

The quality of workmanship is about par with that of Feathercraft and Klepper. Durability is good, as befitting a boat used by the military, although its fittings do not hold up well.

Cost/Depreciation.

The Raid 2 is priced between the Folbot and the top-of-line foldables. Depreciation has been a bit less favorable than for other foldables because spare parts were hard to find. Improvements in distribution and the availability of a repair service should help bolster the resale value of older Nautiraids.

Pouch Eureka 2

This boat is being dubbed the *other* folding kayak from Germany, but it's not a Klepper, at least not a modern one. Its design bears a striking resemblance to the pre–World War II Klepper double.

The Eureka 2 is now being brought into the North American market in a way that shows some promise, especially since it is a very good craft at about the price of a Folbot. The Eureka 2 has frame members similar to the Klepper but their fittings are more primitive. The deck is of lighter cotton, and the hull consists of a reinforced vinyl material.

Assembly/Portability.

Assembly can be difficult, and disassembly even tougher—until you figure out the knack. Even when everything goes smoothly, it will take you 20 minutes to do each of these jobs, particularly disassembly. The boat lacks air sponsons, which ease these processes in other foldables. The skin fit is tight, which makes the insertion of frame halves very exacting, and removal is also a chore, since the parts tend to wedge inside the hull. The boat is fairly light, but its bags are awkward to carry and their straps aren't padded.

Stability/Seaworthiness.

The Eureka 2 excels in both these departments, which makes up in part for the difficult assembly process. It is extremely stable and rides over swells and waves with abandon. However, the boat is cut very low

Pouch Eureka 2.

and may take on water, especially since the spraydeck is not strong enough to deflect anything but spray.

Tracking.

This boat tracks beautifully, cuts cleanly through the water, and is not affected by crosswind or side swell.

Maneuverability.

Despite its extra length, the Eureka 2 turns well and responds well to its rudder.

Speed/Efficiency.

The Pouch double is a very fast boat that requires little effort to get up to top speed. Once there, it cruises efficiently. It's easy to paddle, because its low sides allow clearer swing room for your forward stroke.

Versatility/Access.

Its stable platform gives plenty of versatility for sailing, fishing, and attaching a motor. The rather large cockpit enhances your ability to engage in these activities. The Eureka 2, however, is somewhat harder to paddle solo because of its length. Access below deck is on par with other open-cockpit foldables.

Quality/Durability.

The workmanship is good but not on a level with the better double foldables. The wood appears to have less varnish than the others and has rough edges. The vinyl hull is not likely to give it as long a life as would Hypalon or to hold up as well under a variety of conditions.

Cost/Depreciation.

The Eureka 2 is low priced, but its array of accessories cost extra. Depreciation is an unknown factor, because the boat is only now being brought into the market in any numbers.

Single Folding Kayaks

Single folding kayaks offer you a world of personal discovery. They have all the seaworthiness of folding doubles but are generally more responsive than their bigger cousins. The single foldables bring you into closer contact with the elements around you than can any double, whether rigid or folding. The single-seat folding kayaks come in two classes: full-sized craft that range from 15 to 16 feet in length; and mini-foldables that average 12½ to 13 feet. These two classes share many attributes but are different enough to be examined separately.

Full-sized Singles

The three foldables in this class are every bit as good as their rigid-single counterparts at providing that sports car feel of the sea. And they have the added advantages of foldability, stability, and inherent seaworthiness.

Contrary to popular opinion, these foldables are not slow. If you're on a demo beach at some sea-kayak gathering, you can count on any of these three being as fast as, if not faster than, at least 80 percent of the single rigids being demonstrated. In competition, and in

BOAT	PRICE	LENGTH & BEAM	WEIGHT	OPTIONS	KEY FEATURES
FOLDING DOUBLES					
Feathercraft K-2	$4,060 Feathertex $4,230 Hypalon	19'3" X 33"	87 lb. in Hypalon; 79 lb. in Feathertex	comes standard with spray skirts and sea socks; $95 each for special backpack	longest foldable, fast, deck hatches
Folbot Greenland II	$1,700	17" X 35"	65 lb.	$100 for rudder; $125 for spraydeck and skirts	inexpensive, easy to assemble, zippered deck access
Klepper Aerius II	$3,250 Classic $4,390 Expedition	17' X 34"	75 lb. Classic, 83 lb. Expedition	$190 rudder; $395 for spray deck and skirts	thick hull, highly seaworthy, reputation for durability
Klepper Quattro	$5,490	17' X 34"	89 lb.	$395 for spraydeck and skirts	military-grade craft; extra air sponsons allow changing hull shape
Nautiraid Raid 2	$2,950	16'5" X 35"	70 lb.	$200 solo spraydeck	versatile, easy to convert to solo use
Pouch Eureka II	$1,690	18'2" X 33"	72 lb.	$190 spray cover; $115 for rudder	inexpensive, fast, roomy cockpit
FOLDING FULL-SIZED SINGLES					
Feathercraft K-1	$3,335 Feathertex $3,555 Hypalon	15'11" X 25"	55 lb. in Hypalon, 48 lb. in Feathertex	$90 special backpack	fast, seaworthy, deck access hatches
Klepper Aerius I	$2,850 Classic $3,590 Expedition	15' X 28"	56 lb. in Classic; 62 lb. in Expedition	$295 for spraydeck/skirt; $190 for rudder	seaworthy, easy to assemble
Nautiraid Raid I	$2,450	15'1" X 29"	55 lb.	everything standard	fish-form shape, moderate price
MINI-FOLDABLE SINGLES					
Feathercraft Short Touring	$2,620 Feathertex $2,745 Hypalon	13'6" X 27"	48 lb. in Hypalon, 42 lb. in Feathertex	$90 rudder or $62 for a skeg	very maneuverable, very strong frame
Feathercraft K-Light	$1,570 light Hypalon $1,800 heavy Hypalon	12'10" X 25"	29 lb. in lightweight Hypalon, 33 lb. in heavier grade	$90 rudder; full harness back-pack comes standard	lightest foldable, stable, easy to carry
Folbot Aleut Klepper Aerius 2000	$1,200 $1,995	12' X 30" 12'6" X 26"	39 lb. 40 lb.	$115 rudder; $100 spraydeck $295 for spraydeck/skirt	easy to assemble very fast, responsive, strong
Nautiraid Miniraid	$1,600	12'6" X 29"	37 lb.	everything standard	small cockpit, very maneuverable

Feathercraft K-1.

capable hands, they come in toward the front, especially if the water is choppy and the distance long.

Feathercraft K-1

This model is the longest of the single foldables and the fastest in potential speed. Like other Feathercrafts, it has a rigid kayak-type cockpit rather than a more open one. The K-1 has a nice feel on the water.

The K-1 has an aluminum and polyethylene frame. It's available in the same array of hull options and deck colors as the K-2.

Assembly/Portability.

Assembly requires some strength and leverage. Assembly times will exceed 20 minutes for most people. The K-1 comes in one bag, so to carry the disassembled boat more comfortably, opt for the special backpack with full load-bearing harness.

Stability/Seaworthiness.

The K-1 is the narrowest of this class and has a bit less initial stability. Its seaworthiness is superb, as the K-1 clings beautifully to the contours of the sea. For greater safety, the K-1 comes with a sea sock.

Tracking.

The K-1 has little rocker and tracks as straight as an arrow in flight. It will not be pushed around by side winds.

Maneuverability.

The K-1 does not turn quickly because of its lack of rocker, so its turns tend to be wider unless you're skilled at body lean and turn strokes. The rudder works well and, as an advantage, can be pulled out of the way onto the deck when not in use.

Speed/Efficiency.

The K-1 scores well on both counts. It moves out fast with your first paddle stroke with little inertia and can cruise efficiently at high speeds.

Versatility/Access.

Versatility is limited because of the cockpit arrangement. It also lacks customizing potential. Underdeck access, however, is great because of the Feathercraft deck hatches that allow you to insert gear and shift it around for optimum use of space.

Quality/Durability.

The K-1 shows top-notch workmanship and great attention to detail on the deck layout of tie-on points, grab lines, and similar features. The Hypalon hull is more durable than the less expensive Feathertex hull, but the Hypalon hull is heavier.

Cost/Depreciation.

The K-1 is high on the singles price list, but it comes standard with just about everything. Depreciation is low, except for an earlier version that had an integral spray skirt that is no longer considered desirable.

Klepper Aerius I

This kayak has been with us almost as long as the Aerius II, and it enjoys a similarly long track record of achievement and owner satisfaction. The Aerius I

Klepper Aerius I.

has been around Cape Horn and been paddled on nearly every waterway from pole to pole. This stellar performer is capable of delivering broad service.

The Aerius I comes in two models, the lighter-weight Classic and the heavier-duty Expedition.

Assembly/Portability.

Assembly is slightly more difficult than for the Aerius II because added torque is needed to form the frame's radical lines. But the Aerius I has the fastest assembly time in this class, 10 to 15 minutes. Its two carrying bags have padded straps but require some juggling, especially if you're porting lots of other gear.

Stability/Seaworthiness.

The Aerius I defines stability and seaworthiness for single boats of any kind, rigid or folding. It is amazingly at home in the sea under any conditions.

Tracking.

Because of its considerable rocker, this boat has fair tracking ability. Many paddlers prefer to use a rudder to keep the boat straight, especially in beam winds and waves. But if you work at developing good technique, you'll need a rudder only for sailing.

Maneuverability.

The Aerius I will turn on a dime and has been used in Class III whitewater because of this quick-turning ability. You can lean it on its side in open water and carve some very sharp turns to maneuver through the waves.

Speed/Efficiency.

The Aerius I has some inertia on takeoff, so you need a few strokes to get it up to speed. Once at cruising speeds, it doesn't take much to keep it going. This boat has proved itself in a number of open-class races, where it has beat out numerous fiberglass and plastic sea kayaks.

Versatility/Access.

Almost as versatile as the Aerius II, the Aerius I offers the best sailing ability of any of the singles. Access to underdeck cargo space is adequate, and you have room for plenty of gear around you in the cockpit area.

Quality/Durability.

This model is top-of-the-line in both areas. The quality of its workmanship is flawless. For durability, even the lighter-weight Aerius Classic I will hold up well.

Cost/Depreciation.

The Aerius I is expensive, especially the Expedition version, and accessories add to the cost. However, its depreciation is very low, thanks to its high demand on the used-boat market. This isn't a kayak you find at garage sales, where you may find used doubles.

Nautiraid Raid 1

The Nautiraid regular-sized single is made of a wooden frame and Hypalon hull with a polyester deck. The boat's shape has a fish form rather than the Swede form typical of other foldables and of most hardshells. The Raid 1's radically different design puts the widest part of the boat forward of its midpoint, which creates unusual handling characteristics that affect some of the factors below.

Assembly/Portability.

The Raid 1, like its bigger brother, has numerous subassemblies, and tight skin fit. All the precautions mentioned for the Raid 2 apply for this boat. And its

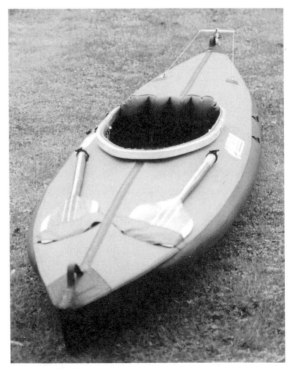

Nautiraid Raid 1.

assembly can take longer than normal if not done correctly. The boat is the lightest of the regular-sized singles and now comes in two bags that are manageable to carry.

Stability/Seaworthiness.

The Raid 1 is highly seaworthy, thanks to the added stability of its flexible frame and external sponsons.

Tracking.

Going straight with the Raid 1 can present a problem because the fish form tends to make the rear end want to swing around. To track well, you'll either have to develop finesse or add a small weight in the aft end to keep the tail from sliding around. Its rudder also will do the trick.

Maneuverability.

The fish form helps the Raid 1 turn fast on open water or in tight quarters. It's the most maneuverable of the larger single foldables.

Speed/Efficiency.

This kayak's sleek look doesn't disappoint you when you paddle it. The Raid 1 will accelerate fast, because the cockpit position forward of the center of the boat allows you to apply power to your paddle stroke.

Versatility/Access.

Although it has an open cockpit, it's not quite as versatile as the Klepper. For example, it won't sail as well, partly due to its fish form. Access to the rear cargo area is difficult because of the long aft deck, again the result of the fish-form shape.

Quality/Durability.

This boat's quality is quite good. The fittings can loosen and come off over time. But its durability is good.

Cost/Depreciation.

The Raid 1 is the least expensive in this class. Depreciation has been a bit less favorable than for other foldables but should improve because of the better distribution setup.

Mini-Foldable Singles

During the late 1980s, hardshell manufacturers began to introduce shorter versions of their most popular boats to meet the needs of a growing segment of the market: women. They've been dubbed women's kayaks, but, whatever your gender, don't be turned off by this sexist term. At least in the folding kayak field, the smaller kayaks, called mini-foldables, are a good choice for virtually anyone. Even strapping 6 foot, 2 inch, 220-pounders will be comfortable in one of several models of mini-foldable singles.

The new folding minis can keep up with the traditional-sized foldables under most situations and, in some instances, actually will cruise with less effort. The mini-foldables have much more to offer than the small rigid kayaks. They weigh about the same as their fiberglass counterparts and are lighter than the plastics. One, the K-Light, is actually the lightest sea kayak of any type. In waves and wake, the mini-foldables seem to thrive playfully and are much more stable than their short, rigid counterparts.

The typical folding mini packs into one bag that is manageable by virtually anyone. The minis can generally be assembled more quickly than can their larger counterparts, because the radical lines of the larger boats create tension and torque resistance that must be overcome in the assembly process. Once assembled, the minis are easier to put on a roof rack and carry down to the water. Also, the minis tend to cost less. All of the minis make good day-use boats. And, if you know how to pack small and light for camping, will see you through a week-long camping trip.

Feathercraft Short Touring (ST)

Feathercraft started the mini-foldable movement with what it first called the River Kayak, now called the Short Touring model or ST. It was designed for the Japanese market that demands light, maneuverable kayaks. The original ST sold in Japan weighed 39 pounds, but now, with a beefier hull and other components, the ST is the heaviest of the mini-foldables, yet still a manageable 44 pounds or so.

Assembly/Portability.

Assembly is a very fast and relatively straightforward operation. The ST carries well when you're using the optional backpack-harnessed carrying bag.

Stability/Seaworthiness.

This Feathercraft mini is very lively on the water and moves well with the action of the sea. Its stability is especially good for lighter paddlers.

Feathercraft Short Touring.

Tracking.

The ST shows its river origins—it doesn't track well. Almost everybody who paddles one must use a rudder or skeg to keep the ST moving straight. The best choice is the Feathercraft skeg, basically a stationary rudder, because it's less complex than a rudder and causes less drag.

Maneuverability.

With its rudder or skeg lifted out of the water, the ST turns in tight circles at your command. Even with the skeg in position, it responds well to leaned turning movements.

Speed/Efficiency.

Although the ST is the longest of the minifoldables, it's not the fastest. The ST's large amount of rocker creates a shorter in-water length that doesn't promote speed. It does paddle efficiently, however, so you can cruise with little effort.

Versatility/Access.

Versatility is limited; you paddle this boat, period. Underdeck space is reasonably accessible.

Quality/Durability.

The ST is built to the same fine quality standards and materials specifications as the larger Feathercrafts. The all-Hypalon hull will give you more durability, but this does push the ST's weigh up to the top of what might legitimately be considered the minifoldable class.

Cost/Depreciation.

The ST is the most expensive of the minifoldables, and it has a good depreciation record.

Feathercraft K-Light 1

Weighing in at 29 pounds (a thicker-hull version still weighs just 33 pounds), the K-Light is unbelievably light. You can lift the assembled boat with what seems just one finger, and the bagged boat hefts easily onto your back and carries well in its special backpack bag.

Components are lighter than those of other Feathercrafts, which saves weight and production costs and keeps the price low. The aluminum tubes are lighter, as is the Hypalon hull, and the crossribs are polycarbonate, not polyethylene.

Feathercraft K-Light.

Assembly/Portability.

Assembly is easier than in the K-1 because leveraging is called for in only one place. The K-Light takes portability to a new level; you can't get much lighter and still have a sea kayak.

Stability/Seaworthiness.

Under most sea conditions you're likely to encounter, the K-Light resists tipping. It allows that nice one-with-the-water feeling.

Tracking.

The K-Light tracks much better than the Short Touring and does not require a rudder or skeg. Only the most severe of beam winds is able to nudge it a bit off course.

Maneuverability.

This mini-foldable responds well to leaned turns. It doesn't require a rudder.

Speed/Efficiency.

The K-Light has a nimble feel and will cruise almost effortlessly. Like other minis, its top speed is not as great as that of regular-sized foldables, but, since few paddlers can maintain their boats' potential top speeds, the K-Light won't leave you behind.

Versatility/Access.

The K-Light is on par with its larger brothers. Access to gear underdeck is through the cockpit area and is no more difficult than in other minis.

Quality/Durability.

The K-Light involves less hand-crafted labor, which is a departure from Feathercraft's norm. But it is still a quality product with attention to important details. You're never likely to drag such a light boat on land, so that factor should enhance its durability.

Cost/Depreciation.

The K-Light's price includes accessories. Depreciation should be good, since used K-Lights are likely to be in high demand.

Folbot Aleut I

The Aleut is the least expensive foldable kayak on the market today. Like the double in the Folbot family, the Aleut is designed for the mass market, for people who aren't performance-minded but simply want to enjoy paddling without much fuss. For that market, the Aleut I delivers the essentials of any folding kayak—foldable convenience and stability.

Folbot Aleut.

The Aleut's frame consists of aluminum long pieces and polycarbonate ribs. Its hull is Hypalon and its deck is coated polyester.

Assembly/Portability.

Assembly is a snap; the Aleut has only three ribs and only about 14 parts. Some parts are already held together in subassemblies. You can get the Aleut either in one or two bags, but take the convenient two-bag option because the single bag is awkward to carry.

Stability/Seaworthiness.

The Aleut's stability cannot be overstated. No kayak can be termed untippable, but the Aleut goes a long way in that direction. It handles well in open water, and its nose refuses to dive in all but the highest waves and wake.

Tracking.

The Aleut tracks extremely well. It refuses to turn into any wind or water force on your beam. In following seas it resists broaching or being turned sideways.

Maneuverability.

This is the downside of the Aleut's terrific tracking ability. The boat is hard to turn because it wants to go straight. Turns require lots of stroking on one side and plenty of body lean.

Speed/Efficiency.

The Aleut is the slowest of the foldables. It's hard to get moving, and effort is required to keep its speed up.

Versatility/Access.

The Aleut's versatility rating is high because of the great underlying stability of the boat. Access to underdeck areas is not especially restricted, because the rib openings are big and, in this short boat, there isn't much deck to begin with.

Quality/Durability.

Quality and durability are on par with the Folbot Greenland II, i.e., good enough for most purposes—but not normally for heavy-duty use.

Cost/Depreciation.

This is the least expensive foldable you can buy. Depreciation suffers because of the low cost of buying a new Aleut.

Klepper 2000

The Klepper mini is a no-compromise, shorter version of the time-proven Aerius I. It is lighter by far than its larger sibling but just as tough. If anything, it feels more solid because Klepper basically compressed the Aerius I's frame to form the 2000's frame. The Klepper mini also seems to have inherited all of the good sea manners of the Aerius I and developed some unique performance virtues of its own.

Assembly/Portability.

The 2000 can be assembled more quickly than the Aerius I, because it has less torque and fewer parts. The 2000 is Klepper's first one-bag carry, and it works well. The single bag incorporates a full backpack harness that can be detached for checking as airline baggage.

Stability/Seaworthiness.

The 2000 has an initial stability that may feel a bit "tippy" or "tender" to some paddlers, but its final stability is excellent, i.e., it won't easily capsize. It handles beautifully in open water and has a lively, responsive feel.

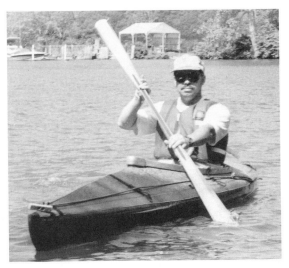

Klepper 2000.

Tracking.

The 2000 tracks better than the Aerius I. It will go as straight as you want without being affected by beam seas and winds.

Maneuverability.

It won't turn quite as quickly as the Aerius I but will respond to body lean to get around in a hurry.

Speed/Efficiency.

The 2000 is fast off the mark and has phenomenal glide. It keeps going and going even after you stop paddling. This trait makes the 2000 a delight to paddle at normal cruising speeds. It may be the fastest of the minis; in effective top speeds, it gives up one knot, at most, to the larger Aerius I.

Versatility/Access.

The 2000 has a provision for a sail mast, but the boat may lack the stability needed for aggressive, full-range sailing. None of the minis is as good a sailing vessel as a regular-sized foldable. Its below-deck access is on par with the Aerius I.

Quality/Durability.

Klepper did not compromise anywhere when making the 2000. Frame dimensions and specifications are identical to the rest of the model line. The hull is expedition quality.

Cost/Depreciation.

The 2000 is within the price range of the other mini-foldables. The only standard equipment included in the price is the wooden paddle, so other accessories will add to your cost. Depreciation is likely to be remarkably low, as this boat will be in high demand on the used-vessel market.

Nautiraid Mini-Raid

The Mini-Raid is an extremely appealing kayak—from its sleek lines to its curved oval, five-ply wooden coaming surrounding its small cockpit. It offers a tight, personal fit and is extremely responsive.

The Mini-Raid has an all-wood frame like other Nautiraids. The deck is polyester-coated on the outside and the hull is made of reinforced vinyl.

Nautiraid Mini-Raid.

Assembly/Portability.

The Mini-Raid can be quick to assemble because of all its subassemblies, but, like other Nautiraids, you may get hung up because of the tight tolerances in its skin-to-frame fit. This kayak is very easy to carry in its one bag, despite the lack of padded carrying straps.

Stability/Seaworthiness.

External sponsons make the Mini-Raid a very stable sea kayak. In open water, the boat gives you a secure feeling, and its responsiveness allows you to take on all but the most severe conditions.

Tracking.

The Mini-Raid does not track well. It has lots of rocker, which tends to make the boat turn into anything beyond a beam breeze. It has no provisions for a rudder. To keep it going straight, you'll have to learn good paddling technique or rig up your own rudder substitute. (Feathercraft's rudder will fit with a little fiddling—see Chapter 15 for suggestions.)

Maneuverability.

The Mini-Raid turns on a dime; you don't even need much body lean to coax it around a turn.

Speed/Efficiency.

The Mini-Raid has a fast, nimble feel on the water. Paddling it requires very little effort, and at cruising speed, it will paddle efficiently.

Versatility/Access.

This kayak is meant to be paddled and nothing much else. For pushing gear inside, its access is tight because the decks are low and the ribs small.

Quality/Durability.

Nautiraid's quality is quite good in general, but because the Mini-Raid's hull is made of vinyl, it is likely to be less durable than other models in the company's line.

Cost/Depreciation.

The Mini-Raid is in the middle of the price range for mini-foldables and comes complete with spray skirt. Its depreciation, like that of the rest of the Nautiraid line, has been a bit less favorable than that of the leaders in the field. But that should change because of a better distribution system.

CHAPTER 5

Equipment and Accessories That Work Well in Foldables

Folding kayaks can make good use of most of the equipment and accessories made for hardshell kayaks. But foldables differ enough from hardshells that you should use special care when selecting some of these items, and you may want to consider a number of products that are made just for folding kayaks.

As you read through this chapter, keep in mind that you don't need to purchase everything at once. You can stock up on items as you get accustomed to your boat and your horizons and needs broaden. It's better to start off slow, go easy on your pocket book, and keeps things simple.

Basic Equipment from Folding-Kayak Manufacturers

Some decisions about add-ons will already have been made for you. How so? A manufacturer may have only one option for a specific item, and your foldable's requirements in that area may be so specialized that there simply aren't any aftermarket alternatives available to you. Your only other choice might be to make your own substitution. Several suggestions for do-it-yourselfers are covered later in Chapter 15.

Here are the key pieces of equipment that your folding-kayak company is likely to offer.

Spray Coverings

Spray coverings (spray skirts, spraydecks, or both) keep out ocean spray and rain, but you'd be surprised just how dry you can remain in some folding kayaks, especially doubles, without such covering.

It's not unusual for a paddler to go out without any spray covering for a few hours into the middle of a large bay that's being churned up by wind and powerboat wakes and find that only a few cups of water have gotten into the open folding kayak. Much of that water is kept out by higher sides and the flare-out overhang created by the air sponsons. However, if that paddler were in a hardshell without a spray skirt in such conditions, he or she would be taking on enough water to be in danger.

In warmer weather, the little water that does splash in from chop or drip off your paddle can feel refreshing on your body. Many folding kayakers, especially in boats with large cockpits, never use spray coverings.

But a spray covering is a wise investment. Not only will it keep you from getting chilled in cold weather, but you should be concerned in a general way about having an open boat in open water. A large, breaking wave could dump gallons of water into your foldable, potentially getting you in trouble; that same wave would very easily be deflected by a spray covering.

When shopping for a spray covering, you'll find yourself hemmed in by proprietary equipment that is difficult to find substitutes for elsewhere. The spray-covering options differ by company. Here are your options:

Feathercraft.

All of this company's folding kayaks have individual cockpits designed to be covered by spray skirts that attach to the paddler. (An original version of the K-1 came with an integral spray skirt built into the

49

boat; although that version isn't recommended, it's still available as a special-order boat.) Feathercraft's only spray skirt is top quality and worth your consideration.

Some paddlers don't like the suspenders on Feathercraft's spray skirt, because instead of fastening with snap buckles, the straps must be threaded through. Some aftermarket spray skirts that fit the Feathercraft coaming do offer the fast-snap feature and even a chest pocket for holding such things as sunblock, sunglasses, and snacks. (Feathercraft also will offer a chest pocket, if you ask for one.) But before you buy any aftermarket spray skirt, be sure to get the right size by first measuring the cockpit's opening.

Folbot.

You have little choice but to buy Folbot's own spraydeck and spray skirt setup. No aftermarket company makes the spraydeck, and the skirts are of a peculiar size for the cockpit hoops in the Folbot spraydeck. And Folbot's setup is so inexpensive that making your own custom substitute would cost almost as much as the original spray equipment.

Klepper.

This company offers you some real choices in spraydeck/spray skirt arrangements—three variations for both singles and doubles. The options offered for

the doubles, described below, are a good representation of the singles options as well.

The least expensive double, the Touring Spray Cover, is a one-piece affair with chimney-type openings for each paddler. You wrap the chimney material around yourself and secure it with snaps. The Touring cover connects to the coaming with stainless steel clips. This covering is not recommended, because it won't keep a dumping wave out of the boat, and if you ever capsized the Klepper, the cover would be hard to get back on.

The next spray-covering option is the Expedition Clip-on, which consists of a deck with a ringed opening for each paddler and separate spray skirts. The Expedition Clip-on is better than the Touring because of the individual spray skirts, but its clips won't hold securely if hit with heavy wave action. If the boat capsized, you would have a problem attaching the spray covering, and meanwhile more water could get dumped into the boat.

The preferred Klepper spray covering is the Arctic Tuckunder. It has a spraydeck and two spray skirts like the Expedition Clip-on Cover but relies on a tuck-under feature rather than clips. The hem of the deck has a bead that tucks under the coaming and into a groove on the hidden side. To attach the Tuckunder spraydeck, you partially inflate the sponsons with a

Klepper spraydeck and skirt.
(Walther/Klepper)

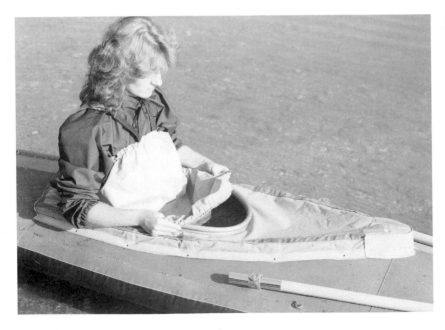

few puffs of air, tuck the bead into that underside groove—making certain to get all the hem into place—then finish inflating the sponsons. The cover stays tucked so tightly you can almost lift the boat by the spray cover alone. The downside to the Arctic Tuckunder is that you'll find it hard to access your stashed gear through individual cockpit openings. In the Clip-on version you can release a few clips and have ready access.

Klepper also offers a zippered spray skirt that allows access to things around you. This military-derived option costs more and is probably overkill. If you have to reach things, you can just pop the regular spray skirt to find what you need, achieving the same effect as a zipper.

Nautiraid.

Like Folbot, Nautiraid has only one offering in the spraydeck department, and it is peculiar enough not to be found on the aftermarket. You could use commercially available substitutes for the Nautiraid skirt if you want features like easy-release suspenders and handy stash pockets as described above under Feathercraft options.

Rudders

Most of the manufacturers don't offer you much choice here. Folbot, Klepper, and Nautiraid offer only one rudder option for their boats, both singles and doubles. You could make your own rudder but would probably have to buy a component or two to complete the job. (See Chapter 15.)

Feathercraft offers a top-notch rudder. Feathercraft is a major supplier of original-equipment rudders to numerous hardshell companies, so it has a good reputation in this department. Its flip-up surf rudder is a classic and comes as standard equipment on most Feathercraft models. It is easy to operate and comes with a device for lifting it out of the water from your cockpit. Once lifted out, the rudder lies securely out of the way in a holder on the rear deck. This is a distinct difference, because although the rudders on other foldables can be lifted out of the water, they aren't stowed on deck and out of harm's way. Instead, they hang a few inches above the water where they can get slapped around by waves and provide unwanted windage.

The other Feathercraft option available is a skeg, basically a non-turning rudder meant to help keep a boat tracking straight when hit by beam winds and waves. The skeg is the preferred option for the Short Touring Kayak.

The Feathercraft skeg can also be retrofitted onto other brands of foldables that don't come with rudders. The Nautiraid Mini-Raid accepts the Feathercraft skeg and requires only a few minutes to customize the attachment.

Sails

Generally, folding kayaks are good sailing vessels. All the manufacturers underline this fact by listing sails in their catalogs. Except for Klepper's, all of the sail offerings are downwind rigs, but for your convenience some manufacturers are happy to point you to outside sailmakers who can provide a full-range sail.

For example, Folbot has an excellent downwind sail that is capable of broad reaching (the wind coming from 45 degrees aft of the beam) and almost beam reaching (the wind coming from directly on the kayak's beam, or 90 degrees off the bow). It originally came from Balogh Sail Designs and was called the Twins, but it's now being made by another sailmaker directly for Folbot.

The big advantage of buying your sail rig through your folding-kayak manufacturer is that you'll know for certain that the rig works on your boat. If you buy from the aftermarket, you'll have to make sure the supplier has fittings to adapt their sail to your particular boat. Check on this before going through the expense.

Klepper's sails, which are made by the Klepper factory itself, give you a stepped-up approach to sailing; you can buy increasingly complex components as you build up toward a full-range sail rig capable of beating (going into the wind). The system revolves around one common mast and leeboard setup. You'll need the leeboard to do any beam reaching and beating. You can buy a jib, which will give you the ability to reach and to run downwind comfortably. Or you can get the M-1 sail, something like a mainsail, which is strictly a downwind affair. Then, the M-1 can be mated up with the jib to start giving you some upwind range. Better upwind performance comes from replacing the M-1 with a larger mainsail. The full sail rig is called the S-4.

The S-4 is a classic gaff-rig sail with a jib. Many thousands have been sold, especially years ago when the cost of buying both the boat and sail rig was so little that it made sense to go all the way. The S-4 is the most widely used kayak sail in recent kayaking history. It's a good sail that, like any rig, has its tricks. (See Chapter 12.) The S-4 has recently been facing some stiff competition from the aftermarket, which we'll look at later in this chapter.

Klepper is now making an interesting proprietary sail called the Freewind. It's basically a small downwind rig that can broad reach. Its key advantages are that it uses half of a paddle for its mast and is simple to set up. The sail area is small, but it's large enough to give any Klepper, even a loaded double, a boost when the wind is cooperating.

Carts

All the manufacturers offer boat carts that can be used either to move the assembled boat for long distances or to cart around the disassembled boat in its bags.

Unless you're buying one of the lightweight mini-folding kayaks, you'll probably need a cart at some point in your folding-kayak's lifetime. This type of cart is made to knock down quickly and stash away in your boat until it's needed again. It's especially handy for moving a cargo-laden folding kayak, and when you're traveling by train, a cart allows you to walk long distances through train stations with minimum effort. Look at Chapter 11 to see how to make best use of a cart for this and Chapter 13 for how to avoid damaging your boat when carting it assembled.

Boat cart, compass, anchor. *(Walther/Klepper)*

You're probably best off buying the cart offered by your own folding-kayak manufacturer, because you can be confident it will work with your boat. Some aftermarket carts may not function as well, and they may not withstand salt water. Carts designed for canoes are primarily meant for freshwater environments.

Essentials from the Aftermarket

Some of the essential equipment you'll need for paddling your foldable is best purchased in the aftermarket. While most of the folding-kayak companies offer paddles, you're better off getting them from other sources because they'll likely perform better.

However, if you deal with sources for non-folding kayaks, be aware of the differences between hardshell kayaks and foldables. Their advice about essential equipment may not always be the best for your foldable, because it's mainly geared to the requirements of hardshell paddlers.

Paddles

After purchasing your boat, which paddle you choose is your next most critical decision. Your paddle is what will put you in contact with the water and move your boat. Just as you would want the best hiking boots you can afford for the kinds of terrain you're likely to traverse, you shouldn't be thrifty when it comes to purchasing your paddle. A good paddle can make the difference between a pleasant day out on the water, covering great distances effortlessly, and a miserable time getting nowhere and hurting at the end of the day.

Paddling a foldable narrows your range of choices of this essential piece of equipment. First, obviously, you'll have to go with a take-apart paddle. No use having an eight-foot, one-piece paddle when you're planning to carry your boat in bags that measure half that length or less. Next, you'll have to select a longer paddle than you would for a rigid boat.

Paddle-length choices.

Since foldables tend to be a few inches wider than their hardshell counterparts, you'll need the longer length in order to clear your deck. For example, a typical single hardshell might be paddled with a 7½-foot paddle, perhaps even a smidgen shorter, while a folding single will require a half foot more. Double rigid kayaks rarely need even eight-foot paddles, while foldables may require paddles as long as 8½ feet.

Paddle length for foldables hinges on how much of the paddle is blade and how much is shaft. For example, Klepper's standard wooden paddles for its doubles are eight feet in overall length. The Camano is a great paddle, made for the aftermarket by Werner. But to use the Camano effectively with a double Klepper, you'll have to get an 8½-footer. The reason is that the blade portion of the Camano is not only narrower, but, more critically, it's longer. So all that extra blade length will hit the side of the Klepper—unless you get a longer Camano paddle.

One way to know how long an aftermarket paddle should be is to measure the shaft length of the paddle sold by the folding-kayak manufacturer. As long as the shaft lengths match, you can be sure to get the right length of paddle from an outside source.

You may find some shortcomings when using a longer paddle. You might not be able to keep up as great a stroke rate as you could with a shorter paddle because you have to swing through a wider arc. The longer paddle will also put more stress on your forearms. To compensate for both arc and stress, you'll have to develop some good paddling technique, which will be described at length in the next chapter.

What about paddles from folding-kayak manufacturers?

With the exception of Feathercraft's paddle option, you'll probably want to avoid what the manufacturers have to offer. Let's take these one at a time.

Klepper's wooden paddle is made by an outside source, and it's been used by many thousands of paddlers. But a Klepper paddler who tries one of the better aftermarket paddles usually buys one despite the high cost. Why? The Klepper paddle is heavy. Until recently, the shafts were round and on the fat side, making an awkward grip for your hand. Their shafts have now been made slightly more oval, but if you choose to feather your paddle, it will still be awkward and troublesome. (More about this in the next chapter.) The feathering angle built into the Klepper paddle is 90 degrees. This forces you to crank back excessively with your control-hand wrist to get the opposite blade in position, more so than you would have to with a feathering angle of 75 or 80 degrees.

Folbot's paddle shares some of the same handicaps. It is heavy and feathers at 90 degrees, not the wrist-saving 80 degrees or less you'll find in better paddles.

Feathercraft's optional paddle is significantly better than what the other folding manufacturers have for their customers. Made for Feathercraft by a well-respected Canadian paddle maker, it is light, has a better feathering angle, and breaks down into four pieces. Since Feathercraft's storage bags are shorter than those of other foldables, this paddle's shorter take-apart length is important. Also, you may not find as reliable a paddle as you will with the Feathercraft offering. The company has extensive experience with four-piece paddles. Another paddle manufacturer may offer to cut a four-piece for you, but you can't be absolutely certain this would be done in a manner that will hold up as well as the time-tested Feathercraft one.

Which are the best of the outside sources?

You can spend a lifetime trying out what's available from the many manufacturers, but your best bets are the few that have proved to work well with foldables.

The Camano by Werner, which we've already mentioned, is becoming the choice of folding kayakers who want the best in performance and rugged durability from their paddles. It also happens to be one of the top choices for hardshell paddlers as well.

The Camano is not inexpensive, but it's worth every dollar you spend on it. It has a fiberglass shaft and reinforced fiberglass blades that are asymmetrical so they don't pick up water when being lifted out at the end of the stroke—as would a more rounded or squared-off blade end. The shaft's springiness helps put more power into your stroke. The shaft is oval and slim, which helps your paddling technique and promotes a more relaxed grip on the paddle. It is also available in Kevlar for greater weight reduction, albeit at equally greater cost.

Another top choice in paddles is the Eddyline, either the Sea Swift, which is eight inches wide, or the Wind Swift, which is five inches wide. Both are lighter than the normal Camano. The shafts have gone through some changes and are now round instead of oval, but they're still choice paddles for foldables. Be careful about the length. Ordinarily you can't get them in anything longer than eight feet. The Sea Swift works slightly better with a double boat than does the Wind Swift because its blade is slightly shorter.

Personal Flotation Devices (life jackets)

Next to your paddle, your Personal Flotation Device, or PFD, is your most important boating acces-

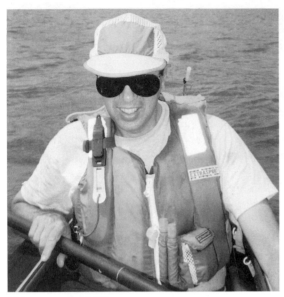

PFD, a must. *(Ian Giddy)*

sory. It may well save your life someday—*but only if you're wearing it.* It's an essential piece of safety equipment. Regardless of the nature of the water you're paddling, always wear your PFD. Otherwise, at that critical moment, it can't possibly work.

Unfortunately, paddlers who think of their folding kayaks as invincible don't always wear their PFDs. Why? The sensation of stability one gets in a large foldable lulls them into thinking that nothing can happen. Some paddlers will wear a PFD in a hardshell kayak but insist they don't have to wear it in a foldable. *Not Smart!*

Though foldables are certainly more stable than other sea kayaks, they can tip over. And, though folding kayaks are easier to climb back into than are rigid ones, why not gain the extra boost a PFD's buoyancy gives to your reentry effort? If you were injured in a capsize, wouldn't you appreciate that extra measure of protection keeping you afloat?

The common excuse some people give for not wearing a PFD at all times is that they can be uncomfortable in foldables. Folding kayaks have higher spraydecks and higher seats than do rigid kayaks. When you wear a spray skirt in a folding kayak, your PFD will often ride up uncomfortably.

However, there's at least one fine PFD on the market that works well in foldables—the Extrasport Seaker. The Seaker has several features that make it a great PFD for sea kayaking, especially in a foldable kayak. It's short body length doesn't interfere with spray skirts and, for the most part, doesn't ride up on the wearer. The Seaker may ride up a bit on some short-waisted people, but not so much as do other PFDs.

The Seaker is nicely set up for gadgets. Its principal pocket can carry an emergency space blanket, signal mirror, waterproof matches, and a small spare compass. It has special sleeves to hold a dye marker and flares, and above that you'll find a slotted tab for attaching an emergency knife or strobe light, whichever you require. The zipper pull is a good place to tie an emergency whistle.

It comes in a wide range of colors. The yellow or orange gives you the greatest visibility, which is important if you're about to be run down by another boat. If you pick another color, you can improve your visibility by wearing a bright hat, taping reflective strips onto the vest, or using paddles with brightly colored blades.

Feathercraft in Canada makes a PFD that compares to the Seaker in performance and comfort. It's as short as the Seaker and has extremely good workmanship, beveled foam panels, fine stitching, etc. The Feathercraft PFD comes only in yellow, because Canada requires that all PFDs be either that color or international orange for optimum visibility.

Unfortunately, the Feathercraft vest isn't sold directly in the U.S., because it hasn't gone through the U.S. Coast Guard's elaborate, expensive testing needed to pass muster for use in the U.S. One problem might be its two very large pockets. When approving PFDs, the Coast Guard assumes the worst—and probably with good reason. When determining how much flotation any particular vest can provide, the Coast Guard fills all pockets with lead weights.

Flotation Bags

Flotation bags, or air bags, are a must for any folding kayak. Foldables do not have bulkheads, which are underdeck walls that create watertight compartments in the fore and aft areas. Fiberglass kayaks generally do have bulkheads and therefore don't require flotation

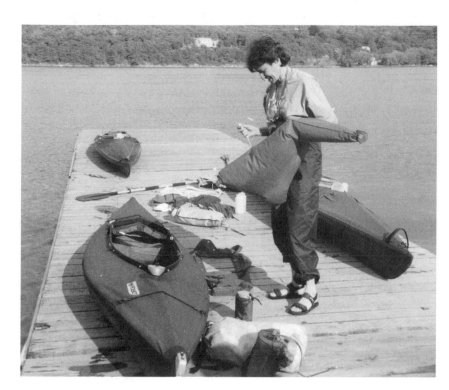

Adding flotation to a Folbot Aleut.

bags. Even so, some hardshell paddlers use them as a back up. In plastic boats, flotation bags are also a must, because their bulkheads tend to come loose and compromise the integrity of their supposedly watertight compartments.

In the event of a capsize, a boat equipped with flotation bags takes on much less water. The upright boat will ride higher and be more buoyant. And emptying it will take a lot less time and energy. A single foldable can fill up with more than 80 gallons of water; a double can take on 150 gallons or more. That's a lot of pumping.

Many people don't use air bags because of their naive belief that the air sponsons are enough. They are not. Read Chapter 10 for the details about rescue drills and dealing with a swamped boat. The only time you can safely venture out without air bags is when you have the underdeck areas so completely loaded with camping gear that the gear will displace any water that might want to enter the boat in a capsize. Of course, the gear can only do that job if it's stowed in waterproof storage bags.

Some manufacturers sell air bags for their boats, but they tend to be of marginal use. Folbot's are simply too small; they wouldn't displace much water. Klepper's are also on the small side. Both are constructed of lightweight vinyl that appears flimsy.

For flotation bags, turn to the aftermarket. Two good choices are Aquaterra and Voyageur. Aquaterra sells a fairly inexpensive set of air bags called Sea Kayak Standard Flotation Bags that work well in double and single folding kayaks. They won't fill all the underdeck area, but they're large enough to reduce the amount of water that would need to be pumped out after a capsize.

Voyageur's flotation bags are more costly but better-made than Aquaterra's. Voyageur is heavily into the dry-bag business and has a good reputation in this area. Voyageur air bags come in several sizes. Measure your foldable's underdeck area, then check with Voyageur for the appropriate size. Voyageur specifies sizes for hardshell sea and whitewater kayaks but doesn't seem to chart requirements for foldables. Go for a bag that will fill the length of your underdeck area. Don't worry if the Voyageur bag may be wider than your underdeck width, because you can compensate by not quite filling it.

Bailers and Pumps

Bailers and pumps are necessary safety items for any kayaker. They're doubly important in a foldable, because, in the event of a capsize, the relatively large interior space could fill with a huge amount of water. If the flotation bags covered above are "preventive medicine," then pumps and bailers are your "first aid" or remedial measures. They should always be on board.

A bailer is a handy way to extract water quickly, but you won't find a single one on the market. Make your own from a pail, plastic bleach bottle, or almost any large, unbreakable beverage container made for refrigerator storage.

Hand pumps are available on the aftermarket and are inexpensive. Look for one with a cylinder large enough to do some good, about two inches in diameter. The hand pump should also have a flotation collar in case it falls overboard. Aquaterra makes a good one that is available just about everywhere.

Electric pumps are sold in marine-supply stores as electric bilge pumps for small craft, and they cost more than hand pumps. Operating on flashlight batteries, an electric pump is good for getting rid of several hundred gallons of water, that is until its batteries need replacement. The pumping rate is less than you can do by hand, but because it requires no effort on your part, an electric pump will work while you

paddle for shore. Like anything electric or electronic around a small boat, electric pumps can fail. Some cynics store them in their bailing buckets.

Klepper makes a hand-operated bilge pump that fits into a special cut in the keel board of a double, just in front of one of the paddlers. This is a military-specification item. If you feel you absolutely need one, you can probably coax it out of the company as a special order.

Handy-to-Have Items

The wise paddler would never venture out without the basic gear discussed above. But, depending on what you are doing, you might also want to include some of the handy items discussed below.

Side Bags

One advantage of a folding kayak is that you have accessible storage room around you for things you might want to get at while on the water—without having to land to dig them out from underdeck areas. The crossribs in the cockpit area are ready made for attaching specialty side bags that can keep such needed items handy.

Two good side bags are available on the aftermarket. The first is made by a company in Alaska and goes under the model name Kaipak bag. It comes in two widths, one to fit in Nautiraids, the other to fit in the rest of the foldables that have greater space between ribs. The Kaipak attaches to the crossribs alongside you with Fastex snap buckles and adjustable straps. The Kaipak is made of waterproof nylon with no seams at the bottom, so the bag can take splash and even sit in bilge water. However, its two-way zipper is not waterproof, so you must use Ziploc bags to protect any items you need to stay dry. Each bag can hold almost as much as a day pack. You can keep handy a rain jacket and pants, rain hat, a wool hat, socks, and gloves, plus a medium-weight polypropylene top, bottom, and gloves. You'll probably want a pair of these side bags, so you can keep the second bag filled with sunglasses, sunscreen, repair kit, lunch, flashlight, flares, toilet paper, first aid kit, and other items from the 38 essentials you should always have in any sea kayak (see sidebar).

SealLine, formerly Cascade Designs, offers a similar but less cavernous one, The Access Bag. It's made

Military pump for Klepper Quattro. *(Walther/Klepper)*

of vinyl and has a zipper that's almost waterproof. The bag attaches just like the Kaipak does. An earlier version of this bag failed to hold up in the zipper area, was withdrawn from the market, and has been reintroduced. It still may not be as good as the Kaipak in overall performance and durability.

With its boats, Klepper issues small canvas bags that fit on special hooks built into the cockpit area. At best, these small bags can carry some sunscreen, sunglasses, and a pair of gloves. Klepper sells a larger bag to fit in the same area, this one made of waterproof material, but because it closes with just snaps, water will definitely find its way inside—under some conditions. The larger bag is not available in North America, but you may get a pair by beseeching your local dealer.

Compass mount with a Silva UN 70 compass. *(Michael Skott)*

Dry Storage Bags

All the camping gear you take on a trip should be placed in watertight storage bags. This is true not only of folding kayaks, which have no waterproof compartments, but also of hardshells, which invariably let in some water—no matter what their manufacturers claim.

Numerous dry storage bags are common on the aftermarket, where they range in price, durability, and effectiveness. SealLine, Voyageur, Colorado Kayak Supply (CKS), and Northwest River Supplies are among the reliable brands. You can find specific advice on using storage bags in Chapter 13.

Compass and Compass Mounts

You should have a compass with you, even if you don't plan to be far from the sight of land. A sudden fog or rain squall will quickly limit your sightlines. At such times your compass will be your only means of finding your way. Because you can't permanently mount a compass to a foldable as easily as you can to the deck of a rigid boat, the task is more complex. Luckily, foldable-kayak owners have a range of compasses and mounting methods to choose from.

Start your search by seeing what your folding-kayak manufacturer has to offer. Because its compass comes with its own device for mounting to your boat, choosing that brand will save you the hassle of improvising something. For example, the Silva UN 70 is an excellent steering compass that you can also pull out of its holder to use as a hand-bearing compass.

(You can also buy this excellent compass at marine supply stores.) Klepper sells various compass boards for using this compass on either single or double boats.

Some of the smaller marine compasses can be mounted to your deck with bungee cords. If you have D-rings around your cockpit area, attachment is a cinch. If not, you'll have to improvise. On some foldables with spraydecks, you may be able to permanently attach a light compass to the fabric by screwing it through to some backing material that will keep the compass in position and water out of the cockpit.

Anchors and Sea Anchors

Anchors and sea anchors are handy devices. In some situations, they become not only handy—but eminently necessary.

Don't get a heavy anchor, because you'll be lugging it around when traveling with your foldable. The type of light dinghy anchor found in marine shops will work well. Avoid any anchor with sharp ends that could poke at the fabric of your foldable. You could also improvise a utility anchor by filling a small stuff sack or mesh bag with rocks, but you'll have to remember to pick up the rocks before you shove off from shore.

Sea anchors have proved their worth in many circumstances by helping you hold your position and rest when the wind is trying to push you back. During a rescue situation, deploying your sea anchor

What Should Always Be in Your Boat

You might get away with bringing along very little. Just jump in your foldable with a can of Coke and a couple of sour balls in your pocket, and on many of your outings you'll be okay. But what about other times? Sour balls and Coke can't repair anything, won't help you find your way if you're lost in fog, and make lousy signaling devices—unless you can make enough noise by rattling the sour balls in the Coke can.

To meet all of the vagaries of kayaking, you'll either have to carry the essentials listed below or travel with someone who does.

Some items need explaining. First are the **absolute essentials.** The assumption is that, like your American Express card, you should never leave your launch site without them. These are the items that keep your boat floating, and moving, water on the outside. They keep your internal engine fueled and lubricated, and let you know where you are and where you're headed.

All items on this list that could be damaged or compromised by getting wet should be packed in whichever form of watertight bags or containers you prefer. The special side bags previously mentioned in this chapter are a handy place to carry these absolute essentials. Or, if you want to put them in a large fanny pack, you can keep the pack either strapped around you or very accessible and easily removable. Or you could thread the strap of the fanny pack through the arm holes of your PFD, thus keeping the pack on your back.

In the **repair section**, the Leatherman tool is an unusually important component. Much better than a Swiss Army knife, this tool has real screwdrivers, pliers, wire cutters, a functional file, and a knife. For any folding kayak—with all kinds of fittings and brackets—the Leatherman is an all-in-one must. Gerber makes a similar device.

Other spare parts listed in the repair section will depend on which model of folding kayak you have and which of its components has the greatest probability of breaking. Your dealer or distributor may help you with this. The dental floss isn't just for your nice smile, and the leather laces aren't just for your shoes. Both these items can be used with duct tape to secure or repair broken ribs, stringers, and more. (See Chapter 16.)

Extra clothes are a must, even in the blazing days of summer. If you've ever been caught in a July hailstorm, when you're chilled to the bone by plummeting temperatures, you'll understand why extra clothes become essential.

will help stabilize your boat by keeping it pointed into the wind, which is the least vulnerable position for reentry.

Many sea anchors are available, some quite cheaply at marine shops. Your best bet, however, is the more costly Drift Stopper made by Boulter of Earth. It works well in a kayak and has proved its durability. The Drift Stopper is easy to deploy and retrieve. Many hardshell kayakers are using them for keeping their position in heavy winds. There are various ways to mount the Drift Stopper to your boat. With a large-cockpit foldable, the best way is to snake the sea anchor's holding line under your spraydeck and connect it to a rib. On Feathercrafts, loop the connecting line around the coaming.

Other Sail Rigs

Folding-kayak manufacturers usually list sails in their catalogs, as mentioned earlier. However, if you want a rig from the aftermarket that performs exceedingly well, look at what Balogh Sail Designs (BSD) has to offer.

BSD has become a supplier to hardshell manufacturers because of its reliable outrigger system. Known as B.O.S.S., for Balogh Outrigger Stabilizing System, it allows the hardshells to be sailed upwind

It's a big list, 38 items altogether, and that's just for ordinary day trips. Major crossings might require a marine radio, running lights, and other additions. The items listed weigh as much as five to eight pounds, not counting any of the absolute essentials. Since you have to heft all this on your back, it's easy to say, "Why bother?" But consider this. In the fickle environment that is the sea, these items will give you an edge and make an uncomfortable situation more tolerable. And once in all your paddling days, they may make the difference between life and death.

Absolute Essentials
- PFD
- spare paddle or paddle leash
- extra flotation
- water
- food
- chart and compass
- pump, bailer, sponge
- spray skirt

Extra Clothes
- bandanna
- wind or spray pants
- wind or paddle jacket
- socks
- shirt
- warm top
- gloves or pogies
- hats, wool and rain
- sunscreen, lip balm
- sunglasses
- toilet paper
- weather radio

Emergencies
- windproof/waterproof matches
- fire starter
- small tarp
- energy bars
- space blanket
- signal mirror
- flares
- flashlight
- whistle
- first-aid kit
- knife

Repair
- boat repair kit
- spares for break-prone parts
- Leatherman tool
- parachute cord
- dental floss
- leather shoelaces
- duct tape

using the Balogh Batwing rig. Balogh also specializes in fitting the Batwing to foldable kayaks. It provides mounting hardware for all the major foldables that have open cockpits, i.e. Folbot, Klepper, and Nautiraid. BSD has also experimented with fitting the Batwing to Feathercrafts. By the time you read this, you may be able to fit one to your boat.

The Batwing is a very powerful sail that is cambered like a windsurfer's sail using adjustable battens. The Batwing comes in various sizes to suit both single and double foldables. Its reefing zippers and snap-buckled straps allow you to decrease the sail area in a hurry if winds get too strong for the full sail.

Balogh also makes an excellent downwind sail called the Twins that is extremely stable because most of its power face lies low on the mast where it's least likely to unbalance your boat in a wayward gust. This sail rig looks like a child's kite, but upside down. You can double it over to make a triangular sail that can broad reach and almost beam reach.

Other Items

Every other sea kayaking manual will tell you that you'll need a paddle float for your kayak. A paddle float is an inflatable bladder that you attach to one end of your paddle to use as an outrigger for getting back into your boat after a capsize. A paddle float is necessary with hardshells, which otherwise would be nearly impossible to reenter after a capsize, unless a second boat is positioned to stabilize the first. But because foldables are easier to reenter from the water, paddle floats are largely unnecessary for them. However, you may want to have one in case of extreme conditions.

You should have deck lines. This safety device allows you to grab onto your boat when you are in the water. A few foldables—Feathercraft Elite models and the Klepper Quattro—come equipped with deck lines. If your boat doesn't, consider buying your own. While the decks of foldables give you more grabbing surface for hanging on than do sleek hardshells, you'll find that deck lines give you added insurance. Tie the line at one end or the other, loop it through the deck fitting at the opposite end, and then back to near your position in the cockpit area. This will give you something to hang onto while you disembark for landing.

Protective Clothing for Winter Paddling

Paddling in northern climates can always involve the possibility of hypothermia unless you're equipped to be immersed in cold water. All too often folding-kayak paddlers who somehow feel immune to the forces of nature don't prep for cold water—don't even wear PFDs—on the theory that nothing bad can ever happen in a folding kayak because of its great stability.

Not true. Folding kayaks go over. Perhaps it's only infrequently, but if it happened to you, you'd certainly wish you had been prepared.

Canoeists have long been fond of wearing woolens and rain gear during cool-weather paddling. Some of this gear has a long history behind it. Shackleton's expedition survived several years of Antarctic travel after its ship was crushed in polar ice. The explorers wore heavy woolens and Burberry rain gear.

Even if you are as hardy as a polar explorer, don't bet your life on rain gear and wool fibers. When the water is cold (experts vary on the precise cautionary level, but below 50°F to 55°F), you've got four choices:

Don't venture out.
Wear a neoprene wet suit.
Don a dry suit.
Wear a special diver's suit.

Wet Suits and What They Do

A wet suit is your cheapest and most basic survival alternative. It is made of 3-millimeter-thick neoprene. Farmer John-type wet suits generally cost about $100-

$120 and come with a front-entry zipper. They allow a thin layer of water to penetrate the material and be held close to your skin, where the water is warmed by your body heat and insulated by the neoprene.

A wet suit must be tight to keep the layer of water thin. How tight? You should be unable to gather the material when you clasp the suit with your hand, except in the crotch area and behind the knees. But it shouldn't be so tight that your breathing is severely hampered.

For comfort, wear a thin polypropylene or polyester (Thermax, Capilene, etc.) shirt underneath the top portion of the wet suit. Don't wear long-john bottoms underneath, because they won't help insulate very well and also make it harder to put on the wet suit in the first place. Slick Lycra tights will work OK if you feel a need for an extra layer. To keep warm while paddling in cold weather, wear insulation layers, such as a pile jacket, over the wet suit. Over that wear a paddling jacket (waterproof material, neoprene neck and wrist gaskets) or a dry top (waterproof material, latex gaskets). For comfort when on land, wear pants that are windproof or waterproof. Neoprene has a chilling effect when wind blowing across its surface rapidly evaporates any water or sweat.

The Dry-Suit Phenomenon

Dry suits work on an entirely different principle—they keep the water out. They're made of loose-fitting waterproof material with tighter gaskets at the neck, wrists and ankles. In one-piece suits, access is generally through a waterproof front zipper. A two-piece suit has a means of mating the top and bottom, usually overlapping latex material that is rolled tightly for waterproofing.

Some water may enter a dry suit, but you're more likely to get damp from your own sweat than from the half cup of water that will creep in during a day's outing. You are insulated from contact with the cold by your layers of insulated clothing. Synthetic tops and bottoms worn inside the dry suit can be of varying thickness, depending on the water's temperature.

Dry suits cost about $300-$350 each, but they're worth the expense for at least two reasons: 1) they are more comfortable to wear, since they're less restrictive than neoprene; 2) they will protect you longer if you're exposed to cold water.

You may tend to build up sweat within the suit, but you won't feel cold or clammy because no air can pass over you to cool you down. You hit what dry-suit paddlers call "a relative, happy humidity level" within the suit. One fabric that seems to work well as an underlayer to keep you feeling drier is Polartek 100. The fabric, which is available in a number of brands of clothing, does a fantastic job of wicking moisture away from your skin surface to the product's outer layer. The layer next to your skin will always feel dry.

Dry suits also come in Gore-Tex, which is breathable and theoretically will keep you drier. Some comments: It's more expensive, about $500 per suit. Salt water has long been thought to contaminate Gore-Tex, rendering it useless. While the manufacturer claims this problem has been solved, there have been reports of such leakage. Instructions that come with the suit recommend you rinse it with fresh water after each use. Your PFD will reduce the advantage of Gore-Tex by reducing its breathability, as would your spray skirt. Gore-Tex works by letting moisture out through microscopic membrane holes that are too small to let water molecules in. But it takes heat

to drive the moisture through the membrane, your precious body heat. You'll chill faster.

Light Scuba Suits

You have another option beyond wet and dry suits—one of the miracle products that are being sewn into special suits for scuba divers. Two viable choices for kayakers are suits made by SSA (818-376-0402) that use three-layer Darlexx Thermalastic, and suits made by Henderson (609-825-4771) and others that are based on a special three-layer fabric that incorporates Polartek 100.

These special diver suits are sometimes called tropical diving suits to distinguish them from those meant for cold-water dives. Don't let that throw you off. The suits are equivalent to two millimeters of neoprene in the protection they provide, and can be brought up to the same three-millimeter protection as normal wet suits by adding special vests, bought separately. Your PFD also adds insulation.

The specialty suits have several advantages over wet suits. They are less restrictive, virtually windproof, and breathable, while being somewhat waterproof. They cost just a bit more than wet suits, around $150. The two types (Darlexx and Polartek) consist of three layers: an outer shell, a waterproof barrier sheet in between, and fuzzy insulation material next to your skin.

They seem to be more of a viable option for folding kayakers than for rigid ones. The odds of going over in a folding kayak are much slimmer than in rigid kayaks. And, the quicker rescue possible in a foldable means less time hanging out in cold water risking hypothermia. Even the two-millimeter versions of these specialty suits (i.e., sans vest) will give enough measure of protection for survival. Since so many paddlers are reluctant to put on confining wet suits, the specialty suits are a reasonable and practical answer to safety needs. If you go this route, opt for a looser fit than a dive shop is likely to specify. Such shops are thinking of divers, not kayakers who need to have freedom of upper-body movement while paddling. Even slightly loose, the suits will work in cold

(continued)

water to keep you alive until you can get back into your boat.

Other Considerations

Although pogies (special mittens that attach to the paddle) are great protection for your hands while paddling in cold weather, they'll be useless if you capsize. Neoprene gloves tend to be awkward and constrictive. If using neoprene gloves, get a larger size to compensate for this. Dish-washing gloves with liners are another possible solution.

For protecting your feet, wear neoprene booties. Most people like to wear liner socks inside the booties. A synthetic liner with a wool middle layer would be a good idea. The non-zippered booties work best, because they let in so little water. Zippered booties leak but are easier to put on, and they can be dried out more quickly.

Regarding headgear, wool hats and detachable non-down-insulated hoods from winter jackets are fine. Hardshell paddlers wear neoprene hoods, because they plan to roll to self-rescue in a capsize. As a folding kayaker, you'll come out of your kayak and, for the most part, your head will remain out of the water.

Bring along a thermos full of hot tea, soup, or cocoa. Plan trips that cover smaller areas or that don't require too much time. Cut short your trip if there's any possibility of adverse weather. Stormy winter seas are more fierce than their summertime counterparts.

- *Become a Competent Sea Kayaker*
- *Benefit from a Foldable's Inherent Seaworthiness*
- *Learn How to Paddle Efficiently for Sustained Time on the Water*

PART TWO

Handling Skills for Foldables

A folding kayak helps make you a better sea kayaker from the moment you step into one. Freed of worry about balance and stability, you are quickly on your way to becoming a proficient paddler. You can concentrate on developing the most important paddling technique of all, an efficient, sustainable forward stroke.

When the chips are down, a folding kayak enhances your efforts to weather rough conditions. Built-in seaworthiness magnifies the effectiveness of your repertoire of support and maneuvering strokes. If you're in situations over your head, these boats will help see you through, as they have thousands of paddlers before you.

If catastrophe calls and you do capsize, folding kayaks greatly simplify the recovery process. They are exceptionally easy to reenter without the aid of other boats or the need for special devices.

This section of the book aims at making you a competent sea kayaker. It focuses not only on the single paddler but also a group generally overlooked in most manuals, those who venture forth in double kayaks. Paddling techniques, maneuvering strokes, and rescue routines are explained for both singles and doubles. This section will also help you in the life-long process of becoming a savvy mariner, one who grasps that knowing how to avoid trouble is more important than knowing how to get out of it.

CHAPTER 6

Paddling Techniques: The Forward Stroke and Other Essentials

Learning to paddle a folding kayak involves goals and considerations that are very different from those needed to paddle a rigid boat. The gulf that exists between the two worlds is vast.

Other sea-kayaking manuals, which teach paddling skills exclusively for rigid kayaks, devote several chapters and many pages to the often-needed *defensive* paddling strokes for those boats. They go into elaborate descriptions of bracing strokes (high and low) that keep you from tipping, various ways of sculling to keep your rigid boat afloat on its side for severe conditions, and a number of variations of the Eskimo roll needed when you do capsize.

Although these instructions may be fascinating reading, they don't apply as much to a folding kayak, because its first line of defense is its inherent stability and seaworthiness. You can't reliably roll a folding kayak, certainly not as a real-life self-rescue method. (The air sponsons along each side of a foldable tend to resist the action of an Eskimo roll, as does the basic width of these boats.) And because its wider beam positions you so far from the side of the boat, sculling is difficult beyond a certain angle. When you try to put a foldable on its side to scull, your body is higher than your paddle, which creates a precarious, plunging angle to the sculling motion. Bracing strokes, while useful to learn, are less applicable to a stable folding kayak. Besides, the bracing strokes you may want to use in a foldable are more simple.

It's too bad most manuals have you dedicating so much time to defensive strokes such as the Eskimo roll. While trying to perform these strokes correctly, you may get distracted from perfecting the most important stroke in sea kayaking, the forward stroke, the motion that gets you where you want to go. The forward stroke lies at the heart of sea kayaking and is one of its chief sources of pleasure. Being on the water in a foldable allows you to concentrate on the forward stroke without worrying about the arsenal of defensive moves required by a rigid kayak.

The forward stroke looks deceptively easy but has many subtleties that you'll also learn in this chapter. You'll learn the brace strokes you may find handy in a foldable, particularly a smaller one. And you'll learn how to use your paddle to make quick turns without a rudder. The strokes described below are meant to be used with single folding kayaks (that's a Feathercraft K-1 in the photos in this chapter). Chapter 8 explains how to adjust them for doubles.

The Forward Stroke

Anyone who looks at paddling as a chore, a necessary evil of venturing in a touring kayak, is missing one of sea kayaking's less obvious pleasures. The forward stroke is a form of enchantment. It involves fluid and powerful movements of the body that make you feel alive and that blend your landbound being smoothly with the watery element that makes up most of our planet. When you have the forward stroke right, the miles and hours pass in an intoxicating trance of dance-like rhythm. A folding kayak is an especially good place to fall under this spell, because you can concentrate on forward paddling with less concern for balancing your boat.

Not as Simple as It Seems

The forward stroke looks simple enough. You hold both hands out in front of you on the shaft of a two-bladed kayak paddle. Dip Blade A in the water and move it alongside you while swinging Blade B forward through the air. Then the process is repeated, only this time Blade B dips into the water and Blade A gets airborne.

Many novice paddlers do it just that way, without much thought or control of the process. After a short time on the water, they tire, they hurt. Though they may be getting a kick out of being afloat and communing with nature, they're not enjoying the paddling experience itself, because they've failed to grasp the underlying complexity of the forward stroke.

Newcomers are not the only kayakers who, lured by the deceptively simple appearance of the forward stroke, overlook its intricacies. Many seasoned paddlers also miss the nuances, particularly those in folding kayaks. Since the boats are so simple to enter and take off in, it's easy to forget to develop basic skills, starting with the forward stroke. Paddlers may go along for years puttering through the motions but not

Feathering May Have the Edge in a Foldable

Early on, you'll have to make a choice between feathering your paddle or using it unfeathered. This decision is generally a toss-up, but feathering may actually have the edge when you're paddling a foldable.

A feathered paddle has its blades roughly at right angles to each other, and you use your control hand to turn each blade for proper entry into the water. The shaft rotates freely in the non-control hand. Whether you're right-handed or not, feathered paddles are generally right-hand controlled, only because you seldom can find paddles that make provision for feathering with left-hand control.

Unfeathered paddles have the blades in line with each other. You use each hand to turn the blades to the correct entry angle.

Supposedly, feathering is rough on the forearm and wrist on your control-hand side. That's why some people unfeather their paddles. However, the damage that comes with feathering is more the result of two different factors, not overuse of the control hand.

One, the feathering angle could be too great. You can avoid arm injury if the feather angle is less than 90 degrees. More paddles now come with feathering of 80 degrees or less. This reduces how much you have to cock back your control hand to get the opposite blade into the correct water-entry angle.

Two, incorrect paddling skills cause stress. If you learn good paddling technique as described in this chapter, you're not likely to hurt yourself even when paddling long distances. Proper balance of the elements of the forward stroke and relaxing both hands will reduce stress on the control hand and forearm.

Feathering may be your best bet for paddling a folding kayak because a foldable heightens feathering's key advantage, and at the same time it reduces your need for the benefit of unfeathering. Even foes of feathering recognize that a feathered paddle gives an advantage to any kayak paddling into the wind. The feathered blade running through the air has its edge forward to slice through the wind's resistance. Feathering in these conditions is more efficient. Unfeathered paddling into the wind is harder because the broad side of the upper blade is being pushed through the wind. Because folding kayaks require longer paddles and wider and higher arcs, unfeathering is even tougher.

In hardshells, feathered blades increase the risk of a capsize in heavy crosswinds, because the wind can catch the broad side of the blade as it swings through the air. Unfeathered paddles offer less surface area for crosswinds to bite on. But since foldables are inherently more stable than rigid boats, there is less risk of being upended by crosswinds if feathering.

really getting the power and enjoyment they might if they were to perfect the stroke.

A lot is happening in the forward stroke; it's not just muscling through the motions. Onlookers from the deck of a powerboat may laud what they think is your enormous upper-body strength making your boat move. Go ahead, bask in the macho image, but don't pump up those muscles. Relax them and put your mind into the stroke.

The description that follows dissects the forward stroke into its components and analyzes what is going on at each step of the movement. Even as you study the points, though, try to remember that the forward stroke takes place as much in your head as in your body. You have to be thinking it to get the most out of the technique.

One of the thoughts that should be going through your mind is that, during the forward stroke, your blade has very little longitudinal movement in the water. Instead, you are attempting to use your whole paddle to pry your boat forward through the water. The key to a good forward stroke is enhancing whatever leveraging force you can apply to that prying effort.

Your Physical Components

Many parts of your body come into play during the stroke. Here's what each part should be doing to get the most sustained and powerful output from paddling a foldable boat.

Torso or trunk.

Most manuals start off by talking about your hands and arms, but the true center and most critical component is your trunk. Your torso should be relaxed, loose enough to rotate freely with each stroke.

You should be thrusting one shoulder ahead into the *push* part of the stroke, swinging from the hip. It's more like throwing a punch than a swimming motion. Your other shoulder should be moving back, leading through the *pull* part of the stroke. Your shoulders should never remain perpendicular to the line of travel of the kayak. They should be pivoting around an imaginary rod running down through the center of your head to your seat.

Always paddle from your trunk, because your biggest muscles—lower back, shoulders, hips, stomach—are located here. These big muscles are less likely to fatigue than are your arms and forearms.

Arnold Schwarzenegger would give out before Mother Teresa if he were using just his arms and she were putting her full body into her paddle stroke.

Since the deck of a foldable is usually higher than that of a rigid boat, more of the paddler's body resides below the cockpit rim. Therefore, foldable paddlers are less prone to using their full bodies, instead relying heavily on arm movement. Don't forget body rotation in your paddling movements.

Legs.

These too should figure decisively into the stroke. Your legs should be flexing and relaxing with each stroke. To use your legs properly you must brace or press your feet against some support.

You should be pushing or pressing on the foot *opposite* the shoulder that is pushing the airborne blade. This bracing action by the foot locks your body in position to deliver all the power of the stroke to the forward movement of the boat. Avoid thinking of this foot action as pressing on the same side as the blade being pulled through the water. That thought could make you focus too much on pulling the paddle and not enough on the upper-body push on the paddle shaft. *Diagonal thinking* is better than linear thinking in this case.

Feathercrafts have adjustable foot pedals to press against, even without using a rudder. Most other folding kayaks do not. It is important that your feet be pushing against some rib, and your knees should be bent or flexed, not straightened out fully. If, while your knees are bent, your feet don't rest on a rib, you should talk with your dealer. He or she may already have a device that fits the purpose or could help you improvise something.

Hands.

Keep your hands relaxed at all times, except possibly when heavy winds threaten to steal your paddle from your grip. Use a flat palm to push the shaft on the side cutting through the air, and keep your fingers open as if you wanted someone behind you to count them. Rest the shaft in the cupped fingers of the other hand to pull the blade that's going through the water. Don't have all your fingers of either hand tightly wrapped around the shaft. At most, let your thumb crook around the shaft.

A death-grip on the paddle tires the muscles of the forearm and biceps. Hand relaxation is a bit easier in a folding kayak, since you don't need to keep as tightly gripped for possible bracing as you would in a hardshell.

You should also keep your hand, wrist, and forearm in a fairly flat plane. Avoid cocking your wrist too far back at an acute angle. Look at it this way: a watch on that wrist should be more visible to God than to a paddler behind you.

Arms.

Many people try to paddle with their arms crooked throughout the paddling motion. That's a waste of your muscles and will lead to fatigue and possibly injury.

Your pulling arm should actually be fairly straight for moving the blade that is in the water. Pull the paddle by using your rotating shoulder and trunk to move the straight arm backward. By keeping the arm straight with the elbow almost locked, you make effective use of muscles in your stomach, back, and shoulder. The straightened arm acts like a lever to transmit the power of these strong muscles to the pulling motion. The straight arm also discourages heavy dependence on the weaker arm muscles for power. Rely on your arm's bone structure more than its muscles.

Your pushing arm obviously starts from a bent position, but you should straighten it out as you move the upper blade through the air. Then let the upper shoulder continue to push the extended, straightened-out arm as far as is comfortable. Again, as in the pulling process, the straightened arm transmits the power of your back and shoulder through bone structure while making only minimal use of arm muscles.

The Control Center

Your head is the control center, the computer that tells all the physical components what they should be doing at every moment. Your head should be making minute adjustments throughout your hours on the water, and it should be keeping some factors constant. You don't have to be thinking about every step all the time. But do think them through enough so that you can put everything on automatic pilot.

You'll be adjusting the physical components in two ways. One, obviously, will be accounting for changing winds and sea conditions to keep your boat moving smoothly. You'll also be making small changes to shift the workload among all the muscles in your body. Sometimes, for example, you'll be using your legs strongly for a few minutes to reduce the load on your torso. Or you may let your arm muscles do the work for a two-minute burst in order to rest other parts of your body.

The factors to keep constant are elements of the stroke that give good prying grip in the water to move the boat ahead.

Here are some of the principal things your brain will be monitoring and fine-tuning:

The push and pull phases.

You may have picked up from some instructor or manual the need to be doing both pushing and pulling at the same time. They usually suggest some fixed amount of effort for the push and so much for the pull, such as 35 percent push, 65 percent pull. Don't lock yourself into any static split of effort.

You should be making constant adjustment between pull and push. Sometimes the push will be 80 percent, other times the pull will be 80 percent. See what feels good, stick with that for awhile, then adjust the split so you don't fatigue any particular muscle group. Play with the tuning knobs feeding those push-pull instructions to your body, just as you might adjust the sound balance on your stereo tuner.

Even within each part of the stroke, do some monitoring and adjusting. For example, in the push phase, stretch out your arm a bit farther than normal for a few strokes. Or for a few moments don't rotate your torso quite as much as you've been doing.

You may gain some mastery by thinking solely of either the pushing or the pulling during your stroke. For example, concentrate for a few strokes on just pushing the blade through the air, and ignore the pull. You'll be pulling anyway to some degree. This focus will sharpen the powerful pushing phases. Then think for a few moments of just the pull. Switching your tuner will help you get a feel for the right balance for prevailing conditions. If you're paddling into the wind, which is covered in greater detail in Chapter 7, you may find that a greater proportion of push works better than a 50-50 balance. The ratio should never be constant for any length of time.

Fluid versus explosive movements.

Some manuals tell you to be smooth and fluid in your motion. True, your motions should be fluid, but they also should be explosive. Both can exist in the same plane, and you should be training your body to do both.

Overall, you should have fluid movement in all parts of the forward stroke. Fluid motion is easy on the muscles. But explosive motion is easy on the muscles, too. It gives them rest during non-explosive stages.

As your blade gets set in the water and your leverage is right, as explained below, you should move the paddle through with an explosive burst of power. Then relax all your muscles as you get set to place the other blade smoothly into the water. Meanwhile your muscles begin coiling up for their next burst of explosive power. You can vary how explosive you want these bursts to be. It's a good idea to keep power bursts short and to concentrate on staying relaxed between them. You can also go long periods without power bursts. But do make certain to put some bursts into your stroke.

Explosive power with rest periods as the muscles wind up is similar to what marathon runners and long-distance cross-country skiers do. The marathoner's foot hits the pavement with an explosive burst and takes off; the shoe seems hardly to touch the ground as the body floats relaxed to the next explosive foot plant. Cross-country skiers explode off each split-second planting of their skis with split-second rests in between.

Zone of power application.

Some paddlers get confused about this topic probably because they are thinking of arm muscles instead of full trunk. The conventional wisdom says don't apply power right away as the blade enters water and don't continue power beyond the point where the blade is back parallel to your hip. However, torso rotation actually gives you a surprisingly wider zone than this.

If you have rotated your on-side shoulder forward with the blade, you have plenty of leverage to start applying considerable power as the blade dips into the water. If you were using just your arms to paddle, you couldn't.

The same is true for knowing when to let off the power. If your body has rotated back and the arm pushing the blade through the air is fully extending with the full force of your torso, then you can continue power to a point where the in-water blade is just going behind the line of your seat. At that point,

your effort will be tapering off and your blade knifing out of the water. Your real cue to turning off power is not when the blade is parallel to you but rather when the pulling hand is coming almost parallel to your torso.

Think of this in degrees. As the blade hits the water, apply force at a rate equal to 80 or 90 percent of what you plan to be doing during that stroke. In the middle of the zone—say, from the point the paddle is catching well in the water—go to 100 percent of the effort you plan. Then as your hand gets in the vicinity of your seat, taper off to 50 or 75 percent of that effort as you bring the blade out of the water just behind your seat.

Obviously, these figures are too precise to monitor or control in real-life paddling. They're just intended to illustrate the varying levels of exertion during the stroke, starting with pretty close to full effort right away and tapering off later than usually prescribed.

Placement of blade in the water.

The blade should be placed as far forward as you can comfortably rotate your torso and extend your arm out straight on that side. With the shaft parallel to the water's surface, dip the blade vertically down into the water. The blade should make little or no noise as it enters. This is one clue that you are placing it correctly.

Placement should also be as close to the boat as possible, but be careful not to bang the deck fabric or hull. Your best leverage is close to the boat where it takes full advantage of your torso rotation. You may, however, at times want to place the blade a bit farther out, to work your muscles a little differently.

Hand placement on the paddle.

Instruction manuals too often get hung up on precise measurements for where the hands should rest on the shaft. Their advice is that they should be shoulder-width apart. It's okay to start your first few strokes from that position, but be ready to change it often.

Hand placement is part of your throttle. Wider spacing between the hands can give you more power, but it leads to a lower cadence. Closer placement increases your paddle pace but is tiring. Play between the two extremes, even at the extremes, for a few minutes at a time. During the course of the day, your hands should be all over your paddle shaft.

Some paddles have special areas on the shaft designed for your hand grip, and some even include finger grooves. These paddles might serve for a short sprint, but if you're paddling a touring kayak, they wouldn't allow you to comfortably run your hands to other areas on the shaft whenever you need to adjust for speed and prevailing conditions.

Pivot point of the paddle.

The pivot point should generally remain constant. To find this point, hang your arms at your sides and bend your elbows until your forearms are horizontal. Notice where this puts your hands. The point around which you should be rotating your paddle is about eight to 10 inches in front of where your hands ended up. If you try to paddle with your hands and arms tucked too close to your body, your torso muscles will not wind and unwind fully into the stroke. If your hands are too far ahead of you, you'll waste energy and lose some of the leverage you need for a good forward stroke. Also, never let your hands cross over beyond the center line of your cockpit. This too wastes your energy and decreases your leverage.

Height of the airborne part of the paddle.

Much of this control depends on the width of your boat, the height of the coaming, and the length of the paddle. Generally though, remind yourself to keep the airborne blade as low as you can, even if this means having the in-water blade farther from the side of the boat. You're definitely not going to get much

power out of the pushing side of your body if its hand is thrusting out above the level of your nose.

Blade angle and depth.

Your thinking should be sharp on these crucial considerations. The blade should be held as vertical as possible throughout the stroke. Be careful not to change the angle as you take the paddle out of the water. If you do, you'll scoop up water and tire your muscles.

The depth of the blade in the water should be shallow. None of the shaft should go under, just the blade. Digging the paddle in too deeply is hard on your body, because it takes more effort. It also complicates knifing the blade out of the water at the end of the stroke.

There is an exception to this vertical angle and shallow depth of the blade. If you're feeling a bit unstable in beam seas or wind, you may want to skim the blade through the water at a different angle and to lead with the top edge. This semi-bracing stroke is more often performed in hardshells, seldom needed in foldables. Bracing strokes are discussed in more detail later in this chapter.

Putting It Together

Let's go through a full forward-stroke cycle to see how you control the physical components so that they work together as a sustained, powerful lever for prying your boat forward. A good place to start is just where Blade A is about to enter the water.

Forward stroke—full extension.

Forward stroke—straightened arms.

Forward stroke—finishing up.

Side B is coiled up to put power into pushing airborne Blade B as the torso completes its backward rotation on Side B. The foot on Side A begins to push on a crossrib or foot brace as Blade A enters the water to act as a levering point to diagonally support Side B's pushing effort and to directly counterbalance Side A's pulling effort.

Side B's shoulder begins to rotate forward with power as Side B's arm quickly straightens out ahead at a slightly lifting angle. Side B's open hand pushes the paddle, with the shaft resting on the fleshy part at the base of the fingers. The wrist stays fairly horizontal, i.e., barely bent. Side B's straight arm and uncoiling shoulder push ahead until its hand comes to the centerline of the boat.

While Side B is going through its push motions,

Side A simultaneously pulls on Blade A with backward rotation of the torso and straight arm with little or no bend in the elbow. Side A's hand pulls the paddle with fingers loosely cupped over the shaft, wrist flat and horizontal. As this hand comes almost abreast of the torso, Side A's arm bends at the elbow to lift Blade A out of the water.

Side A is now coiled back for its turn to push on the airborne end of the paddle. The foot on Side B pushes on a crossrib or foot brace as Blade B enters the water, repeating the process.

This is a powerful forward stroke that you can keep up all day. Pay attention to torso and shoulder rotation, keep arms straight, hands loose. Follow all the earlier suggestions on form such as blade angle and depth, height of paddle on the side away from the water, etc. And make certain to fine tune such variables as how much push and pull, and where your hands rest on the paddle.

Turning Strokes

You'll have to turn your kayak from time to time, and you may need to apply the brakes hard every once in awhile.

You could turn simply by paddling only on one side for a number of strokes. Or you could just put twice as much effort on one side. But these are rather inappropriate methods of turning.

The strongest turns generally involve some boat lean and laying your body out to one side over your paddle. Your foldable's tremendous stability allows you to lean out more aggressively than you'd want to risk in a rigid boat. Many folding kayakers resist doing this, but once you've learned the turning strokes with sharp lean, you'll see how crazy it is to think folding kayaks lack performance.

Even if you have a rudder, you should learn to turn without it. Rudders depend on cables, yokes, pins, hooks, and other mechanical devices that have a way of giving out when you most need them.

The basic turns we'll look at are described as though you were using a single folding kayak, but they apply to doubles as well. More details about how to turn a double folding kayak appear in Chapter 8, along with variations for their specific needs.

As you master these strokes, you'll also be developing confidence for learning the basic brace strokes that work well in a foldable. Braces and how to apply them are detailed later in this chapter.

Forward Sweep Turn

You'll use this turning stroke constantly. It works for turning while on the move and for coming about

Forward sweep turn.

when you're standing still. (See discussion below.) Your turning radius will vary with how much you're willing to lean your boat and put your body over your paddle in the water.

If you're moving, here's how to get into the sweep turn from your normal forward stroke. As you prepare to dip the blade on the side opposite the direction you want to go, lean your boat slightly on that side. Instead of placing the blade close to the boat, dip it farther away and not so far forward as you normally would. Turn the blade so that the top edge leads the motion through the water in a slight skimming angle close to the surface.

Lean for a second on that skimming blade and sweep out to the side with your paddle rather than straight back as you would with the forward stroke. As the blade approaches a point in line with your seat, push off the blade as your hip and lower body level out the boat beneath you. As in the forward stroke, use your torso rotation and other key elements to power you around.

As you complete the sweep on one side, continue with your normal forward stroke on the other side. Then if you need to turn more, repeat the sweep stroke again. This will keep up your momentum and forward motion. The sweep stroke is part of the forward-stroke pattern, and you miss not a beat.

Few folding kayaks offer a tight enough fit for you to put your boat on its side with just hip movement and raising the knee on the side you're turning toward, which is the way it's done in tight-fitting rigid kayaks.

But you can take advantage of the tremendous final stability a foldable offers to accomplish almost the same effect. What you wind up doing is not advisable for rigid boats but is perfectly safe in a foldable: Lean with your upper body so that its center of gravity is close to the side of the boat. Inherent stability in a folding kayak will keep you from capsizing so long as you don't hold that position for more than a second.

Before achieving the ideal sweep turn described above, you may want to begin by just sweeping the paddle out beyond the normal forward stroke arc, thus leaving the boat and your body upright and the blade vertical. This will turn you, but it takes strength. Next, sweep the blade out through the arc, but with the top of the blade as the leading edge. Also, lean a bit on the paddle shaft. You'll find that the skimming blade gives a good amount of support. Keep practicing, and eventually get the boat onto its sponson for a second or two as you sweep out with the angled blade.

You should be getting the feel for your boat, a sense of body lean, and a good idea how much support a shallow-angled blade gives you. Play with the angle between vertical (without leaning on the blade!) and 45 degrees off horizontal. You'll find an angle that suits your body size, your foldable, and your paddle's length and blade shape.

This turn works; by putting the boat slightly on its side, you raise the ends and change the effective keel line of the boat from the centerline to a point higher up on the curved side of the boat. This temporarily gives you a "new" rockered keel line that helps the boat turn swiftly. Also, by leaning out on the paddle, you widen the sweeping arc and increase the power it gives the turning maneuver.

Stern Rudder Stroke

The sweep turn described above takes lots of room, so it's good for open water, and it won't cost you momentum. The stern rudder stroke described below will turn your foldable more quickly and securely, but you'll lose speed.

The stern rudder stroke turn is simple. You place your blade into the water behind you, toward the stern on the side you wish to turn toward. Have the blade perpendicular to the line of travel and fairly vertical. The power face should be toward the back or toward your kayak. Hold hard onto the shaft, and you'll turn quickly. Continue it long enough, and it'll stop your kayak.

Because the stern rudder stroke slows you down, you generally use it in moving water such as a following sea or wake from a passing vessel. If moving water is threatening to send you sideways, this stroke actually is your rudder to keep you going straight. In such conditions, the stern rudder stroke acts as a security blanket to settle you and your boat down. (More on this in Chapter 7, about handling open-water conditions.)

Reverse Sweep Turn

The reverse sweep turn is like the sweep turn except that you sweep the blade from the rear forward. It will turn you in a hurry and with force, faster than

Reverse sweep turn.

support. Let up on the braking action immediately and quickly repeat the same forceful action on the other side. You should be able to do a full braking motion to two sides in less than a second and a half each. When you master this, you can come to an abrupt stop from full speed within about four strokes.

Maneuvering When Not in Motion

Here are the best methods to get your single kayak moving from a complete standstill. These require some of the turning strokes described above.

Turning Completely About

To turn in the opposite direction from which you are facing, you simply combine reverse and forward sweeps on opposite sides of the boat. For example, do a forward sweep on the right side once, then a reverse sweep on the left. Do that a few times and you'll turn 180 degrees, especially if you aggressively lean forward and out on the forward sweep strokes and stretch back and out for the reverse strokes.

Backing Up

In effect, you do reverse sweeps on both sides. It pays to twist around your torso, not only for power but also to take a glance at where you're going as you back up. Do not change the direction your blade is facing; keep it just as you would while paddling forward—its power face facing back. Some people turn their blades around on the mistaken notion that they can't paddle with the back of the blade. Actually, you get more than enough power from using the "wrong" side of the blade. More importantly, you'll be ready to move ahead quickly if you find yourself backing into any obstacle. If you had to stop to reverse the blade face, you might not be able to get out of the way fast enough.

Going Sideways

When coming alongside another boat or pulling up to a dock, you'll need to know how to make your foldable go sideways.

To maneuver sideways or broadside, you must use the draw stroke. First, turn your body toward the side you wish to move. Raise your paddle until the blade is out about three feet from amidships, with the power

the forward sweep can. But, unlike the forward sweep, the reverse sweep will tend to slow you down.

The reverse sweep looks very much like the stern rudder stroke at the start. But it has two differences. In the stern rudder stroke, the paddle is held fairly static with just some adjustments in the blade angle, and the reverse sweep starts farther out from the side of the boat.

The reverse sweep turn is also similar to the forward sweep in two aspects. In the reverse sweep, the blade sweeps forward, similar to the way the forward sweep stroke moves the blade back. And you also lean on the paddle shaft somewhat and rotate your torso.

When making the reverse sweep turn, keep the power face of the blade pointing back. Fine tune the angle of the blade—somewhere between vertical in the water to sweeping at an angle—as the top edge of the blade leads the motion. This technique works well in a folding kayak to get you turned around fast.

Braking

To avert hitting something ahead of you, you can use the turning strokes described above in some combination that will take you to one side. Or you can apply the brakes. The best braking stroke requires severe reverse sweeps applied quickly on both sides.

Dig the paddle into the water about 45 degrees behind you with the blade out about two feet from the side of the boat. Slap its non-power side down hard on the water and dig it in with a powerful reverse sweep, with the shaft pressing into your stomach for inboard face toward you. Lean out a bit and have the blade enter at about 45 degrees.

Now, pry the blade toward you by pushing on the shaft with your upper hand and pulling with your lower hand. Don't let the blade come up to the side of the boat. Instead, about a foot from you, cut the blade out of the water, toward the stern, and then keep repeating this draw stroke until you get where you want to be.

Bracing

Bracing, sculling, and Eskimo rolling are required skills when venturing out in a rigid kayak, because these tricks of the trade counteract the underlying instability of most hardshell kayaks, especially when sea conditions worsen. Folding kayaks, while not untippable, are so stable and seaworthy that you may never have to use these defensive strokes. In fact, you'll find that when conditions have rigid-kayak paddlers low bracing and modifying their forward strokes into semi-braces just to maintain their balance, you can confidently put down your paddle to eat lunch! Still, learning the basics of a few defensive strokes is worthwhile, just in case you ever need to add to the inherent stability of your foldable.

The problem is that it's a little difficult to put a folding kayak on its side in order to carry off high bracing strokes and sculling movements. Air sponsons resist the sideways motion, and the final stability is so strong that a folding kayak being tipped drastically to one side will often pop back up as if righted by some invisible hand. Even if you can get the boat on its side, the greater width of a foldable gets in the way of exercising some of the strokes.

Advanced high-brace sculling for extreme conditions depends on having your body stretched out at the water's surface with support from your paddle, which is sculling at a shallow angle to the water. In a wide, buoyant foldable, your body's position is significantly higher than your sculling blade, so the resulting angle lends little or no support to your body—and may plunge you in.

The Low Brace and Folding Kayaks

The low brace is a paddle stroke that uses the back of the blade, the non-power side, to give you support to recover from a potential capsize.

Here's the basic movement. Hold the paddle shaft low, your hands positioned at the normal forward-stroke rest position, and then push down on the non-power face directly out to your side. Water is dense enough for you to lean strongly on the blade at least momentarily and, with some variations, have sustained support.

The low brace differs from the more advanced high brace in its hand and arm positions and in which side of the blade provides the support. In the low brace, your arms are in front of you (or to one side as you lean on the shaft) and generally held low. Your wrists are horizontal and facing down. In the high brace your arms are held closer to your body, generally up about chest height or slightly higher. Your wrists are turned back to vertical or near vertical. For the high brace, the power face is down, unlike the low brace in which it is up.

The high brace is preferred by rigid kayakers in extreme situations. It gives greater support than the low brace and allows more radical lean, even to the point of lying prone in the water on your moving paddle, if you are one of the few who get to that expert level.

The low brace is almost as effective in a folding kayak as a high one for rigid boats, thanks to the foldable's greater stability and resistance to capsize. Those characteristics also allow you to push low bracing beyond the limits it has in rigid boats. Looked at another way, a folding kayak already comes equipped with the stability that you can only achieve in a rigid boat through low bracing strokes without you doing a thing. Add low bracing to a foldable and you achieve a level of stability that you can only get in a rigid boat through high bracing techniques.

The only place you may need—and can work—a high brace effectively in a folding kayak is in surfing conditions with waves higher than three feet. And that brace would be such a modified version that, in effect, it would be a low-high brace. It's used so rarely in folding kayaks that it will be covered in Chapter 7, which covers operating skills.

Practical Low-Bracing Techniques

Below, in ascending order of difficulty and support, you'll find the low-bracing techniques that work well in foldables and take advantage of their inherent stability. The strokes include a turn stroke you may find handy that relies on a low brace for support.

Low slap brace.

Slap brace.

The low slap brace is a quick-recovery technique that is often used to steady rigid boats. Since a foldable is more steady to begin with, you'll seldom need it. But if you do resort to a slap brace, it'll be doubly effective, reinforcing the boat's natural tendency to pop back up from extreme tipping angles. This pop-back tendency acts almost like the hip snap used as part of any brace in a rigid kayak.

You could use the slap brace if you were suddenly jarred over to one side. To begin it, you reach out in a lean with the paddle, then slap the non-power side down hard on the water and push off from the rebound created by the water's resistance to the impact of the blade. To gain the most effect, your outer arm is held straight and your inboard hand is kept low. This angle assures a flat slap on the water, so there's very little danger that the blade will plunge in. The slap brace gives you, at most, about a second of support before the blade sinks, unless your boat is on the move.

To use it effectively, the slap brace should become second nature to you. Practice it on every outing, even in calm conditions, and on both sides of your foldable. It will help you develop the instinct to use paddle support to bring your foldable back from extreme tipping angles. The normal instinct for folding kayakers is just to right their boats by throwing their weight to the side opposite the potential capsize, something you can usually get away with only in a foldable. The slap brace is much more effective and almost guaranteed to get you back from extreme heeled-over angles.

Sweep low brace.

Rigid kayak paddlers normally need more than a second of support afforded by the slap brace described above, so they depend on the following technique.

Sweep the flat blade along the water's surface in a small arc, starting with the blade out to one side at a point a few feet behind you. Then sweep the flat blade forward with the leading edge slightly up. The moving blade planes on the surface, giving enough support that you can lean on it without capsizing. When you have the blade about parallel to the seat, push up on it the way you would in a slap brace.

Since your foldable kayak gives you a far more stable platform from which to work the sweep, you can do the same sweep low brace with less of an arc and with greater lean, if you wish. Make certain to keep the paddle shaft as flat as you can, because, with the greater width and buoyancy of the air sponsons, your leaning position in your cockpit is higher than it would be in a rigid kayak. Your paddle blade may want to plunge in if the shaft is at an acute angle to the water.

Low sculling brace.

Sculling low brace.

This a hybrid brace. Sculling is generally considered something you do off the high brace, not the low brace. But sculling in folding kayaks is best done from the low-brace position, because a high brace might tend to dig the blade into the water.

Start by holding your paddle in the normal low-brace position. Reach out alongside you with your outstretched arm straight and the paddle low in the other hand. With the power side up, sweep the paddle back through a three- to four-foot arc that starts slightly in front of your body. Then, in a continuous motion, sweep the blade forward again to the start position. Keep doing this at a steady, unhurried pace. As you sweep in either direction, the leading edge of the paddle should be slightly raised. Do not run it absolutely flat.

Bear down on the paddle shaft as you go through the sweeping or sculling arc. The moving paddle will support your weight. Keep your body as low as you can and your arms as far down as possible.

Telemark low-brace turn.

This low brace produces an elegant, fast turn when you're on the move, and it has all the grace of the ski turn after which it is named. You can turn to point almost directly back in the direction you came from. It looks very impressive and gives you a nice way to come up sideways to a landing spot. It works very well in a folding kayak, because the sponsons lend stability throughout the turn and their round sides slip around smoothly with little drag.

To begin executing the telemark low brace turn, you should already be moving with a current or paddling hard to build up some steam. Lay out a low brace on the side you wish to turn toward, and have the blade about 45 degrees behind you, with its leading edge raised as in the sculling sweep motion. Water pressure under the back of the slightly angled blade will give you enormous support. The more aggressively you lean on the skimming paddle, the faster and sharper you will turn. You should also be placing the boat on its air sponson on that side to get more rocker in the hull for the turn.

As you come around, your boat will slow down. You can continue the turn by finishing with a sweep of your paddle toward the bow as you level out the boat.

Practicing Braces

To get a feel for the fundamental movement, first practice the low brace in shallow water, about a foot or so deep, i.e., enough to float the boat. If you're not doing it right, you can at least push yourself back up when your paddle touches the bottom. This practical experience will teach you just how far over on its side your foldable can go before it finally goes completely over.

Telemark turn.

The slap brace should be firm, but it shouldn't sound as if someone has belly-flopped off a high diving board. Keep leaning the boat farther over each time before you slap brace.

You'll notice that it's harder to push off the paddle brace if you're keeping your body erect or trying to lead the recovery with your upper body and head. Lead with your lower body, and keep your head down and trailing your body as you right. This way, you're letting the boat level off and bring you up with it.

Doing the exercises first in shallow water will encourage you to be more daring in leaning your body out and in stretching farther to your side with the outbound blade. After you gain confidence in how far you can get the boat over and still pop back, you'll be ready to do this maneuver in deeper water.

CHAPTER 7

*O*perating Skills: From Launch Site to Open Water and Back

Some people think folding kayaks come with "Handle with Care" stickers plastered all over them, that they'll self-destruct on the first rocky beach or splintery dock. They think folding kayaks are fair-weather friends, not up to the performance required in heavy seas and winds. Both these impressions are so false that they'd be laughable—if it weren't for the fact that many paddlers believe them, and therefore miss getting into a breed of vessel that's innately one with the open sea, that could give them decades of hardy service without kid-glove care.

Landing or launching a folding sea kayak is pretty much the same process you'd use for a rigid sea kayak, but with a big exception—you can get in and out of a foldable much more easily. You'll appreciate that characteristic difference when you try to land alongside a high dock or on a beach that's being slapped by the massive wake of a passing tugboat-barge combo. If you treat your foldable's skin as you would the hull of a fiberglass kayak, with perhaps a bit more care, you'll be able to enjoy all of its 30-year life expectancy.

Here's some sound advice for handling your foldable in launching and landing and for dealing with most conditions you're likely to meet in open water and coastal areas. These techniques are aimed at single folding kayaks, but they basically apply to doubles as well. Chapter 8 describes the specific ways you use these techniques when paddling a double folding kayak.

Launching and Landing

One of the first things you'll notice about launching a folding kayak is just how easy it is—you just step in. Nothing precarious about landing either, you just step out. Here's exactly how it works under launching and landing conditions that range from the easiest to the toughest.

Calm Beaches and Shorelines

If you were using a rigid kayak even under such benign conditions, you'd first have to learn how to use your paddle to stabilize your boat to avoid an embarrassing spill a foot offshore. Fortunately, you don't have to use this technique for a foldable, except under certain circumstances.

This method, you'll note, is hard on paddles and occasionally leads to a chipped blade, broken shaft or both. Place the shaft behind your seat at a right angle to the boat and rest one blade on shore or in shallow water. Grab the braced shaft and, with your weight on it, use the paddle to support you as you climb into your tippy rigid kayak.

To launch a foldable from a shore or beach, you don't need to do anything with your paddle, as you see rigid kayakers doing. Simply place your foldable in water that's deep enough for it to float with your body weight aboard and step in. The boat can be parallel to shore or pointing out, whichever is easier at the time.

Landing is the same process, but reversed. Step out with the boat just at the water's edge. You don't ram the bow on shore, as in a fiberglass boat.

There are exceptions. When you first get one of the narrower mini-foldables, you may want to use the braced-paddle entry method described below. This is what rigid kayakers must do every time they climb in, even in calm conditions.

Lay the paddle's shaft behind your seat at a right angle to the boat, and rest one blade down in the shallow water. Grab the shaft, put your weight on it, and use the shaft to support you as you climb in.

But the odds are that once you get used to the balance of your new boat, you'll hardly ever need to use a braced paddle for launching or landing. In any of the foldables, you might want to use a bracing if a choppy wake is slapping the shoreline. Even if you do, you don't have to put potentially damaging weight on the paddle while using it as an entry support. Just having the paddle resting in the braced position will suffice for entering your foldable.

High and Low Docks

Docks keep your feet dry but are trickier to handle, because any kayak tends to move out and away from the dock as you enter and lower your feet into it.

The open cockpits of Folbots, Kleppers, and Nautiraids are easier to get into than Feathercrafts, but if you have your spraydeck attached to any open-cockpit foldables they'll be a little harder to enter as well.

Lower your boat into the water carefully so it won't drift away, and hang on to the coaming or a line. Then, here's what you do, depending on dock height.

Low docks.

If the top of the dock is less than about two feet above the water's surface, first sit down on the edge of the dock, then place your feet in the boat forward of your kayak seat. Twist your body onto one buttock

on the dock with your weight on your arms and lower yourself in. Keep your weight off your feet as much as you can during the process, so you don't push the boat out from under you by your entry movement.

When landing at a low dock, reverse the process. Get a grip on the dock's edge first. Once your arms are on the dock and supporting your weight, lift yourself out of your seat and get up into a seated position on the dock. Your feet are in the boat keeping it from drifting away. Lean over to get a grip on the boat and take your feet out.

High docks.

The process is similar to that for low docks—only harder. It requires agility, upper-arm strength, confidence, *and* commitment.

Here are several things to remember before starting. If you have the boat tied off, make sure you can loosen your tie line from your seat in the kayak after you're sitting in it. Set your paddle near the edge of the dock so that you'll be able to reach it. If the dock is very high, you may want to secure your paddle onto one of your boat's deck lines before lowering the boat.

Sit at the dock's edge with your feet suspended over your kayak's cockpit. Then, twist around to one side facing the dock. With your weight totally on your forearms, begin to lower yourself until your feet are touching the floor of your foldable. Continue to lower yourself in with your arms stretched up, if the dock height requires this. Your foldable isn't likely to tip

Even unorthodox methods work in a foldable! *(Wolfgang Fischer)*

on you, but it might want to push away as you move your feet forward into a seated position.

Landing at a high dock can be complex. A deck line tied to the bow will be handy for hanging on to your boat after you get onto the dock. If you have to pull the boat up, you may have quite a reach down to retrieve it, so that a line becomes even more necessary. What about your paddle? Throwing it up on the dock might backfire if you find that you can't manage to get up onto the dock right away. You may want to leave your paddle tied off on the boat.

Let your foldable's stability enhance your exit. You can stand in most folding kayaks even without the support of a dock. It's one of the confidence builders covered in Chapter 10, on rescues. Stand up slowly while holding firmly on to anything on the dock; if you merely hold an open hand against some vertical surface, you might push your boat away as you stand. Raise yourself with your arms to a point you can either sit on the dock or throw yourself up there in a prone position.

Paddling Out Through Surf

Surf conditions can be hard on any boat. Much depends on the nature of the rough water you're encountering. If conditions are fairly calm, merely foam or low lapping waves near shore and larger ones breaking further out, you'll have at least enough of a paddling start to build up momentum to deal with the larger waves. If big waves are breaking right at the shoreline or close to it, then think seriously about

picking a better launch site or waiting for better conditions.

If you study the general shoreline you're hoping to launch from, you'll probably find a less vulnerable stretch that's free of large breaking waves. Exactly where depends on the depth of the water, the width of the beach, the proximity to offshore obstacles, which direction the beach faces, a host of variables. As a general rule, you're most likely to find the more hospitable spots away from the dead-on center of a beach, toward the sides of a cove or bay. But not too far to the sides. As you go farther out toward the points of land that define a cove or crescent beach, conditions can be even rougher than at the center

When you find a better spot, study what's happening out to sea. You may be able to detect the wave pattern. Some people believe they can count the sets or groups of waves so they can make their entry or exit during the break between groups of waves. But even if you can't get a fix on sets, you'll get a clue as to when big waves are building up. Note the height and shape of big waves when you first spot them offshore. While you're watching, you're almost guaranteed to see calmer areas, perhaps where the water is deeper or where waves are being deflected away. Also, notice how the water pulls out from the beach.

If you have time, it may be better to wait until another part of the day when the surf is less formidable, at either a lower or higher tide, for instance. If you're on a camping trip and have the equipment to stick around comfortably, you should wait. What's

Coming through surf in a K-1.
(Feathercraft)

more, handling a gear-laden boat through surf is a daunting experience.

Getting into your boat.

If you must launch in surf, the stability of your foldable will come in very handy here, because you won't have to lose time bracing your paddle behind you to get in. But if all you're dealing with is foam from waves washing ashore, you can take a running push-off start.

Moving out.

Don't bother to attach your spray skirt at this point, because you don't want to lose the momentum built up by your push-off start. Paddle hard at a sprint pace. Don't let up even as you confront the first wave, but keep your paddle low. Pry the blade into the face of the wave to give it purchase and pull yourself through or over the wave. Keep this up until you're clear of the surf zone.

Several tricks: keep your body low and lean forward if possible; be conscious of meeting the wave with the blade's edge, not its flat back; don't raise your arms in triumph as you go over that first terrifying wave, because there are probably others on their way.

You have at least these two things going for you. While you're paddling out, you can see the waves coming toward you, so you're not dealing with anything unseen. Also, pushing into waves is a very stable position for any kayak, even more so in a buoyant foldable.

Landing Through Surf

This is the toughest condition you're ever likely to encounter. Any boat is at its least stable when running in the same direction the waves are moving, because it tends to want to broach, to be moved sideways to the face of the wave. From seaward, it's difficult to judge the height of waves or how and where they're breaking. Some of the pointers for launching your foldable into the least problematic surf area also apply for landing it in the surf.

If you can wait to land, it may pay to do so, especially if you're only marginally confident about handling the challenge at that moment. A folding kayak permits you to wait for the better moment, because

Push-off Start

The push-off start in a foldable isn't hard to learn. In effect, it looks like you just push your boat alongside of you and, while it's still moving, jump in. You could never do this in a rigid boat, but it's handy for launching a folding kayak in anything from a dead calm to foamy water stirred up by light waves. Learn it and practice it in calm conditions.

Here's how you do it. Start by leaning over your boat in shallow water with one hand on each side of the coaming just about a foot ahead of the backrest of your seat. You'll be balancing yourself on your hands and arms, so make certain you have a good grip and the position feels secure. The far-side hand should also be grasping your paddle, which is laid along the opposite side of the boat. Push your boat forward and, while it's moving, throw your weight onto your hands and—suspending yourself over the cockpit opening—swing both legs in. Pivot your body in. You may first want to just see if you can vault into your boat from this position while it's standing still.

The movement is similar to the way you push a bike ahead with two hands on the handlebars and throw one leg over the bike as you get on. The secret is to hunch over your boat and keep your body as low as you can, allowing just enough clearance to swing your legs into your moving boat.

As you practice this moving start, you'll find that entering from one side may feel better than the other. It's alright to develop such a "sweet side" for this maneuver; calm or foamy-water conditions aren't likely to dictate that you be able to perform it equally well from either side.

Low-High Brace

If a wave is taller than two feet or so and is too high for you to place your paddle on, you'll need to do a low-high brace. This is a form of high brace that uses the power face of the blade, but you use a radically different arm position than rigid kayakers use in their high brace. You'll use the low-high brace only when broached on a high wave.

If broached, put your paddle into the face of the wave with its power face down. Your hands are hanging on to the shaft for support, your wrists are cocked back and not flat as in a low brace, and your elbows should be kept down, tucked in close to your body. The shaft should be held low near your chest, about nipple-high. All your weight should be on the shaft and pushing down on the power face of the blade, which is planted in the face of the wave. The power of the wave will keep you upright as long as you lean into it on the blade.

Do not raise your elbows. If you do, you risk damaging your shoulder blades as the force of the wave pushes on the blade.

The low-high brace allows you to have your wrists in a better support position than can be maintained with a low brace. If you tried using a low brace on a high wave, you wouldn't be able to hold your paddle against the force of the wave. By keeping your elbows low and almost locked to your sides, you have your whole body counteracting the wave's force.

you can lay out a sea anchor while you're still well offshore and just hang out. You can even take a rest in your foldable by kicking any gear out of the way and stretching out.

Even if you can't see enough of what's happening with the waves, you have some judgment options. Remember how waves generally tend to hit strongest at the center of a beach and weaker toward the sides? Is this true where you are? Since you're already out on the water, you're probably able to paddle on to another stretch of beach where there's a more sheltered landing spot, perhaps caused by an island, a headland, or bottom contours. Try to remember what the coastline looked like a few miles back. Were there some better landing sites?

Once you've determined that you're about to paddle in through the surf, these pointers should see you through in one piece.

Paddling in.

Unless you're very skilled, you are always better off with a cautious approach rather than coming in hellbent-for-leather on the crest of a wave. Begin by trying to stay on the back of waves, not ahead of them or surfing them, at least not when you're getting closer to the zone where they may start their curl and break. If you're riding a wave, leaning back in your seat will help keep your bow up, thus counteracting any tendency for the bow to plunge under.

Use the stern rudder stroke to help keep your boat moving straight and to avoid broaching. Back paddle to keep from being pushed faster than you're comfortable going. You can back paddle to keep off the front of a wave, even one that seems about to break. It's amazing how well this works for controlling your kayak.

If you do broach, you may be forced to ride the wave in sideways, because there's little chance of getting straightened out again. When broached on a low wave (less than two feet tall), lean your foldable toward the wave and use a low brace to support you by placing the blade onto the top of the wave. Your foldable's buoyant sides will help you with this. If the wave is higher, you'll need to do a low-high brace (see sidebar). It could be a long ride.

Although you won't be able to get yourself straightened out so that you again are facing shore, you may have a chance of getting yourself pointed seaward, depending on the wave. Being turned to seaward is not a bad position to be in, as discussed below.

About face.

At some point though, you may have to commit yourself to paddling hard to get out of the near-shore part of the surf zone and onto the beach. Make certain you have the room and time to do so. And, remember that water washing out from shore will retard your progress.

Here's an alternative landing approach that works especially well when your boat is so laden with camping gear that it's hard to maneuver and build up speed. Go in backwards. It's not a sissy thing to do—actually, it's pretty smart. You can see the waves coming, because you're facing seaward, just as you are when launching. No monster wave is likely to sneak up without your seeing it, and you're in no danger of broaching if you're paddling into the waves. Your forward stroke is more powerful than your "rear-ward" stroke, so you can keep from being propelled too quickly toward the beach.

The hard part is seeing where you're going. But turning around to take a peek toward the beach is much easier and safer in a stable folding kayak than it would be in a rigid boat, where you'd have to brace to one side for that important peek. A rigid kayaker rarely considers backing in, but for a folding kayaker, backing in is quite a viable, if undramatic, way to come in through surf.

Getting out of your boat.

You'll want to do this in a hurry, so the next wave doesn't hit you. Once you're in the backwash foam near shore, jump out quickly, taking advantage of the stability of your foldable. Get your hands on your coaming on either side and arm-press yourself out of the cockpit—to the seaward side of your boat if it's being turned parallel to shore. This will keep the boat from being pushed against you by the end of the next wave and knocking you over. Hang on to your boat and drag it on shore. Over time, dragging it very far can be rough on the hull, so do it only if wave action at the water's edge is likely to bang it up worse.

Out on the Water

On open water, folding kayaks have good sea manners. And they have some special tricks up their sleeves that you'll find handy on a storm-tossed sea.

Open water conditions present many challenges. You'll encounter a wide variety of winds, waves, swells, boat wakes, and currents, especially as you paddle in and out of close coastal quarters.

Wind

Wind is an ever-present companion for the sea kayaker, part of being out on the water. It affects the way you paddle and what you're able to do on any given day.

Wind quite often is predictable. Monitor your weather radio forecast of wind conditions. What you learn from the forecast may help you decide to paddle a northerly course that day instead of a southerly course, or vice versa. You may even want to postpone your trip until the winds die down.

Two conditions to be wary of are heavy winds and winds blowing against the tide or current. When a wind is blowing at more than 15 or 20 knots, it can present a problem no matter which direction it's coming from. If the wind is coming from the direction you want to head, you're in for a physically demanding time. Coming from your beam, the wind will force you to alter your paddling style. From behind you, it could be unsettling. If a heavy wind is predicted to be coming from behind you, avoid the temptation to take a free ride in the morning, because your return trip in the afternoon will probably be against that same wind.

Wind in opposition to the tide and current always results in one thing—heavy seas and breaking waves. This is especially true in coastal areas such as bays, estuaries, and rivers. Since the direction of most tides and currents changes every six hours or so, what was a calm sea with an annoying little breeze in the morning can become a washing machine later in the day, due solely to the tide changing into opposition with that breeze.

Here's how to deal with wind and its consequences.

Head winds.

Wind coming straight at your bow is the easiest to contend with because it has no effect on your boat's tracking. Every boat will go straight when paddled into the wind. But it does require a certain mind set to conquer a head wind.

As a rule of thumb, when the wind exceeds 10 knots or so, it will cost you one knot of speed for every increase of 10 knots. So 20 knots of winds will slow you down two to three knots. In effect, you may find yourself paddling in place.

Your only solution is to paddle harder. An interesting phenomenon seems to occur. If you're paddling only at a moderate level, you don't move. If you increase your effort 25 percent, you start moving not just a little, but a lot. Your progress will be significantly more than that 25 percent increase would normally get you in calm conditions. It's as if you have broken through some barrier and are once again free.

How do you get that extra burst to buck the wind? Try leaning forward more than you would for your normal paddling stroke. Leaning does three things. One, it cuts down your surface area that is resisting the wind. Two, it reduces the resistance of your paddle blades, since leaning also gets them lower to the water's surface. Three, you're able to reach even farther with each paddle placement, which will elongate the zone of power application of your stroke.

Another strategy is all in your head. Get angry at the wind, consider it a challenge, do something to work yourself up mentally to fight the wind. A few ounces of sheer determination equal many pounds of muscle when you need to slug it out for long hours against heavy wind.

Beam winds.

These seem to present less of a challenge to folding kayaks than to rigid ones. Unless beam winds are very severe, they won't unsettle your foldable. Even if you're paddling with feathered blades, side winds catching their flat surface will not threaten to tip your boat, although they may rip your paddle out of your grip. Beam winds are one of the many reasons to either carry a spare paddle or use a paddle leash.

Beam winds can throw any kayak off track. Most kayaks tend to turn into the wind like a weather vane, so many people respond by paddling extra strokes on the upwind side to keep their boats running straight. A rudder can be handy at such moments, but good paddling technique is a better solution. Try the following:

Lean your boat a bit toward the upwind side. This is very easy to do and maintain in a foldable with no risk of a capsize. Leaning reduces your windage a bit and, if maintained over a distance, will help most kayaks track better. Or you can lean it only momentarily to windward when pulling the windward blade through the water. In effect, this becomes a quick turn toward the downwind direction that compensates for the boat's tendency to point upwind.

Choke up on the downwind side of your paddle. This extends its effective length on the upwind side. It allows you to paddle at a normal pace while the slightly extended paddle adds force on the upwind side, thus keeping the boat from turning into the wind.

Following winds.

Your boat might want to turn into the wind coming from behind, but only if you slow down or stop. In that case you may find your boat turned upwind within a few seconds. If you're paddling at a normal pace, you'll enjoy a nice boost from the wind and will need to make, at most, minute steering corrections. The problem with a following wind is that it often creates a following sea. More on that below.

Waves

The word "waves" has a dangerous sound to it, but waves needn't be scary. Many of the waves you'll encounter in open-water paddling in large bays and off shore are ocean or current *swells*. These elongated bumps seem to pass along the water's surface, and any rigid or foldable kayak will ride over them gently. As the big ones pass under your boat and you can see down into the chasm between them from high up, you may feel a little apprehensive—but they present no danger.

Where they can present a problem is in closer quarters near land and in estuaries. As the swells move into shallower water, they start developing *crests* and they eventually break. In narrow confines at the mouth of smaller bays, they can start stacking up to create either turbulent seas or *breaking waves*.

A *boat wake*, that V-shaped trail of disturbed water that streams out behind bigger vessels, is another type of wave you'll encounter. Ferries can send off wakes as high as five feet, particularly near shore, and these may tend to break. Throw in the wake of other vessels passing by and you get a confused sea situation in which waves collide, crisscross, and come at you from different directions.

Here are some common wave conditions and how to operate in them with your folding kayak.

Straight-on waves.

Just like when you paddle out through surf, this is one of your least worrisome wave situations. You can see what is happening, you're not likely to be thrown off course, and your kayak is in its steadiest position. As when paddling into a head wind, you have to tough it out by putting some determination into your stroke.

Beam waves.

These can be very unsettling in rigid kayaks, so their paddlers flatten out their paddle blades for stability on the wave side of the boat to be ready to brace into beam waves. But in a foldable, you can relax in all but the largest of beam waves, taking them broadside and just riding over them. The sides of a foldable have considerable buoyancy that resists the tendency to sink sideways, a trait that requires a hardshell kayaker to low brace. In a sense, the folding kayak's buoyant sides provide you with an automatic form of low brace. The same principle holds true in boat wakes. But do be careful if caught in shallow water without a spray skirt, because beam waves or boat wakes from the side could break and give you a lapful of water.

If beam waves are large, however, you may want to change course slightly to take them at a different angle, just to avoid getting knocked around or getting water splashed into your boat. You don't need to change course so much that you're heading straight into them; a shallow angle will usually suffice.

Waves from behind.

Following seas are not a problem unless they develop powerful waves. As in surf, such following seas can throw off your tracking, and your boat will try to turn in the direction the waves are coming from. To counteract heavy following seas, use correction strokes such as the stern rudder stroke and forward sweep. Also, at the top of each large wave, you can straighten out your boat quite well, because its ends will momentarily be out of the water. This allows you to turn your boat by pivoting on its center.

Confused wave patterns and stacked-up water.

Here's probably the worst position to be in: fresh waves and wakes are coming at you from one side, and on your other side, earlier waves are coming back at you after having bounced off of bulkheads and rocks on shore. On top of that, you're in a narrow estuary that is feeding water from a large sound into a small bay and it is stacking up.

Your problem may have been avoided if you had read your charts and tide tables (see Chapter 9). They would have suggested that you avoid being in that location at specific times. But you do have some outs.

Paddle out from shore a few hundred feet if you can, because reflected waves usually have less force the farther you are from the shoreline. Also, if you just keep paddling hard, keep up your momentum, you won't be tossed around so badly by the confused seas. Relax your mind. The odds are minuscule that such conditions will capsize a folding kayak. Its flexible skin will absorb much of the force of the confused water, and your boat will remain steady with minimal banging around.

CHAPTER 8

Paddling and Operating a Double

Double folding kayaks are a world unto their own. Not only is the experience different from that of the singles, but so is the way you operate a double. The pleasures and benefits a double bestows on its two crew members often exceed what they'd receive from paddling two single kayaks.

Within a double's close proximity, you and your fellow adventurer will be experiencing this new world at the same time, intimately. When either of you spots interesting and unusual things, it's easy to point them out. You're in the perfect position to talk about the discoveries you're making. Since your partner is within normal conversational range, you can even whisper to each other so you won't startle the wildlife you're observing. A double can even give you two different views of the world around you just by switching seats. The change in perspective is uncanny.

A double also lets you share the paddling load. One partner can slack off for a spell while the other continues to paddle. Often a double allows two people to go farther than either one could individually.

Doubles do involve compromise. In a double you and your partner are literally "in the same boat," so you both lose some of your independence. You have to agree whether to dawdle or move fast. One person can't go ahead and wait for the other to catch up, as you can in two singles. You must adjust your paddling pace and style to those of your partner.

But, even as you lose some independence, you gain something of immense value: a sense of satisfactory social intercourse that comes with the teamwork needed to power forward, make turns, and deal with the natural elements. As you learn the techniques that make possible moving as one, you'll find yourself bonding closer to the friend or loved one in the other seat. This feeling of wellness that comes with team-work is foreign to the solitary world of the single kayaker, even one who's operating in a group.

Safety is another consideration. You'll never get separated from your paddling buddy by wind, waves, or fog, wondering where the other person is. A double foldable is inherently more stable than even a foldable single, and if capsized, a double is much easier to reenter than a single.

Doubles often require such distinctly different techniques than you would use for single kayaks that they warrant separate consideration. Below are pointers about how to paddle doubles and about handling them in certain launching and landing situations.

Paddling, Turning, Bracing Basics

To gain the benefits, camaraderie, and safety of a double, you and your partner must become proficient in coordinated paddling and teamwork. For starters, make certain that you have absorbed the driving lessons covered in Chapter 6. These are also the fundamental building blocks for paddling and maneuvering a double. Then, consider the following suggestions to help you and your partner become a more effective crew.

The Forward Stroke

All the principles needed to develop a good forward stroke in a single apply equally in a double. You use your body components in the same way. You should be rotating your torso, using your legs, adhering to the suggestions for hand position and looseness, and keeping your arm straight in various parts of the stroke.

But, clearly, paddling in tandem can put some restrictions on your movement. For example, if seated

Forward stroke in a double.
(Walther/Klepper)

in the back, you're limited in just how far forward you can swing your paddle. Doubles generally seat the two crew members close enough that they have to avoid clanking paddles. The exceptions are the Feathercraft K-2 and the Pouch Eureka 2, both of which have more than enough room between the paddling positions to permit less coordinated paddling strokes.

In other boats, you'll want to synchronize your paddle strokes for at least three reasons: clanking paddles together can be hard on them; jerky movement through the water causes drag and wastes the energy of both paddlers; and paddling in unison is aesthetically pleasing—it certainly looks better than two individuals flailing about.

Here are some suggestions for getting the most out of your forward stroke in a double.

Put your more powerful paddler in front.

Your double will move better if your stronger team member is in front, because this position offers greater clearance for a powerful forward stroke. Double kayaks narrow toward the bow, beginning at the front cockpit area. This gives the front paddler a chance to place the blade in the water closer to the boat where it can deliver greater straight-back power. Less deck interference also means the front paddler can reach farther forward for a longer zone of power application.

Very few teams follow this advice, however. In many couples, the man wants to be in the back seat, where he can be in charge of turns and course. The rear position controls the rudder and usually does more in rudderless turns.

When you paddle in the rear position, you're responsible for coordinating your stroke with that of your partner up front. Paddling in tandem is like dancing. One partner leads and the other follows—or you risk stepping on some toes.

Only the person in back can see what the other person is doing, so it naturally becomes that person's job to follow any change of pace set by the person in front, and also to avoid hitting paddles. Whenever paddles clank, it's probably the fault of the person in back.

If you're in back, try to anticipate what the front paddler is doing. Play these games with yourself: try to match the exact angle your partner's blade is slicing through the air, or try to place your paddle in the water at the same moment. Think of tandem paddling as a contest in which you are being judged on synchronization.

If you're in front, recognize the limited range of motion your rear partner has.

When you set a paddling pace, be aware that your partner may not be able to match it. You're in the better position to paddle at a faster beat because of the extra room you have. Your partner cannot extend forward as fully as you can and is also concentrating on not hitting your paddle.

Signal any major paddling changes you are about to make.

If you're in back and want to stretch farther forward into your stroke, let the front person know so he or she can give you a bit more room. If you're in front and intend to pick up the pace, warn your partner.

If you're the front paddler and you need to put down your paddle, place it far enough forward that your partner still has clearance to continue paddling unimpeded.

This occurs when you stop paddling to check a chart or take a drink. If your rear partner has to quit paddling just because you didn't leave clearance, your kayak will lose momentum.

Turning a Double

Doubles differ radically from singles in the way you turn them. Tandems generally are longer than singles and track better, i.e., they run straighter. So they often don't respond as well to the turning tricks. But when you develop the skills and good teamwork, you'll be surprised how maneuverable a double can become.

Teamwork is the big key at all times. The person behind doesn't get the undisturbed panoramic view, but he or she does control the rudder. The front person can see obstacles better, but he or she shouldn't be initiating turns. So the two paddlers must constantly be in communication to decide on turns.

Your position in the tandem determines what you can and cannot do in turning strokes. For example, if both partners tried to do the forward sweep the way they would in a single, that turn could be largely ineffectual in a double. Leaned turns are also harder unless each team member makes the same adjustment for relative position in the boat.

Rudders are practically a must in double kayaks. They help keep a double going straight when partners are mismatched in their paddling styles and strength, and they're very useful for making turns.

Even though you might never use a rudder to turn a single boat, you'll find it very handy almost all the time in a double.

Even so, you and your partner should learn to turn by paddling technique, without a rudder. That way, if your rudder gives out, you'll already have the team coordination to maintain control of your boat. Good turning technique is useful in conjunction with your mechanical rudder to shorten the radius of your turn, complete turns more quickly, and even avoid obstacles.

We've looked at some of these standard turning techniques when talking about singles, but let's see how they should be applied specifically in doubles:

Sweep turn.

Several differences apply to doubles. First, you may want to be more careful about how much you lean out. Doubles are more stable than singles, but you don't want to push your luck. Two people leaning in one direction can throw each other off. Second, if you're both doing a forward sweep on the same side, you should adjust the zone in which you are applying the sweep, depending on your position in the tandem.

In leaning out on your paddle, start by doing so only about half as much as you would in a single boat until you and your partner get a feel for how far over your combined lean takes the boat. To be on the safe side, angle the blade a bit to work a form of brace into the sweep. Remember, the top edge of the blade should be leading the blade's movement through the water.

If both partners are forward sweeping on one side, you should do the following. If in front, do your sweep stroke mainly ahead of you. Reach forward

Stern rudder turn in a double.

close to the bow with your paddle and sweep back no farther than your seat. This assures that you are, in effect, moving the bow away sharply from the side on which you are doing the sweep turn stoke. If you're in the rear, start your sweep at a point level with your seat and continue the sweep stroke as far back as is comfortable. If you try to sweep in the zone forward of your seat, you'll be attempting to move the broad side of your boat around, which is largely a wasted effort.

Working plenty of torso rotation into the sweep will make the stroke doubly effective in a double, no matter which position you're in.

Stern rudder stroke.

Since you're not alone in a tandem, you can actually improve on the stern rudder stroke. While the rear person is doing a stern rudder move, the front person has two choices: do a forward sweep on the opposite side (not a reverse sweep) or continue normal paddling. A sweep will turn the boat sharply toward the side of the stern rudder stroke. Continued paddling will reduce the loss of momentum that ordinarily results from stern ruddering.

Some instructors suggest using what's called a bow rudder stroke in conjunction with either a stern rudder stroke or a sweep by the rear paddler. The bow rudder, however, is a difficult turn stroke to get right; it depends on a certain angle of the blade, its exact placement, the distance from the side of the boat, and other factors. Many people find it too strenuous to hold for long against the water pressure that builds up, especially since the bow rudder takes place in front, where they have the least leverage. So, the best advice may be to avoid it.

Telemark turn.

Though this is a bracing stroke, it is probably best thought of as a maneuvering one. As in any lean out for bracing in a double (see below), you should exercise caution not to let two overzealous partners go too far over to one side.

The telemark turn done in tandem looks stunning. But to be on the safe side in the beginning, the telemark should be performed by the rear paddler only. The front person should let up on paddling and enjoy the feel of the turn.

Once you have gained confidence, you both can participate. The rear person can be quite aggressive

in leaning out, and the front person can do some leaning on the paddle to help see the telemark through. The rear person should call out the direction of the telemark, the side he or she wishes to turn sharply toward. Paddle once on the off-side and then start the telemark. Try to keep the paddles wide apart for greater effectiveness.

Maneuvering a motionless double.

To get turned around 180 degrees, you can take advantage of the fact that there are two of you. One does a reverse sweep, the other a forward sweep. Who does what? Let the front person do whichever is thought of first. The rear person, like any good dance partner, follows the lead and does the opposite turn stroke on the *opposite* side of the boat.

Backing up is done as in a single. Both of you back stroke and look around. The back person gives directions.

The draw stroke is performed pretty much the same as in a single. Again, be careful how much you're leaning out in placing the paddle for the draw stroke, so that you don't find yourselves in a precarious position.

Bracing in a Double

The low brace is definitely the only type brace you should be doing in a double, even a hardshell. It's tough for two people to coordinate the degree and timing of their body lean to the point necessary for proper high bracing.

Even the more limited range of lean in the low brace bears watching. In a single boat, you are the only force doing the leaning. In a double, two of you are leaning. How do you coordinate how far you go to one side? How do you determine exactly when to push off the support of the brace to bring the boat upright again? The timing is so acute that you could easily screw things up.

Here's some advice:

Slap brace.

If either one of you senses that the boat is tipping over, do a slap brace. Don't wait for the reflex action of your partner to kick in—or to discuss it. He or she will be thankful you did the brace.

Practicing the slap brace carefully can also be something of a game. To start, you agree that at the count of three you will lean the boat over as if it were being

Learning how to double.

tipped by a wave. One partner counts out loud, one does the tipping action, and both of you slap brace.

Sweep low brace.

If you feel you need to do a sweep brace to gain some support, don't wait for your partner to react—just do it. But do have a prior agreement on which direction you will sweep. Avoid getting tangled up. If you're in front, sweep mainly parallel to your seat and slightly forward, even if this isn't the most powerful spot for low bracing. If you're in the back, you do have room to perform the sweep from behind you up into an area parallel to your seat.

Sculling low brace.

As in the telemark turn in a double, you may want one person do the sculling motion at first. You can both try the sculling motion after you're confident you can coordinate the push-off motion for recovery.

Care should be taken with the surface area each is sculling through. You would not want to collide or crisscross paddles during this sensitive stroke. If you keep the sculling arc small, say about two feet, and directly out from your seats, you shouldn't clash. Again, you should agree beforehand on a signal for when to push off in recovery from the sculling motion. Then, start the push-off as the blade is moving rearward in its arc. Don't forget to keep your heads down, letting the boat come up first, followed by your bodies and then your lowered heads.

Launching and Landing Doubles

Double folding kayaks launch and land even more easily than do single foldables. Two paddlers are better than one for steadying the boat. One can hold on to the boat while the other gets in. Having two paddlers simplifies other tasks as well. For example, one partner can hold both paddles while the other gets in.

Below are some tips on launching and landing doubles, starting with the easiest situations and progressing to the real challenges. You may want to reread

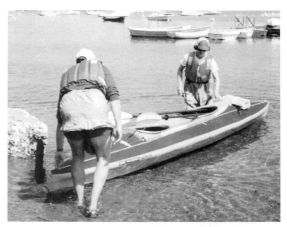

Beach launch.

Chapter 7, which covers how to handle these situations in a single boat.

Calm Beaches and Shorelines

As with single folding kayaks, doubles do not require that you use your paddle as a brace when getting in. You and your partner both step directly into the boat.

Usually the rear paddler holds the kayak steady while the front paddler climbs aboard. Then the rear partner steps in. Only under unusual circumstances would the front paddler need to steady the boat in any way, since his or her weight is already steadying it quite sufficiently. It's best to keep the double parallel to shore, so the front paddler won't have to get in from deep water, which would require a higher step-in.

High and Low Docks

Doubles really simplify this process. Here are several methods to mount from a low dock. In one, both paddlers sit on the edge of the dock with their feet planted in the boat in the vicinity of their seats. The front paddler slides in and gets situated in the front seat, while the rear paddler continues to steady the double with his or her feet, which are still in the boat. The front paddler, seated, grabs hold of the dock with hands or forearms resting on the edge. The other paddler drops down into the rear seat.

Docks that are two feet or higher require a slightly different technique. If you can reach the boat's coaming with your outstretched arms while lying prone on the dock, it's fairly easy for either one of you to steady the double while the other boards the kayak. Follow the boarding procedure for singles: sit on the edge of the dock, turn your torso around so you're facing the dock with your weight on your arms, lower your feet into the boat, and then drop into your seat. The paddler already in the boat holds on to the dock while the other paddler enters in a similar way.

Landing a double at either low or high docks is similar to landing a single, except that you've each got the other person very handy to keep the boat steady. One person gets out and then steadies the boat from the dock's edge while the other person exits. With particularly high docks, the first person to exit can secure taut lines from both ends of the boat to the dock, which helps steady the boat enough for the second person to stand up and pass gear to the first partner.

Paddling out Through Surf

Pick a launch spot that offers the calmest conditions for getting onto the water, just as you would in a single. Remember, on almost every beach you can find calm areas toward the sides of the cove, where wave action is refracted. Not so at its center.

Get your double into a bit of water. The rear person remains outside of the kayak, holding the bow steady and pointing into the direction of incoming water. The front paddler gets in and quickly attaches the spray skirt, so any lingering waves and foamed-up water can't lap in.

The rear paddler stands alongside the rear cockpit area and waits for a break in the wave action. When backwater starts washing out, or during a lull, the rear paddler jumps in with the push-off running start described in Chapter 7. The rear paddler makes no attempt to attach the spray skirt, since little water should get in; it's more important to keep moving before the next wave hits. Besides, the front paddler's body acts as a shield, protecting the open rear cockpit.

Both of you should now paddle hard into the waves. Keep low so you don't create too much surface for waves to crash against and slow down your progress. When the boat's moving into a wave, keep your paddles low and pointed into the wave. This will prevent losing a paddle or getting banged by its shaft. As you enter a wave, use your paddles as prying bars to get through it. You should soon clear the immediate breaking-wave zone.

Coming in Through Surf

Your best bet in a double folding kayak that is carrying a full load is to avoid surfing in the first place. If you've done your homework with charts and have a good estimate of your traveling range, you should be able to avoid getting into a situation beyond your skill level. (See Chapter 9 on common sense sea kayaking.)

However, winds and waves change, and a place that normally is benign can suddenly gather more wave action than you bargained for. When that happens, what do you do? First, study the situation closely. It's not unusual for paddlers, even those with lots of experience, to spend 30 minutes or more looking things over. Being in a double helps this reconnaissance, since you have two sets of eyes to watch and two sets of paddles to keep you from being drawn in by the power of the outer waves. Come in as close as you can under control, because it's harder to read waves from seaward than it is from land. Is any part of the beach not being hit hard or maybe getting only small-wave action?

When you do decide to attempt landing, you have the same choices you would in a single, to come straight in or go in backwards—facing the oncoming waves. Coming in backwards allows you to see the surf as it builds up and comes toward you, so you can position yourself much better in respect to each wave. Also, since you won't want to use a rudder while coming in anyway, you'll have an easier time of steering while facing the waves than if you were running with them.

If your double is loaded with gear and you're not confident you have the waves figured out, landing backwards may be your safest choice. When going in backwards, allow yourself to be pushed in a bit toward shore, paddle hard against the next big wave, get pushed in a bit more, paddle hard again, and so forth. This routine can be tiring, but it gives you terrific control.

If you decide to come in facing the beach, get your rudder out of the way, if possible. Plan to make most of your movement toward shore on the backs of the waves rather than in front of them; the front side is where they may move you in so fast that you lose control or where they might break right on you. The front paddler should be alternating between two types of strokes under command of the rear paddler: quick

forward strokes to move into good position on the backs of the waves, and sweep strokes to keep the boat perpendicular to the wave's direction of movement. The rear paddler should be paddling and applying rudder strokes.

Paddle hard enough to keep up with the speed of the wave. It helps to be throwing your body weight forward a bit. If you find that the nose of your double is starting to dip into the water, both of you should lean back hard to counterbalance this. If the nose continues to dive, then let the boat broach or go sideways to the wave rather than pitchpole down.

When your double is sideways to a wave, go into a brace, leaning into the face of the wave. If the wave is less than two feet high, use a low brace. If higher, use the modified low-high brace covered in Chapter 7. Either way, both of you should lean the boat into the wave, supporting yourselves on the blade that in turn is being pressed up by the wave's force. While there's no logical reason for this, whenever you go into a brace on a wave, your boat will seem to slow down, and this in itself can help you regain your composure.

No matter which way you go in through the surf—backward, forward, or on a broach—when you near the beach get ready to jump out fast. If possible, both paddlers should jump out on the seaward side of the boat and move it quickly ashore. In a double foldable, it may be easier for the rear paddler to jump out first. The reason is that the front cockpit area is generally higher and more restricted, making it a bit harder to exit than the back. Your objective is to move fast to get the double out of the way of incoming waves and away from the sucking out-action of water as it returns to sea.

CHAPTER 9

Sea Savvy—A Guide to Commonsense Sea Kayaking

Becoming a competent sea kayaker requires more than just paddling and operating skills. It goes beyond proficiency at self-rescue in the event of a capsize (see Chapter 10). To be truly adept in the watery environment upon which your kayak is afloat, you need to have the whole package, which we call sea savvy.

The ability to navigate is part of that package. Navigation is a complex and technical subject that can only be covered adequately in a book dedicated to that subject. One good navigation manual, *Fundamentals of Kayak Navigation* by David Burch, is a seminal work specifically devoted to kayak navigation (see Suggested Reading in the appendices). Your study of such books should be the cornerstone of any of your kayaking endeavors.

Taking a formal course in coastal navigation is another component of your sea-savvy package. Many excellent classes are offered by hundreds of U.S. Coast Guard Auxiliary groups, U.S. Power Squadrons, and private sailing schools. Look for similar courses at science museums, planetariums, and universities. Most navigation courses are tailored for the skippers of vessels that are much larger than yours. But, as a mariner, you too need to know how to use a marine compass, read nautical charts, understand the various aids to navigation, take a fix to establish your position, do dead reckoning, and so forth.

Even with the best navigation skills, you still need another component to steer clear of trouble while underway: common sense. Below are a dozen guidelines to help you develop the necessary smarts. Of course, these guidelines are not all you'll need to know, but they'll start you thinking. They cover three important activities: keeping tabs on your environment, understanding the rules of the road, and making your way.

Keeping Tabs on Your Environment

Unlike the ancient kayakers, you have all the advantages of modern technology at your disposal for keeping track of the natural elements. These modern gauges will let you know what to expect, what to avoid, and how to get where you want to go. Sometimes, they'll even advise you not to sally forth that day. Heed the advice.

1. Listen to Your Weather Radio.

The U.S. government's oceanographic and atmospheric administration, NOAA, broadcasts its local weather forecasts over National Weather Service radio stations throughout the country, and you can pick up the broadcast that's specific to your location on an inexpensive VHF weather radio, which you can purchase at Radio Shack (it sells the cheapest) or in marine supply stores. You should always consult these marine forecasts before you make your plans to set out, because they'll tell you exactly what to expect for large regions of the sea coast or inland bodies of water. Notice their relationship to where you plan to paddle.

It's a good habit to tune in the radio even when you're not planning to paddle. By listening regularly you learn to recognize the normal weather patterns for your local marine environment and also the conditions you should be wary of. Forecasts of five-foot seas may be normal for one location, abnormal for another. The only way to know is to monitor the local marine forecasts.

No radio can substitute for common sense. You have to provide it yourself. If your abilities are no match for the local weather conditions on the day you plan to paddle, have enough humility to back off. Or use the weather information to select a better stretch of coast or bay for paddling that day.

Whenever conditions are changeable, bring the radio along (in a waterproof bag) and listen again at midday; it may be time to beat a hasty retreat before weather worsens. A weather radio is a must on any camping trip.

2. Consult Your Charts.

Marine charts are your road maps. Study them before you start off to identify all available routes and to determine which routes favor you. Consult your charts regularly while underway.

Marine charts are not hard to read. You'll find a guide to the meaning of symbols in what NOAA calls Chart 1, really a small manual. A navigation book or course will help you understand the specific information you'll need to draw from your charts.

As you lay out your chart before a trip, take note of the general lay of the land in relation to the water along your intended course. Look out for ship channels. See if any large bodies of water feed through narrow passages. Look out for those little wiggly marks in the water areas that designate tide rips, whirlpools, etc. Note any land masses that could block the prevailing wind and provide you with shelter, or, conversely, expose you even more to its blast that day.

You should also be looking on your charts for landmarks such as towers, smoke stacks, sea buoys, and so forth, that will help you identify where you are as you paddle. You should be gauging distances and determining whether you are up to the rigors they will require of you.

3. Look Up Tide and Current Information.

This information can make the difference between an enjoyable trip and a miserable one. The U.S. government publishes data about tides and currents, and you can find the information in some newspapers and special manuals put out privately. For example,

Eldridge Tide And Pilot Book is a classic text that covers the U.S. East Coast, complete with a folksiness reminiscent of the *Farmer's Almanac*. Most marine stores have handy, pocket-sized tide booklets that list the heights of the tides for each day of the year.

However, the directions currents take and their timing are generally more meaningful for sea kayakers than are the differing heights of tides. And that's why, unlike skippers of bigger boats, you as a paddler need to know what the currents are doing.

Currents are caused by the movement of water. Along continental coastlines, there's generally a "longshore" current moving slowly in one direction. Another kind, "tidal" currents, are caused by the tides of the oceans and Great Lakes. Freshwater currents are a third kind, these being caused by fresh water flowing from one place to another. Tidal currents reverse their direction once or twice a day, but river currents flow in one direction only. But, wherever tidal water mingles with a freshwater flow, such as near coastal river mouths or in brackish estuaries, their currents affect each other. It is not unusual for an ocean current to overcome a river current for part of the day and flow against it even 100 miles upriver from the mouth. Moreover, wherever a freshwater current gets restricted, such as in a narrow river gorge, the velocity of the current increases. Tidal currents get stronger or weaker not only where they're restricted, such as over an undersea shelf, but also due to the changing height of the tide.

Coastal paddling is greatly affected by the patterns of movement of water in and out of bays, estuaries, and rivers. In many places, you can take advantage of the local tidal currents by timing your trip to flow with them in one direction for part of the day and then be boosted homeward when they reverse. If your favorite coastal passage normally has a southbound longshore current, and if a storm brings winds up from the south, be prepared for the stiff chop that forms wherever wind direction opposes the current direction. Tides also can affect your plans. For example, high tide may let you take shortcuts over sandbars that, when exposed at low tide, would force you several miles out of your way.

The highest and lowest tides intensify during the full and new moons and when the moon is in perigee, the closest to us in its orbit around the Earth. Pristine beaches can become foul-smelling mud flats at those low tides, and leave you and your ladened boat far from the water.

4. Check Your Compass.

Learning how to use a magnetic compass is essential. You'll need a hand-bearing compass or a steering compass, or both. In determining the line of position of two or more charted objects, you hold the hand-bearing compass in one hand and point it at the objects. The steering compass tells you what direction the boat is pointing, because it fits into a mounting bracket that has been lined up with the boat's centerline. You may prefer a steering compass that also serves as a hand-bearing compass, so that you just lift it from its bracket whenever you need to take a hand bearing. Other aids, such as data scopes, can also help you take bearings, but they're costly.

Before you even get started, you'll use a compass to mark your various *course headings* (travel directions) for your trip in conjunction with your chart. Do so even if you know you'll be able to see where you're going, because if fog or a rain squall rolls in, your sightlines will be shortened or blocked out entirely. Your compass heading will be the only guide for which direction to turn to go on or turn back.

Check your compass regularly, even when you think you know exactly where you are and where you're headed. You may gradually be drifting off course without realizing it. The more you use your compass, the more confidence you'll gain. Whenever in doubt about your position or course, trust your compass—not your internal sense of direction.

Rules of the Road

Going out on the water is like going out on a highway where separate rules apply to trucks, cars, bikes, farm vehicles, and pedestrians. In the nautical world, each different type of vessel has its own rights and responsibilities. As a kayaker, you need to understand the limits of your rights, the enormity of your responsibilities, and what to expect from all the other types of boats sharing your environment.

5. Understand Who Has the "Right Of Way."

The complex rules for navigating on inland and international waters are set down in the Navigation Rules, International–Inland. The rules cover the rights of vessels that are encumbered by their commercial fishing gear or limited in their ability to maneuver within a marked channel, about who is responsible to yield to whom in a crossing or overtaking situation, and much more. Some kayakers believe that they're the most encumbered vessels on the water, since they don't have motors or sails, and that they therefore should have the right of way. Theoretically, yes; in practical terms, no.

What applies to kayakers is the unwritten rule of gross tonnage: If they're bigger than you, get out of their way. Since even the heaviest sea kayak is lighter than the average dinghy, it weighs in at the bottom of the pecking order. You may have a right to be in a certain spot, but you risk being dead right if you get run over by a barge operating out of channel. Besides, even though your vessel is merely muscle-powered, you have a surprising range of movement and number of ways to dodge around. Use these advantages to stay out of the way of others.

6. Learn to Judge What Traffic Is Doing.

At all times, as in any traffic situation, you should swivel your head to spot potential danger. In the words of one baseball philosopher, "you can see a lot by watching." The waters and moving boats have clues written all over them about what they will be doing next.

Channel buoys tell you where big ships and barges will be running if they don't want to run aground. Learn how to read buoys, so you'll know if you're inside or outside the channel, and, if you're inside, which lane you're in. Look out for sailing regattas and races; often they set triangular orange markers that should warn you off. Keep tabs of the locations of sandbars and shallow water; you can be pretty sure the larger craft won't come near them.

Take a look at any boat coming into your vicinity. You can generally determine if it's on a collision course with you by looking at the centerline of its bow. If you see equal amounts of boat on both sides of the centerline, it may be a hit. If more boat appears on one side than the other, it's a miss. Unless the current is pushing one of you sideways, of course.

Similar hints are apparent from the water cutting off the boat's bow or at night from its red and green running lights. Study vessels as they pass safely by you to learn the tricks of reasonable expectations.

7. Work on Being Seen and Signal Your Intentions.

Bikes on roadways carry neon-orange pennants on tall rods and their riders wear reflective clothing. You should be doing something similar to make certain you and your tiny craft are visible to the helmsmen of powerboats, sailboats, and merchant ships. Opt for brightly colored PFDs. (It's not by accident that Canada sanctions only the colors yellow and international-rescue-orange for life jackets used in its waters.) You can help other boaters see you by using colorful paddle blades, and yellow is a top choice.

Very few kayakers carry marine radios, but if they did, they could talk to the larger craft, telling them of their intentions to cross busy channels, or to move into docking areas. The worst way to signal your intentions to other boat traffic is to act erratically, turning here and there.

If you're with other kayaks, stay close enough together so that you can operate like one larger vessel made of numerous kayaks. This grouping will help other boats spot you and avert you. If a larger boat seems hesitant about your movements in a potential collision course, you should stop moving. Signal to the other skipper that your "motor" is shut off, that you don't plan to go ahead, by putting down your paddle and crossing your arms. Once assured that you won't dart out in front, the other boat can proceed safely by you.

Making Your Way

These remaining sea-savvy pointers will help you know where you are at all times so you'll be able to control your situation—as much as anything can be controlled on open water.

8. When You Start Off, Make Certain to Look Back.

This seems like such common sense, but an amazing number of paddlers fail to take visual bearings on their launching site. Later, they don't recognize where they put in and can't exit. Looking back starts you off on the right foot for the rest of your trip. As you make a habit of seeing how the world will appear on your return trip, you'll also be spotting any boat traffic that may be sneaking up on you from behind.

Take your first back-sighting about 100 yards off shore. Take note of landmarks that should help you distinguish the spot from its surroundings, such as a prominent house, a flag pole, and so forth. Turn around again after another few hundred yards and you'll start seeing other reference points on the horizon, such as a large water tank or radio tower. Etch these mental images in your head.

9. Read the "Road Signs" You See Along the Way.

You'll find many road signs on land and water that can help you gauge how far you've come, and how much farther you need to paddle. They'll also let you know how weather changes might affect you later as you retrace your route.

Have a clear idea of which buoys you should expect to see on your trip. They are numbered, so you can count them off on your chart as you pass, and get a broad idea of your location. Buoys move around in the current and wind because they're anchored to the bottom of the waterway with flexible chains or cables. So you should use these floating navigational aids only to indicate your general location.

Look for shallows and sand bars that relate to your chart. On your return trip, will they be covered or exposed? Will an incoming tide make the area treacherous as you return?

Keep looking for reference points on the shoreline and in the distance behind. Smoke stacks, church steeples, towns. All of these feed you useful information to keep your bearings. And you don't necessarily have to use your compass for an exact position. Just take note of your general position in relation to these road signs.

10. Keep Track of Wind and Compensate for Its Effect on Your Course.

Wind will almost always shape your paddling day. Strong head winds could change your destination, since they slow you down and limit the distance you cover. Be wary of tail winds. The free ride they give you in the morning will be against you in the afternoon, possibly forcing you to paddle until nightfall.

And if you were planning to ride a favorable current on the way back, that wind would create strong wave action against you.

Beam winds will toss you off course. If you must make a specific landfall on the far side of an open crossing, you should compensate for the effect of beam winds. There are complex formulas for compensating for the side drift. However, you'll be reasonably accurate if you adjust your course 20 to 25 degrees to windward.

11. Be Careful in Judging Distances.

On the water, distances can look deceptively shorter than they really are. What might look like a point of land three miles ahead may be six miles or more in the distance. You could easily over-commit yourself on what seemed like a short crossing to an island. The better way to judge distance is to use your chart, not your eye, until you develop a better sense of distance.

12. Always Leave Yourself an Out.

Have an escape route or bail-out option. It's very easy to get into situations that are over your head. Unless you work out some alternate routes or find places along the route where you can cut short a difficult trip, you could condemn yourself to a hard and possibly dangerous trip. When disaster befalls paddlers, it's usually because they saw no choice but to press on with original plans that got them into deeper trouble.

Look at your chart. Note places where you could easily pull out if you had to. Use the chart to plot out alternate routes that can help you escape from bad weather or unusual winds, just in case you deem such action necessary. If you give yourself an out, you can always come back to paddle another day.

CHAPTER 10

Developing Confidence, Learning Rescue Skills

Any kayak can capsize. Tip one beyond its final stability point and it will go belly up. Folding kayaks give you generous amounts of stability to play with, and they tolerate your inattention to balance and the action of the sea around you. But they all have a tip-over line; cross it and you'll land in the drink.

As a folding kayaker, you need to test the level of stability your boat allows so you can gain confidence in it. Bracing is, of course, one way to feel out your boat's fine line. Even though your ordinary paddling in a foldable hardly ever needs even a slap brace to restore its balance, you should occasionally do some brace strokes anyway. This practice will help you get that feel for how much your boat will heel before bracing is necessary.

Other drills can also give you a sense of balance and stability. You can do things in a folding kayak that you would never dare in a rigid one, as you will learn below. These drills will build your confidence in your boat and prepare you for self-rescue—and even the rescue of others.

Rescues performed in folding kayaks differ from those of rigid boats. The reentry methods are remarkably easy, almost intuitive, as you will also see below. However, you do have to watch out for some common errors that would test even a foldable's ability to support your reentry.

Confidence Drills

How stable is your foldable? How do you find out? Here are some confidence-building drills that can be done in a single or in a double boat by either paddler.

Before you try any of these drills, make sure you and your boat are set up properly. If your boat has an open cockpit, give yourself more room to move around by leaving off the spraydeck. Be near shore or with some other boat that can help you out. At first, try to do these drills in relatively calm water, until you gain confidence to move into wavier conditions. Remove all loose things from your kayak, so if you do have a spill you won't have to chase after your gear as it floats away.

Be prepared for any prolonged immersion. Dress with long sleeves and pants or a wet suit, even if the water is warm. (More about prolonged immersion later in this chapter.)

Most importantly, fill your boat up with all the flotation you can. The built-in air sponsons aren't enough; get float bags to fill the underdeck portions. Chapter 5 has more information about helpful accessories. Float bags will help keep your boat higher, and it will take on less water, making it easier to empty.

Drill #1

Lift your body completely out of your seat. To do so, support yourself with your hands on the coaming or washboards. Most paddlers have sufficient arm strength to perform this confidence builder. It makes getting in and out a lot easier, especially when you do have a spraydeck attached, and particularly if you have long legs. And it will help you do the push-off start covered in Chapter 7 for getting off the shore quickly.

Drill #2

Get on your knees. The hardest part of this drill is not to scratch or bang yourself up on the crossribs, seat, or fittings. (That's why it's best done with long pants and a long-sleeved shirt, even a cushiony wet suit.) Get into a squat, then onto your knees, and move forward a bit in the boat.

Drill #3

Turn around in your seat—totally around. Some people are monkeys and can do this without hesitation. If you're not a monkey, you can turn around one step at a time. Keep low, twist your upper body to one side, lean on your forearm, and quickly get your lower body turned around. You should now be facing backwards with your body somewhat stretched out. Now, tuck your knees up and raise your upper body as much as you feel comfortable doing.

Drill #4

Crawl a bit out onto the back deck. You do this as an extension of Drill #3. You may find yourself in this position during a self-rescue, so it's excellent practice. Make certain to get a good grip on the coaming on both sides of you, balancing your weight on both hands. Keep low and crawl just a little way onto the back deck, just to get a feel for the position and how secure you are.

Drill #5

Change boats while on the water. This trick can be done with hardshells but is incredibly easy in folding kayaks. It's not only a confidence drill but also a technique worth knowing. You may someday have to switch boats on open water, if someone in a single is hurt or feels ill. Switching the individual to a double may be a good safety measure.

First attempt this drill with at least one double. Here's how to do it with one single and one double:

Get the boats side-to-side, facing in the same direction, with their cockpits next to each other. The front paddler of the double and the single paddler should grab the coaming of the opposite boat. The back paddler of the double sits up on the back deck and throws one leg over the back deck of the single. The single paddler can now move into the back seat of the double. If you're the paddler who's switching boats, remember to keep low, crawl over to the other boat on your belly, then turn your body around into the seat when your legs are in that boat's cockpit.

Next, it's the turn of the paddler hanging out on the back deck to be seated. The paddlers presently seated in the double both hold the coaming of the single boat. The person on the back deck of the double shifts his or her weight to the single boat and rolls over, belly first, onto the back deck of the single, facing the stern. Then he or she crawls, feet first, into the cockpit and then flips into a seated position.

Drill #6

Stand up. Yes, stand up. It's amazing how few folding-kayak owners are willing to try this. This is one drill that will impress hardshell kayakers who have

Switching between doubles.
(Dan Chu)

The ultimate confidence test. *(Sean Coffey)*

a hard time even turning around in their boats. You may want to do this in steps.

First, just lift yourself off your seat into a squat position while gripping the coaming or washboard on either side of you. Keep your feet spread out to each side as much as possible to give you a wide base for balancing yourself. Be careful in a Klepper not to get your foot caught under the edge of the keel board, a distinct possibility if you're wearing sandals.

As you get a greater sense of confidence, stand up all the way. Do it for a moment if that's all you can manage. The objective is not to hang around standing in your boat, but rather to prove to yourself how well your boat will balance. A double folding kayak offers as stable a platform as a floating dock, particularly if someone is sitting in the other seat providing ballast. Regular-sized singles are a little hard to remain standing in, unless you're extremely agile. The mini-foldables will tolerate only a quick stand—and an even quicker sitting down.

Self-Rescue Skills

If you look at other sea-kayaking manuals, you'll find reams of detailed information on rescues after a capsize. They suggest that if no other boats are around to give you a hand, you should self-rescue using a paddle float, or better yet, know how to Eskimo roll.

But here you are, the proud owner of a folding kayak that will not Eskimo roll, and you're feeling a bit intimidated, maybe somewhat less of a sea kayaker

than everyone else around you, rolling their hearts out.

Don't be concerned. As a self-rescue technique, rolling is not what it's cracked up to be. After an unexpected capsize, few people who have learned how to roll will succeed in using it to come back up. They blow their roll, have to wet exit, and do a reentry with a paddle float, i.e., they have to get in like the rest of us. Skill at Eskimo rolling requires constant honing in all kinds of conditions before it becomes a dependable self-rescue method. Only paddlers who are willing to put in considerable amounts of time can continuously claim to have a fail-safe, "bomb-proof" roll.

Your simple moves for self-rescue in a capsized folding kayak are easy to learn, hard to forget, and they don't require precise timing or holding your breath. Self-rescue for doubles and singles will be covered first. Then, you'll learn how to participate in a group rescue.

Any rescue, whether assisted or done without outside help, should be thought of in three "gets," which are expanded upon later:

1. Get the boat right-side up (assuming it was hull-side up).

2. Get yourself back in.

3. Get the water out.

Depending on how much water you have in the boat, you may want to get number 3 before you get number 2.

1. Get the Boat Right-side Up

This can seem the most daunting of tasks when you're neck deep in water and a bit scared. Wearing a PFD is a must, because to get the boat cockpit-side up again, you're going to have to push upward. Without the buoyancy of your PFD, every application of upward pressure would only push you underwater—not right the boat.

Here are three techniques for your practice sessions. See what works best for you. The first is probably the only workable one with a fully-loaded single or double. The others will work for light loads in either type boat.

Over the Hull of the Boat

For the first one, begin by throwing yourself over the belly-up boat from the side, reach over to the far

First Things First: Five Points to Remember

1. Be decisive. Use the rescue method that first comes to mind and do it fast. A better method may eventually occur to you if you start weighing options and jogging your memory, but don't hang around deciding. Do something right away.

2. Check the condition of the people in the water. If you and your partner in a double are turned over, the first thing to do is check if your partner is okay. Ask, "Are you alright?" If someone else is in the water and you're the rescuer, establish how the person is. Speak without panic in your voice. Help keep the swimmer calm.

3. Forget about loose, floating gear. Attend to the people, and get them back into their boats. Then worry about that floating hat or lunch bag.

4. Do worry about paddles. If you go over, make certain that you hang on to your paddle. If other paddlers are being rescued, get their paddles immediately, so long as it doesn't hinder the rescue effort.

5. Make sure nobody remains in the water long. While you're emptying water from a rescued boat, try to get its occupants out of the drink and onto the deck of some other boat, at least until they can get back in their own boat. Your goal is to reduce their exposure time in the water—and its inherent risk of hypothermia.

---

side, try to grab the coaming, and, with a snap of your upper body, pull the boat toward you. If done right, it will break the suction and get the boat upright with little water in it. It has to be done quickly; otherwise a slow flip over will scoop up lots of water, especially if your boat has an open cockpit without its spraydeck.

If you're trying this method in a double, you have two choices. Both of you get on the belly-up boat and proceed as above. Remember to time the pull-over maneuver so that you do it together, using a signal if you have to. If both of you can't participate in the pull-over, have one partner assist from the other side, helping find the hand-holds, pushing up, and so forth.

In the Upside-down Cockpit

This second method borrows from how capsized canoes are sometimes tossed right-side up. It will work for either a single or double foldable kayak. Dive under the boat and poke your head into the cockpit. You'll have a huge air pocket where you can breathe and calm down in what is termed "a zone of silence." Then you (and your partner, if in a double) will push

Getting ready to enter the zone of silence.

up forcefully on one coaming side (be sure to agree which one) while pulling the opposite side to keep it from sinking and scooping up water.

A Hybrid Method

This third approach is generally for doubles although workable in a single. For a double, both paddlers should be on the same side of the boat. One reaches under to get a grip on the coaming on the opposite side. At the same time, both people push up on the closer side to begin flipping the boat. As the boat starts to go up, the first person pulls on the opposite coaming to keep it from submerging and scooping water. In a lightly loaded single, you might just be able to push the boat over right-side up. As it is going over, grab the opposite coaming to move it quickly toward you, so it doesn't scoop water or get away from you.

No matter which of these three methods works best for you, try these additional tricks to get the boat righted more quickly. Try rocking the boat a bit to break the suction seal created by the air pocket. Try to break the seal on the side that will be rotating up through the air. Try to maneuver the boat so the side that will be going up is pointed toward the wind, because the wind may help flip the boat over. At least it will decrease the resistance to righting.

2. Get Back In

Here's where the differences between doubles and singles are really evident. The methods below take advantage of the fact that there are two of you in a double, and one can steady the boat while the other climbs in. In singles you don't have that luxury. In either situation, these hints should ease the task.

1. Now that the boat is righted, try to keep it pointing into the wind—its most stable position—so it won't tend to swing around or away from the entering paddler. In the instructions on doubles below, the rear person reenters first to start operating the rudder or using a paddle to control the boat from the best steering vantage point. A sea anchor would also be useful to keep the boat pointed into the wind.

2. Make certain that your pant legs aren't ballooned with water, a distinct possibility if you wear paddling pants that cinch at the ankles. That extra water weight won't help you get into the boat.

3. Keep your body as flat as possible at all times. This even goes for your body position in the water as you attempt to enter your boat. If you have your body straight down in the water you will be dangerously pulling the boat over and down. By keeping your body parallel to the water's surface, you'll glide yourself in with the force of a swimming kick, with little tendency to upset things. Also, when you finally are up out of the water and on your boat, remain low and flat. This will keep the center of gravity (yours and the boat's) as low as possible to prevent tipping. If you use the over-the-deck approach, crawl on the deck until you're in a position to twist your body into your seat.

Reentering Doubles

If you are in a double, you have several options. Try them to see which one would be most workable for you in an emergency.

Over stern self-rescue in a double.

Have one paddler hold the bow while the other gets in.

If you're the person holding the bow, hoist yourself slightly up on the front deck while the rear paddler gets in from either the side or back. If the boat has a rudder, the rear-deck entry means coming in from the rear quarter, not straight over the back. Then you get in from a front quarter or straight up the bow.

Have one paddler on each side of the boat.

The rear paddler climbs in from one side while the front paddler, who is still in the water, holds the opposite coaming. Then the front paddler gets in while the rear paddler low-brace sculls to the side opposite where the front paddler is getting in.

This second method may have several advantages over the first one. The boat is extremely secure when the first paddler is getting in, because the other paddler is on the opposite side, a great position for preventing a re-capsize. It doesn't require as much crawling on decks, which is not an especially stable activity.

Reentering a Single Foldable

Getting back into a single folding kayak is easier than into a rigid one. Except in very rough conditions, you can dispense with the need for a paddle float to steady the boat. You have two approaches for getting back in sans paddle float.

Over the back deck.

Get alongside the rear of the boat and face front. Grab on to both sides of the boat and hoist yourself onto the back deck still facing forward. Your legs should be straddling each side, your feet in the water, and your upper body low to keep the center of gravity down. Now, with your hands reaching forward, pull yourself along the deck. When you have the trunk

of your body over the cockpit, bring your legs in and drop into your seat.

This method can be difficult if your boat has a rudder with steering cables running along the deck's surface. Also, when you are over the cockpit, it is hard to drop in without raising your upper body somewhat. But if you do so quickly, you should be alright.

From the side.

This position offers you a greater amount of stability and avoids any deck cables. Get aligned in the water alongside your cockpit with your belly down and legs and feet stretched out behind you horizontally toward the bow. Grab on to the coaming on the near side, and then try to grab the far side coaming. If you cannot reach that far, get that hand at least onto the back of the cockpit.

Your flattened-out body should be almost parallel to the boat. Start kicking your feet to bring them to the surface. Continue kicking to help lift your body out of the water as you pull yourself up with your hands. Aim to put your head and upper shoulders over the back deck. Now start crawling toward the stern until your feet and legs can drop into the cockpit. Keeping low, twist your body into the seat. The confidence drills should have helped you get the sense of balance you need for this.

Paddle-float method.

If conditions are exceptionally rough or you don't feel you have a good sense of balance at the moment, use a paddle float. The various kinds of paddle floats inflate differently, so be certain to figure yours out on land. In general you inflate a paddle float about half to three-quarters full, then place one blade into the paddle-float pocket. Now it's ready to use. Inflating the float will be easier if you can throw yourself over the cockpit before doing it.

Self-rescue in a single from the side, without paddle float.

Self-rescue with paddle float.

The beginning and end of the paddle-float reentry resembles the over-the-side method covered above. Line yourself up alongside the cockpit. Place the paddle float at a right angle to the boat with the other end across the back of the cockpit. Hold it there with one hand grabbing both the coaming and shaft and the other hand on the paddle about level with the side of the boat. The float will be acting as an outrigger, which will help you pull yourself up on the boat. If you have trouble lifting yourself up onto the boat, put one leg over the shaft to raise your body half way out of the water. Continue to pull yourself up until you get right over the cockpit, similar to the previous method. Then twist into the cockpit in the direction of the float.

No matter how you get yourself back into the boat, you'll probably want to rest there a minute to get yourself settled down.

3. Get the Water Out

If you capsize where no other boat can lend assistance, and if your boat is brimming full of water, you should try getting some of the water out before you climb back in. On the other hand, you may have managed to capsize and right your foldable without scooping up much water. In either case, here's how to proceed.

Whatever you do, don't try bailing or pumping from an in-the-water position. It's too awkward and inefficient. Keep in mind that a double boat is capable of holding about 150 gallons of water (a single around 80 gallons). That's an awful lot of pumping to be doing from alongside your boat. Here are two methods that work to get volumes out in a hurry:

Get the Boat on its Side.

This method works well if you are on a day trip and not carrying much weight in gear. Folding kayaks have wonderfully buoyant sponsons; you take advantage of this unique feature to get lots of water out quickly. Putting the boat on its side places it on one of its sponsons. The sponson will lift the cockpit out of the water and bilge water will come pouring out. At most, what you'll have left to contend with when you're back in is a few inches of water.

Climb on the Back Deck and Rock the Boat.

Get on the back of the boat once it is upright. In a double, one paddler does this and starts rocking up and down, with the front person at the bow pushing

What happens if swamped and you don't have extra flotation.

up and steadying the boat. The rocking action can get a third of the water out of a totally swamped boat quickly as the water sloshes back and forth and out the cockpit toward the rear. You can also do this with a single boat to get some water out if completely swamped.

There are times when you might not want to attempt to do these steps even if your boat is totally swamped. You might be getting blown into a shipping lane or onto a rocky shoreline. If that is the case get back into your boat right away.

Unlike a rigid kayak, a folding kayak is extremely stable when filled with water. Since the air sponsons run along the perimeter of the boat, they act like a life preserver ring to stabilize the boat. Rigid kayaks have their flotation at the ends (watertight compartments), which makes these boats want to spin like a barbecue rotisserie; they are notoriously unstable when swamped.

In a folding kayak, you can just paddle off even with virtually no freeboard and water continuing to lap over you. You can even paddle the boat totally submerged. It is not the fastest way to be paddling a kayak but you will be able to move out of harm's way. Being in the boat with your spray skirt on will keep you warmer and prevent the cold from sapping the strength needed to pump out water.

If you have added extra flotation at both underdeck ends of your kayak in the form of air bags or waterproof storage bags, you're in even a better position. The air sponsons will stabilize your kayak from rolling over like a swamped rigid kayak, while the extra flotation will give you a few inches of freeboard so water does not keep washing over you.

Pumping and Bailing

Getting water out with a pump or a bailer is better done from inside your boat. If your boat is very full, be prepared for the process to take half an hour or more including some rest periods.

Generally, a bailer will move more water faster than a pump. Scooping and emptying a bailer is less tiring than the piston-like push and pull of a hand pump. But you should plan to have both. A bailer will

Sea Socks

One of the best ways of dealing with water that may get into your kayak is not to let it enter in the first place. A sea sock will do the job. The device is a waterproof fabric bag that fits over the coaming of a cockpit. You sit in that bag within your kayak. The bag, or sea sock, will give you a generous amount of wiggle room within your cockpit and yet not cling to your every move.

It works in two ways. One, in itself the sea sock is small enough that in the event of a capsize it could not take on much water. Two, air pressure from the inside of your boat tends to press out against the sea sock; this resistance helps keep the sea sock from filling up.

If you capsize and have a sea sock attached, there isn't much water to empty out. The little bit that does get into the sea sock can be expelled by simply reaching into the cockpit and turning the sock inside out, which will dump the water out.

The trouble with sea socks is that they hinder your access to things you may need when out on the water. To work, they should be tightly attached to the coaming. This makes them difficult to remove and reattach if you need something.

Only Feathercraft offers sea socks for its models. The socks work well because of the rigid individual coamings the company uses. It is possible to devise your own sea sock for an open-cockpit folding kayak. You would attach it to the same ring in the spraydeck to which you attach your spray skirt. Such an arrangement would not be quite as watertight as that on the Feathercraft but would work well enough.

work well if conditions aren't bringing more water in. If seas are breaking over the deck, you may not be able to bail.

To deal with such conditions, first tighten on your spray skirts. Then push your pump down along the front of your body into the top of the skirt and into the cockpit. Now as you use your hand pump, more water will not come crashing into your boat. In a double, take turns pumping, or pump at the same time if you have two pumps. It's important to keep waves from hitting you broadside, so keep steering into the direction of the sea and wind. Again, a sea anchor would help keep you pointing into the wind. With adequate flotation, you'll be floating high enough not to take on too much water and you'll have fewer cubic feet of water to expel.

Electric pumps are another alternative to hand pumps. These work while you use your hands for better things than pumping, such as paddling. They're not the speediest things in the world but they do work, completely emptying a double in around 20 minutes to half an hour. These were discussed in Chapter 5 on Accessories.

Group Rescues

Having another boat around, a single or a double, greatly aids a rescue. It can even help in flipping the capsized boat over, getting most of the water out, and getting the occupants back in. You should learn how to participate in an assisted rescue from the perspective of both victim and rescuer.

Make certain to heed the five points made earlier about "First Things First" so that you have your priorities straight in making the rescue. Also watch out for other factors mentioned earlier such as the victim's pants cuff gaskets sealing up water in the legs, making reentry extra difficult.

Flipping the boat over and getting water out are part of the same procedure, so will be treated together. Assisting victims back into their boat will follow.

Flip and Empty

The first step is to get water out of the capsized boat fast so you can get its paddlers back in. The steps are a takeoff of the methods used for self-rescue only more quick and effective. Here are a few suggestions:

Get the capsized kayak on its side, alongside and parallel to the rescuing kayak.

If the victim's boat is a folding kayak, you can help get it to ride up on its sponson. The victim pulls up onto the deck of the rescuing boat and pulls on the coaming of the capsized boat to get it to spin toward the rescuing boat. As seen earlier, this will get out plenty of water in a hurry. If the victim's boat is a hardshell, this procedure will be somewhat more difficult unless the boat has flotation bags at either end or watertight end compartments. Give this method a try anyway, because it certainly won't hurt.

Get the two boats perpendicular to each other with the victim's boat bow facing into the rescue boat.

With the victim's boat still upside down, the rescuer pulls the bow up on deck a foot or so. The rescuer then rocks the victim's boat while the victim puts full weight on the stern of the capsized boat to push it down. This motion will force water to run out through the cockpit. The victim's boat is then flipped right-side up. It will have very little water in it.

There's a danger that the weight of the flooded kayak could crack something on your deck. It happens to the decks of fiberglass kayaks when they do rescues; it could happen to your foldable. The top bar might crack or bend. Weigh this potential damage against the urgency of the situation. You can reduce this danger by pulling only a small part of the capsized boat onto your deck and having the person in the water do most of the work. If you feel strong enough, you might just grab the bow while it's alongside your boat rather than dragging it onto your deck. If the rescuing boat is a folding double, you might want to pull the bow of the capsized boat between the two paddlers since this is generally the strongest part of the boat. By the way, hardshellers call this the TX-assisted rescue.

Use two rescuing boats to do the emptying.

If you have two or more boats, you can do what is termed the H-I two-boat-assisted rescue. The two rescuing boats line up side-by-side facing in the same direction. The victim's upside-down boat is floated between the two, bow toward the rescuers. The two rescuers lay both of their paddles perpendicular to, and spanning, the space between them. The bow of the victim's boat is lifted onto the paddles, something like how it's lifted onto the rescuer's deck in the one-boat rescue. The victim, however, has greater leverage to push and twist the capsized boat, because he or she can half sit on the bow of one of the rescuing boats.

As the victim's boat is pushed farther onto the combined paddles, more and more water will pour out through the cockpit opening. Seesawing it up and down will leave the boat almost dry. As the emptied boat is pushed back into the water, quickly flip it right-side up to keep the cockpit area from sucking up water once again.

Getting Back Aboard

To get the victim back in, place the now-emptied boat parallel to yours. Any two boats that are rafted up or held together become a very stable platform. Your body weight enhances the foldable's steadiness even more.

Start by having both boats pointed in the same direction. If you're the rescuer, grab the cockpit coaming of the victim's boat near the back with both hands. Lean into your grip on the other boat; it won't bite you. You now have a platform that is five to six feet wide and will hold through just about anything, as long as you're not timid about using your body weight to keep the platform together.

Or you opt to span the two boats with your paddle. Place it behind you and have it lying across to the back of the other boat's coaming. If both boats were rigid kayaks, you would have to do this just to keep both boats stable. But you don't have to when yours is a foldable. The paddle, however, might serve as a useful gripping point for the person in the water to pull up on when reentering.

Reentry is identical to that of the self-rescue. So if you're the victim, remember to stay flat on the water almost parallel to the rescuing boat, pull yourself up at a low angle toward the rear deck, get your legs into cockpit, spin around, and you're rescued.

Only this time, as the victim, you'll have extra help getting in. For example, as you start lifting yourself out of the water, the rescuer can grab the back of your life jacket or seat of your pants to help you get out. The rescuer can also help pull and aim your legs into your cockpit, or steady you as you turn around into your seat. The rescuer could also assist you in bailing, reattaching your spray skirt, and so forth.

- *How to Pack for the Travel School of Hard Knocks*
- *How to Use One for a Wide Range of Activities*
- *How to Modify and Maintain Your Boat*

PART THREE

Using and Enjoying

Folding kayaks demand little, deliver a lot. They adapt to your needs, not the other way around.

Transport a foldable anywhere in the world by every means from camel to Concorde. Carry it around in its bag or keep it assembled if you wish—your pick. This section of the book will show you how to pack away your foldable to minimize risk to parts and skin during travel.

Enjoy your folding kayak in many ways beyond paddling. A foldable is flexible in spirit, not just in structure. Have an urge to sail? No problem. Folding kayaks are born to hoist canvas and move with the winds. Want to camp? Foldables swallow up gear for weeks of adventure along your favorite water trail or coastline. Have it your way—fish, hunt, row, scuba dive, snorkel, bird watch, take pictures. In Part Three you'll get practical information that will help you enjoy the wide range of activities available to you in a folding kayak.

Accept the boat as it comes from the factory, or customize it to fit your needs. Fiddle, make changes, add do-dads. Your foldable is adaptable. This section will show you modifications that you may find handy and it will tip you off to ways to keep your boat young. Maintenance? Surprisingly little is needed to get scores of years of service from one.

CHAPTER 11

Traveling with a Foldable

Folding kayaks were born to travel. They were first conceived of as boats that could be folded up into portable bags that Alpine vacationers could take aboard trains traveling to mountain lakes and streams. The creators of the first generation of folding kayaks weren't thinking of seaworthiness. But when forced to construct their vessels of collapsible, flexible frames with fabric coverings, they stumbled upon the underlying design principles of the Eskimo kayak, which is arguably the best open-water craft ever built. So its offspring, though aimed at parochial pursuits, unintentionally became globe-trotters—able to be taken and paddled anywhere.

The concept of a folding kayak is mind-boggling. From just a few cubic feet of portable storage space unfolds a fully-formed seaworthy vessel capable of transporting one or two people and all their gear along any waterway in the world, no matter how fierce its seas or remote its reaches. Folding kayaks have been carried by camels across Middle Eastern deserts, by dogsled out to fresh ocean leads off frozen Arctic coasts, and by horseback to high Sierra lakes. A folding kayak recently traveled by llama to a mountaintop lake in the Andes to set an altitude record for paddled craft.

You needn't go to such extremes to enjoy your folding kayak. You can release its potential for pleasure in temperate zones or in any easy-to-reach tropical paradise. And you needn't burden four-footed animals to find your own special world; planes, trains, and cars will do just fine. So will a mountain bike.

But before rushing off to the airport or train station, you should take some travel lessons from the school of hard knocks. Learn how to transport your foldable so that it arrives at your destination in the exact number of pieces it's supposed to.

By Plane

Let's start with planes, since they're what folding-kayak wanderlust is now most associated with. Air travel will transport you the farthest from your home with your foldable. It will open up your broadest horizons, putting you alongside some beckoning shore within a few hours. Add a few handfuls of minutes for assembly, and you will be in a position to paddle or sail off in exploration and personal discovery.

The airport is a good place to learn how to transport your folding kayak by other means of conveyance as well, because flying your stored-away foldable puts it at the mercy of its most rigorous testers—airline baggage handlers. If you can prepare your bags for airline baggage check-in, where they disappear into the dark hole at the end of the conveyor belt, then you can prep them to survive anything.

Folding kayaks have passed muster in air travel with flying colors. They have been kicked, shoved, abused, even tossed from on high, and they've still arrived in the right number of pieces. Several air travelers have retrieved their boat bags and found them adorned with tire marks; the bags had fallen off their baggage carts and been run over. Remarkably, the boats were able to be assembled without problems at the kayakers' destinations.

The funny thing about air travel with foldables is just how few people take added precautions in packing yet get away with it. The parts are just shoved in, the bags are zipped up or tied off, and they're handed

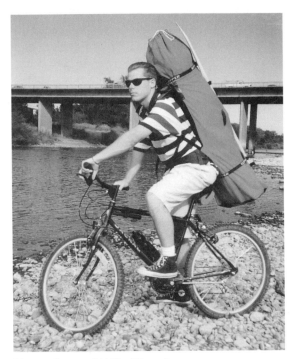

Biking with a mini-foldable. *(Klepper)*

over to the vagaries of the baggage system. Yet they usually arrive in fine shape.

But, why press your luck? Here are some simple precautions to take before traveling on airlines with your foldable:

Check with the Manufacturer

Even if your owner's instruction packet didn't contain additional information about packing the kayak for travel, the manufacturer may have it available through customer service. The company may even offer some add-on product that will help.

But be careful about one piece of advice. One manufacturer suggests that you can use the large flat boxes that are specially designed to carry bicycles on airplanes. It even provides elaborate plans on how to lay the kayak's frame members and skin inside the box. Be warned that these boxes have been known to break and spew parts. Such a box is meant to carry a 30-pound bike, not an 80-pound double boat. Baggage handlers are not ready for the unaccustomed weight of your boat and simply fumble the box. If you plan to use a bike box, you'll have to make your arrange-

ments with the airlines prior to your travel, and they'll require your early arrival and charge you extra.

Follow the Three Key Principles of Packing

Some items need extra protection, others don't. If you understand the principles, you're well on your way to happy packing. Here are the three cardinal rules:

The hull can take care of itself and of some other parts too.

Hypalon and other materials used for a boat's bottom are gluttons for punishment. You need do nothing in particular to protect them.

Take advantage of the hull's toughness to shield other parts of the boat, starting with the deck. Roll or fold up the skin so that the textile deck is shielded by the tougher hull. Depending on the particular boat, wherever possible place frame members within the enfolding hull.

Return frame members to the mass from whence they came.

Wooden frame members came from a tree trunk, aluminum ones from metal bars and ingots. If you pull wooden frame members together in a tight bundle, you return them to the strength of a log. Ditto for aluminum and for any other synthetic structural material.

For example, when packing long wooden frame parts, lash them together mercilessly. Leave them so there is absolutely no wiggle or play, even if you have to bend some flex out of them. Don't worry; it will spring back later. Aluminum tubing parts have far less chance of bending or crinking when tied together to form, in effect, one thick tube.

Some manufacturers provide you with separate straps to lash parts together in this way; use them. If none came with your boat, buy some or tie everything together with cord. If a bag has external straps, tighten them. If not, get some external straps, because they'll help snug frame parts into one fat parcel that can withstand plenty of punishment.

Ends of long pieces and fittings need protection.

You don't want the end of an aluminum piece to get dented. If either the male or female end gets pinched, you may not be able to mate them. Even

Ready to board small-engine plane, Bahamas

boats with wooden frames incorporate tubing to join ends. Cushion these ends with any combination of devices suggested below. The fittings used to connect crossribs to long pieces, though strong, also can suffer damage that would call for repair or replacement. Again, use cushioning. In some models, you'll be able to sneak the ribs inside the hull.

Or, you may want to try another approach toward protection; keep the more susceptible parts out of the baggage check-in system. The oval bag that carries Klepper crossribs is small enough to take on board as carry-on luggage. This eliminates one whole set of parts from your precautionary measures. Camping stores usually have inexpensive versions of this oval bag that can accommodate other foldables. You could also place the ribs in a regular suitcase mixed in with your clothing. Nautiraids don't lend themselves to this; some of their crossribs are attached to long parts.

Cushioning

You have a lot of choices in how to cushion parts from damage in transit. You can pick up some specialized materials or use items that serve a double purpose.

Some people use packing material such as bubble wrap or corrugated cardboard. This works fine for packing protection, but once you reach your destination you'll need to find a home for it. If you're flying to a friend's vacation home or back to your hometown, this material probably won't present a storage problem. But when flying to an isolated take-off point, you'll have to do something with the specialized packing material so that it's available for your return flight.

In that case, you'd be better off with cushioning that wasn't so specialized. For example, towels, which you probably are planning to take along anyway, can also be used to protect the ends of long bags. Shove one tightly folded towel down to the bottom and wrap another at the top of the ends. Or you can use articles of your clothing to do the job. If you're going to be camping, you could use small pieces of closed cell foam, which will be handy as camp seats. Be careful that you don't use so much cushioning that you won't be able to get your two-piece paddles into the long bag.

With any boat that comes in one bag, like the Feathercraft, you may want to shove clothing or towels in here and there. This will help round off the bag and protect end pieces, including the ends of the four-piece paddle.

If you feel a need to wrap crossframe members, you can usually find room to wrap foam sleeping pads around these. The same with long parts.

If you find that the cushion material hinders packing away parts, try thinner dimensions of the stuff. You don't really need a lot of padding. Remember, many folding-kayak travelers don't bother with padding and do fine. You're just trying to buy an extra measure of protection, not build a bomb shelter.

Loose Ends and Other Thoughts

Here are some loose ends to deal with both literally and figuratively.

Loose straps and strings.

You'll want to keep any shoulder harnesses from getting caught in the baggage conveyor belts. If they can be removed or zipped away, do so. If not, lash them in place by tying several belts or cords around the bags.

If your bags tie off, as do Kleppers and some older Nautiraids and Folbots, make sure to secure the knots. First double knot them and then put tape over the knot. This will prevent them from coming loose and allowing parts to spill out. And the tape will discourage any sneaky fingers from opening your bags in transit.

Airline baggage limits.

Some airlines limit the number of bags that you can check in for free, and above that number they charge you for excess baggage. If you have a foldable that is in one bag, no problem. If you have one that comes in several bags, you may get hit with the extra charge. Your first option is to find out which airlines have the more generous baggage limits. Another option is to double up your bags by buying a bigger bag that can carry two smaller ones within. Otherwise, you may sometimes get lucky if you use the airport's curbside check-in service, since porters are not always such sticklers for baggage limits as are the personnel at ticket counters.

Customs.

If you're traveling abroad, you'll have to deal with the U.S. Customs Department and the customs bureaus of other countries as well. Different countries vary in how they treat a disassembled boat being transported inside a bag. And within any country, one customs officer may be more harsh than another. There are no hard and fast rules.

When dealing with customs, the less said is probably the better. Put on a nonchalant smile as if everyone traveled with a boat these days. It's just another personal item like a tennis racket—only bigger. However, if you are pressed to explain what's in the bags, be prepared with descriptive information.

Make clear that this is your personal sports equipment that will leave with you when you exit the country. You intend to use it in the meantime, while staying at some luxury hotel. This shows that you are going to be enriching the local economy with your spending. Be careful about mentioning camping; campers may be looked upon as deadbeats who don't spend much locally.

Be prepared to open a bag and show its contents. If questions persist, it's a good idea to have with you some photos showing how the boat is assembled. These should be personal photos, not a manufacturer's brochure. A professional brochure could be interpreted as sales literature intended to help you sell the boat in that country, which would either be a no-no or require you to pay import duties. You may want to show the customs agent this book as an illustration of what folding kayaking is all about. (But *not* this page!)

Lastly, make certain to have your bill of sale with you. It could come in handy when returning to your home country to show that you bought it there, not abroad.

Shipping.

Instead of carting your boat through the airline systems with you, you might want to consider shipping it ahead. The cost of shipping a folding kayak via United Parcel Service (UPS) from the U.S. East Coast to the West Coast is between $40 and $60, depending on the weight and size. If you ship it a week or so in advance, the boat is sure to beat you to your destination. This will save you the hassle of dragging it through airline terminals on both ends, getting the stuff into cabs, and so forth.

To package your folding kayak for shipping, it's best to use the boxes that it originally came in. However, you could get away with using the carrying bags themselves. In a sense, they are duffel bags, and UPS will accept them as such for delivery.

By Car

You have three main choices when it comes to traveling by car. You could carry your boat in its bags inside the car, tie the bag or bags on the roof, or tie the assembled boat onto your car top and drive away, just as you would with any other type of cartop boat.

Your kayak is always best off inside your car. This keeps it out of the elements and relatively safe from theft, especially if it can fit into your trunk where it's out of sight. Even the largest of the doubles will fit into almost any car trunk, even that of a sub-compact car. So generally you won't have to put the disassembled boat on your roof unless your trunk is loaded with all your other gear. A disassembled boat will need to be made, but that is a 15-minute process once you get good at it. (See sidebar on speed assembly.)

A cartop boat will have to be untied and lowered, and since that will take you a few minutes anyway, it's not much of a time savings over the assembly process. And when first placing it on the roof you have to make certain it's fully secured, even locked. More and more rigid boats are being stolen from roof racks. You would have to protect a cartop foldable just as you would a rigid boat.

It's okay to cartop a folding kayak. This certainly

won't hurt the boat. You could drive thousands of miles at top speed with no negative effect—except on your gas mileage. Cartopping is sometimes handy at the end of a long day, when you're tired and don't want to wait for your boat to dry. Carrying it on a roof rack will dry it thoroughly in the rushing air. If you want to cartop your assembled foldable, here are some pointers on how to do it.

Getting It On

You get a foldable loaded onto the roof of a car just as you would do with a rigid boat. If you're strong enough and your roof is low enough, get your foldable up onto one shoulder.

The way to start to pick up a single boat is to stand along side the cockpit. Crouch down. Pull the boat onto your knees. Place your arm into the cockpit and swing the boat onto your shoulder. Use your other hand to help balance the boat. Stand at the car side with the cockpit facing away from it. Lift it onto both roof-rack bars at once, if you can, or first onto one bar, then onto the other. This procedure works well with a light mini-foldable.

If you have a heavier single foldable, a high roof, or both, do the following. Place a car mat on the ground alongside the car about even with its rear bumper, and place the boat alongside the car with its stern on the mat. Pick up the boat from around the middle toward the bow, pivoting it on its stern, which is protected by the mat from abrasion. Put the front half up onto the front roof-rack bar, then lift the stern end and put it on the rear bar.

With doubles, both partners lift the boat from the ground holding the ends of the boat. They can try to do it all at once onto both racks or do one rack at a time if needed.

If you're having trouble getting your foldable up from alongside the car, try it from behind the car. Have the boat angled 45 degrees from a point about half the length of the boat from the rear bumper. Put a mat on the ground at the stern. Lift the front and pivot the stern on the mat until you can get the bow onto the rear bar of the roof rack. Go to the stern and start lifting the boat onto the rack and pushing it forward until it slides onto the front bar.

Tying One On

Unless you're cartopping only occasionally, for only a few miles, and only at slow speeds, you should use a roof rack. An assembled boat that's simply tied onto a bare roof, with just a blanket protecting the boat and the roof metal, will tend to slip off to one side—or to come flying off.

If you already have a roof rack, you can purchase special kayak cradles that fit onto the roof-rack bars. They offer some added measure of protection, and so too do the windsurfer-rack pads that are made of nylon-covered rigid foam. If you use just the pads, an additional worthwhile investment might be what is termed a kayak stacker-bar set. Stacker

Cartopping a foldable.

bars go in the middle of the roof-rack bars and keep the boat from sliding around when the car is traveling at high speed. The stacker bars also give you a good point to tie the straps that secure the boat to the rack.

Carry your cartopper with the cockpit facing skyward. This is its strongest position and will put less stress on the kayak deck than would carrying it upside down. Pointing the bow toward the front of the car helps reduce wind resistance.

Use webbing straps to secure the boat at both roof-rack bars. Also put one line from the bow to the front bumper and a similar line from the stern to the rear bumper. The end lines will keep the boat steady

Speed Assembly Instructions

Several sea-kayaking manuals state that assembling a folding kayak is "tedious" and thus put off some would-be buyers. However, putting one together needn't be a chore. And, if you put your mind to it, you can get very fast at both assembly and disassembly. Here are some pointers that can give you an edge. You also might want to look at how the military speed-assembles its doubles.

To start off, make certain that all parts are labeled clearly. You might want to use bright colored tape to distinguish front parts of the boat from rear parts.

Study which is the best place to position your body in relation to the boat so you can do the most number of assembly/disassembly tasks from that one spot. Time is lost by jumping needlessly from one side of the boat to the other.

Experiment with how best to position your hands for attaching fittings, especially ones that may be giving you difficulty. Establish if there is some preferred order of rib placement, say, putting in No. 4 rib before No. 3. Camber and flex of frame parts may dictate this kind of order.

All of these steps taken together will almost guarantee that your assembly time decreases to the 12- or 15-minute range for nearly all the foldables reviewed earlier. If two of you are assembling a boat, try the speed-assembly method that is used by military special-forces teams who can't afford to hang around too long making their boats.

The instructions below are for assembling Kleppers, but you can adapt them to your own boat.

The military designates one person as team member A, the other B. Team member A is responsible for the long bag with keel boards, gunwales, etc. Member B is responsible for the hull bag and ribs. See what the duties below look like, they may help determine who will be A and who B. For example, whoever is handier with the several steps of rudder assembly should take the B role. Here goes:

A empties the long bag, while B does the same with the hull and rib bags.

A sorts the long pieces into front and rear piles. **B** sets out ribs in sequence alongside and spreads out the skin.

A assembles the front half of the frame. **B** assembles the rear half. Both insert their halves into the skin. Together they join frame halves and put in any remaining long stringers. **A** puts in rib No. 3 and grabs the coaming, and **B** places ribs No. 4 and No. 5.

A puts in the masthead end of the coaming. Both connect snap locks of ribs and tuck the black edge piping into the coaming grove. Whoever gets to the rear first puts in the boomerang piece.

Each puts in his or her respective seat and seat back.

Each inflates either a port or starboard air sponson, two thirds full.

A inserts the foot-pedal assembly. **B** places on the rudder, yoke, pins, and cables.

A attaches the front of the tuck-under spraydeck, and **B** attaches the rear. Each tucks under one side. **A** and **B** then finish inflating sponsons.

and are added security in case a strap breaks or a buckle slips.

The roof-rack straps should be tightened hard, even to the point that they indent the sponsons. The end lines should not be guitar-string tight. You should be able to roll the line around a bit of your finger with little effort.

Locking it on.

Get a bicycle cable lock set. The cable should be coated so it can't scratch the boat. Lash the cable around the stacker bar or the roof rack. Then work it into the cockpit and wrap it around a rib, gunwale, or anything it can go around. This will secure it against all but the most determined of thieves.

By Train or Bus

Folding kayaks were made to travel on trains, but few people still use them this way. Few people travel by bus with their kayaks either, because the automobile has replaced them both as the primary land conveyance for foldables.

If you do use public transportation to carry a foldable in its bags, treat the situation as you would if you were carrying your boat in a car trunk. You may not need to do any special packing, because the bags will be handled mainly by you. On a train you'll place them in overhead racks. For bus travel, they'll go into the lower storage area, placed by you or by someone who knows you are watching closely to see how the boat is handled.

However, you have to ask yourself how far you can carry the disassembled boat. You may have to cover long distances through terminals and out onto the bus or train platforms. Two people of average build can carry a disassembled double boat and enough camping equipment for a week's trip. One person can't duplicate that feat, especially with the camping gear.

If you're making overnight trips alone, you'll need a boat cart. Folding-kayak manufacturers offer carts that can carry one of their boats either assembled or in its bags. The carts vary in how easy they are to use. They have the advantage of being able to be folded away into your boat when you paddle off.

You can supplement the boat cart with an ordinary collapsible luggage cart for carrying your camping gear. You may wind up looking like a street person— pulling one cart and pushing the other—but it will help you get to a train that will take you to a week-long camping trip.

CHAPTER 12

Sailing

Don't let anyone kid you; if you want to move under full sail at top speeds, you're better off in a sailboat. No kayak can match its sailing performance. But a kayak, particularly a folding one, can take advantage of the wind, even tack into it pretty nicely. What's more, it will give you the underlying thrill of sailing as you search for wind, find it, and hang on for the ride. You might not be moving as fast as a sailboat, but, being so close to the water, you certainly will have the sensation of speed as bow waves break over the deck and you see the water rushing by.

A sailboat is much better at what it does, because it's dedicated to that pursuit alone. A sailboat has a deep keel or centerboard that allows it to hold position in cross winds and to point higher into the wind than could a kayak with its puny leeboard. Even the smallest sailboat carries at least 100 square feet of sail and can be rigged in all sorts of exotic ways. Kayaks on the other hand hardly ever carry more than around 50 square feet of sail area, because any more would be inviting a capsize.

But folding kayaks have several things going for them. If you're becalmed, you can paddle until you can find wind and take off again. Try doing that in a sailboat. You can sail a kayak in shallow waters in which a sailboat's deep centerboard would run aground. You can beach a kayak for exploration. And, of course, your folding kayak, sail and all, can be packed away in small bags for transport or storage.

Kayaks offer one other advantage that affects some people. If you get seasick on regular sailboats as they roll sharply from one side to the other, then the sailing kayak is your remedy. A kayak doesn't even induce a whiff of this common ailment, because you're so close to the water that your pendulum of swing is much smaller and lower. On the pitching deck of a sailboat, your body can be six feet and more above the water's pitching surface.

Folding kayaks are in keeping with the tradition of the great sailing canoes of the last century. Sailing canoes were among the fastest methods of transportation without the aid of motors. Foldables were almost from their very beginning built with sailing in mind.

Sailing is something you can do very well with a folding kayak, better than with most hardshells, because a foldable gives you a wider platform. All foldables have hull shapes that feature hard chines (angular as opposed to round-bottomed hulls) that help counteract heeling. Contrary to popular belief, heeling (running with the boat tilted up on one side) hurts your performance and opens you to the risk of capsize.

As mentioned in Chapter 5 sails are available from the folding-kayak industry and from aftermarket producers. You have two basic choices in sail types: those capable of tacking into the wind, and those considered downwind rigs, albeit with some ability to go sideways to the wind.

Upwind Sailing Rigs

To simplify sailing lessons for a full-range sail capable of going into the wind, this chapter focuses on two types of rigs, the Klepper S-4 and the Batwing from Balogh Sail Designs. The S-4 is typical of the type of sail rig that incorporates a jib and mainsail. This type of traditional upwind rig is also found on older Folbots, Pouchs, and other boats. The Balogh Batwing is a racier rig that uses a cambered windsurfer-type sail with no jib. The design dates back to a batswing sail seen in the last century on sailing canoes. Any similar type sail adapted from the windsurfing world would work in a like fashion.

Sailing the S-4 Rig

The Klepper S-4 rig is a classic in every aspect of the word. It's been around for half a century and has a very traditional gaff-rigged mainsail.

Here are several things to keep in mind when sailing the S-4 rig:

1. It's a lot of sail that can easily overpower you. The S-4 carries 48 square feet of sail, enough to get an unaware or cocky paddler into trouble. Even highly experienced kayak sailors have run into trouble with the S-4 when caught in heavy winds with gusts off nearby highlands.

2. Thousands of people have learned to sail the S-4 successfully. If the rig didn't work for the ordinary guy, Klepper couldn't have continued selling it all these years. Kids and octogenarians with little experience have sailed it.

3. The S-4's secret is that you can learn to sail it one component at a time before trying the full-blown rig. There are mini-sets of rigs within the system. This allows you to expand your knowledge of your foldable and how it functions under various wind conditions while using increased amounts of sail.

Rig Possibilities

Let's look at the S-4's components, the sailing range of each, and various combinations. The sail has a gaff-rigged 32-square-foot mainsail with a 16-square-foot jib. Also available separately is a 10-square-foot drift sail called the M-1. All use the same mast. The other components, besides a rudder, are a crossbar and leeboards that attach to the coaming. Here are some of the many sail combinations you can try:

Jib alone.

Jib sailing is fairly easy, as discussed later in this chapter. With leeboards, you can almost beam reach with the jib alone, i.e., go about 90 degrees off the wind. Some people just jib sail all the time, getting a boost when going downwind or going off at an angle of 90 degrees or less.

M-1 drift sail alone.

This is strictly a downwind setup with some play possible to 30 or 40 degrees off dead downwind. You need pretty steady winds to make this setup worthwhile and luck that the wind is going precisely where you want to head. The drift sail has a boom that attaches with a hook to the mast and ties off to the top and bottom of the mast.

Jib with the M-1 as mainsail.

This is a pretty neat combination that's not likely to overpower you. It gives about 26 square feet of sail all told, about half that of the full mainsail and jib. Because it has a boom, you get some of the advantages of a mainsail, but without the gaff to catch wind in awkward directions, therefore less possibility of a spill. But 26 square feet is not an awful lot of power for a double kayak, so you'll go ahead slow but steady. You can tack with this rig set up, going to windward as much as 40 to 45 degrees, depending on your skill and other factors.

Klepper S-4 rig.

Jib with full main sail, the S-4 setup.

Here is the full 48 square feet of sail area. It has three battens, a boom on the foot or lower part of the sail, and a gaff that swings up from the top of the mast when the main is raised fully. It's a lot of sail. You can perform the full range of sailing possibilities: run with the wind, reach in the various directions, and go to windward.

Special Tips and Doo-dads

The S-4 has prompted the use of many home-made devices and approaches that make sailing it easier. Bill Lozano of Atlantic Kayak Tours of Saugerties, New York, is an innovative paddler who's put a lot of thought into the S-4 rig, fine-tuning it so it's a lot easier to sail.

These ideas make it possible to assemble the rig quickly while underway and fairly easy to strike it when the weather changes or when you want to switch to paddling. Moreover, the customized setup allows unencumbered paddling, which isn't true of the stock S-4 setup as it comes from Klepper. Here are several ideas:

Go without the leeboard and crossbar attached.

These can encumber the paddling of the person in the front seat of a double and certainly will stymie anyone in a single seat folding kayak. For the most part, your boat won't slip sideways much if you're running flat and not beating into the wind. If you absolutely need the leeboards, you can attach them on the go while in the water.

Don't bother having the battens placed in their pockets in the sail.

Instead, just have them handy somewhere in the boat in case you decide it's going to be a day of all sailing. Having the battens in place makes it difficult to keep the mainsail in a tight roll and ready on deck where it won't interfere with paddling. The battens contribute only a small degree to sailing power, certainly not enough to warrant their interference with paddling.

Place a hook on the port mast shroud and a loop on the starboard, or vice versa if you like.

Shrouds are guy lines on both sides that help support the mast. They attach to D-rings on the deck, so they get in the way of paddling if the mast is kept in place. The hook and loop allow you to pull the shrouds closer to the mast and out of the swinging room of the paddle in front, yet the shrouds still give enough support to a mast not carrying sail.

Make certain that the main halyard is tightly attached to the omega fitting on the gaff.

If you don't, the gaff will not be truly vertical. Instead, it will be leaning to one side or the other, complicating sailing and risking a capsize.

Don't follow the Klepper method of lashing the mainsail to the mast.

Klepper calls for running one continuous line through the eyelets on the luff or forward part of the sail, looping around the mast between each eyelet. Klepper calls for either a simple way or a more complex sliding wrap-around non-knot, but always with a continuous line. Instead, just tie short pieces of line to each eyelet and tie off as many as you want to the mast. Most of the time, you can get away with one or two lashed to the mast. This speeds getting the mainsail in place and greatly simplifies striking the rig and putting it away in a hurry if a storm is brewing.

When rolling up the sail, you can easily create a tight package without needing to put it in a bag.

While the rear person switches to paddling, the front person can roll up the sail tightly by wrapping the mainsail sheet (control line) around it. When it comes to hoisting the sail again, the back person can do the unraveling while the front person puts up the mast or works on various lines.

Work out such divisions of labor beforehand.

What are the duties of the front person when switching from paddling to sailing? What are the duties of the back person? Are they the same when striking sail and switching back to paddling? The S-4 has a reputation for requiring too lengthy a setup and knockdown process. Teamwork and split duties can cut the time to a few minutes.

The Control Panel

Bill Lozano's most important little device, what he calls a cleat board, is worth its weight in gold to any S-4 sailor. The board is made out of ½- or ¾-inch plywood, and all you need is about 10 inches by 4 inches, which you'll cut down a bit. The board contains four clam cleats with fairleads. The cleat board is mounted on deck just ahead of the front person and close to the mast.

The two outside cleats are marked In and Out and control running the jib tack (lower front end) in and out from the bow. The jib that Klepper supplies has a snap hook that the company intends to be hooked directly to the deck fitting on the bow. Modify this by running a continuous line through that deck fitting and back to the In and Out cleats on the cleat board. The jib-tack snap hook is attached to a loop about halfway along that continuous line. Using this modification, you can opt to pull the whole jib toward you and store in it in one of the paddle pockets. Why? Because even if the jib is lying flat on the deck, it can catch water in heavy waves and pull over your kayak. The importance of being able to bring the jib in and out while underway cannot be overstated. It is essential to your safety.

The two cleats in the middle of the board are marked J for jib and M for mast, and control the jib and main halyards. By releasing the J cleat, you immediately cause the jib to fall down onto the foredeck without your having to undo any lines. Likewise, pull the line on the M cleat and it will loosen, pay out quickly, and lower the mainsail. Both the jib and main halyards run through a pulley at the bottom of the mast, and, of course, to a pulley at the mast top. This control panel with its cleats provides a key to safety when sailing the S-4 and getting full enjoyment of it even while underway.

Sailing Tips When Underway

Beyond the usual advice on sailing any small boat, advice that you either already have heard or can pick up from a book, class, or friend, there are some things to keep in mind when sailing the S-4:

When letting out the mainsail, be careful not to let it out too far.

Don't let it press against the shrouds. That's as far as it can go anyway, but you don't want to let it get to that point. If you have it resting against the shroud and a gust of wind hits, you have no more room to pay out the sheet (the line in your hand) that is controlling the boom. You could tip over.

Do let out the mainsail until it flutters, then pull it back in a bit to a taut position.

So much of this is feel. But by doing it this way you can quickly get the feel of the wind and its power.

Try to strike a balance between wind and rudder.

This is true of sailing any small boat but, again, trickier in an S-4 rigged folding kayak. You want to work the right amount of wind into the sail (so it's as taut as you feel comfortable with) with the main sheet and the rudder. But you don't want to over rudder. If you do, the boat will stall and either lose power or play some losing games with the wind in which you can capsize, depending on wind strength and the boat's angle of heel.

Try to keep the boat running as flat as possible.

A boat that is heeled over is losing speed. Again, it's a matter of balancing forces. Either slack the sail to keep the boat flat or hike your body out on the coaming or special seat to maintain a flatter running position. You can also sit on something that will allow you to lean over farther than you can from the regular seated position.

A reduced sail area kept taut is better than a larger sail area sheeted out.

Unfortunately, the S-4 does not come with reefing ties or zippers. You have to add these or, awkwardly, roll some of the lower part of the sail around the boom. That's why using the M-1 rig as a mainsail can sometimes make a lot of sense.

Sailing the Balogh Batwing

The Balogh Batwing is a fully battened, camber-induced sailing rig that is revolutionizing kayak sailing. It's an easy rig to strike and works well in the open cockpit arrangements of foldable kayaks. Unlike in a sloop setup, which generally has a jibsail out on the foredeck as well as a mainsail, the Batwing has only one sail to get down and it's close at hand to the cockpit. When you uncleat the halyard, the battens drop the sail almost like venetian blinds into a neat package that can be stowed away or tied off quickly.

Balogh Sail Design has come up with a major innovation in its patented outrigger setup, dubbed B.O.S.S. The outriggers were originally conceived as "training wheels" for beginners to learn sailing without risking a capsize. The system certainly serves that function but has become much more. Seasoned sailors are using B.O.S.S. for greater performance to windward and to achieve higher speeds.

Balogh Batwing on single Klepper with B.O.S.S. *(Dennis Stevens)*

smooth away any sail wrinkles that run perpendicular to the luff, the leading edge of the sail.

The second area that needs tightening is the battens. Here the objective is to get out any wrinkles that run perpendicular to the battens themselves. Tightening the battens is appropriate for wind speeds from moderate to gale. The exception is light winds. In light winds, too much tension cups the sail in the leech area, where the wind will catch and the boat will stall. Looser is better when the winds are light.

Select an Appropriate Sheeting Point

This is a crucial detail for getting the most out of your Batwing. First, the sheeting point is where the sheet or controlling line is held, and it should be approximately six to 18 inches aft of the clew (the back, lower corner of the sail) when the sail is in a midships position. This is the most efficient place from which to control the sail, giving you the most power out of your Batwing.

Second, that sheeting point should be mechanical, i.e., not just your hand. Use a pulley or cleat. It

Square foot for square foot, the Batwing, with its airfoil cambered construction, is more powerful than anything else around for kayak sailing. Under ideal conditions this is great. But that power must be respected. When the wind picks up, be quick, not tardy, to reef—that is, reduce your sail area. You'll actually move faster and have a safer time of it.

The B.O.S.S. outrigger setup allows for greater boat speed under heeling conditions as well as when sailing in stronger winds, but don't get too cocky. Know your own limitations as a sailor. Offshore winds can put you well out to sea before you know it. Tacking back against such strong winds can be a long, drawn out experience.

Below are a number of tips designed to get the most out of the Balogh Batwing. They would apply to any other similar rig that uses a cambered, battened sail.

Tighten Up All Lines

The first point to watch out for is the downhaul that pulls down the bottom of the sail and snugs it to the mast. Under most wind conditions, the downhaul should be pulled tightly; man-handled, it won't break anything. The idea is to pull it tight enough to

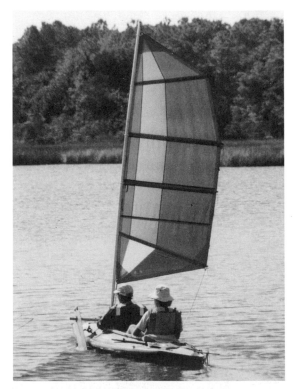

Balogh Batwing on Nautiraid double. *(Dennis Stevens)*

should not be tied off, but a stopper knot can be tied at the end of the sheet to prevent it from running out through the pulley, if that's what you're using. There's an exception to the position described above. If you decide not to use the B.O.S.S., have the sheeting point farther aft. This position delivers less power but more safety, which is especially important protection from unexpected gusts. It gives the sail a greater twist that allows it to spill off any excessive air fairly automatically, so you don't have to be highly attuned to anticipating gusts or to reacting quickly. It's more forgiving if you're going without outriggers.

Use Finesse, Not Force

The Batwing is a high-performance sail that must be handled with subtlety, requiring a feel and touch for the varying wind and sea conditions. Finesse is the key, something that experienced sailors who come from more traditional sails have difficulty grasping. Such sailors almost invariably oversheet, i.e., pull too tightly on the sheet controlling the sail. When they do, they stall the air foil on the Batwing and lose, rather than gain, power.

The Batwing is a radically different type of sail. It's highly efficient, and it has a short outhaul. A sail's outhaul is the distance from mast to back of the sail.

Achieving Various Points of Sail

When sailing, keep an eye on the telltale attached to the upper leech to help your sheeting control. The telltale should be streaming back horizontally in line with the sail. If it's wrapping around the other side, you're sheeting too tightly, so sheet out a bit. If it flutters in front of the sail, you're too loose with your control, so pull in some on the sheet. Also keep your rudder as straight as possible; hard ruddering stalls the boat.

Sailing downwind.

The telltale reading doesn't apply when you're sailing straight downwind. But you should not be going straight downwind, because this course doesn't give you your best velocity made good. When you want to go downwind, tack in a series of broad reaches (45 degrees off downwind). The exception to this rule is very light wind, when you might as well go straight downwind.

Off the wind.

When the clew moves forward in an off-the-wind maneuver, you should pull down and out with the sheet to get more power. Basically you follow the clew. If it's moving into a down and forward position, you follow or mimic this with the sheet control.

Upwind sailing.

When going upwind, don't head directly into it, which is called "pointing too high." Kayaks are light-

Balogh Batwing schooner-rigged Klepper double.
(Dennis Stevens)

weight boats with little inertia, so waves can slow them down and stall their forward motion. Even if the Balogh sail is capable of pointing well up into the wind, this will not give you the best velocity made good. You're better off close reaching and tacking than trying to go too close to the wind.

You may want to try what some paddlers/sailors term "motor sailing." Since you don't have a motor, you paddle to supplement the sailing as you move into the wind. At that point you are working with apparent wind, not actual wind. Paddling moves you enough to feed more air into the sail as you go upwind, thus getting more speed out of the sail. It's a classic symbiotic relationship. The sail is giving you speed between paddling strokes, and your paddling is feeding air into the sail.

Downwind Sailing Rigs

Downwind sailing rigs are much less complicated than their upwind cousins, and are favored by paddlers who are looking for a boost only part of the time. Downwind rigs offer several benefits:

- Cheaper to buy. Downwind sails are about a quarter of the price of upwind sailing rigs.

- More stowable. You can take one along without much fanfare, because it takes up less room in your kayak. Downwind sails have less canvas area, and their masts are often thinner and shorter.

- Easier to rig up. You have fewer lines to deal with when setting up the rig. Hardware requirements are minimal, and very little customizing is necessary to fit a downwind rig to your boat.

- Simpler to sail. Sailing downwind is less complex, as you can only do so much with a downwind rig.

There is a catch. Performance tends to be modest. In most cases, you won't be able to achieve the speeds you can with a full-range rig.

You also are limited in where you can go in relation to the wind's direction. Some downwind rigs can only go within a narrow range of 20 degrees on either side of straight downwind. Others can sail up to 45 degrees off straight downwind, or broad reach. Still other can beam reach or sail almost 90 degrees to straight downwind.

To simplify lessons for using a downwind rig, the following descriptions look at two types: the Balogh Twins and the Klepper jib sail. The Twins is one of the better downwind rigs, because it is so powerful and versatile. Several imitator rigs on the market operate in a similar way. The Klepper jib is a classic setup, and lots of similar rigs are around. Jib sailing has quite a few advocates because of its simplicity and surprisingly good performance.

Other types of downwind sail rigs use kites and parafoils that don't require masts. Their uses are very specialized, and they offer little control.

Sailing the Twins

The Twins rig has a superficial resemblance to a classic design, the Ljungstrom rig, in that it is two triangular mainsails sewn together at their luffs. But the Ljungstrom is mostly an upwind sail, and the Twins is a downwind sail with some upwind capability. Unlike the Ljungstrom, the Twins uses sprit booms under each sail half. The booms are attached to the clew, and they lead nearly perpendicular to the mast.

The Twins rig looks like a child's kite being flown upside down. It carries the widest part of the sail fairly low on the mast, where it is least likely to destabilize your kayak if hit by a gust. The dihedral or two-planed sail is self-trimming. Bridle lines run from the clews to a two-foot-long bridle bar attached to a single sheet. This allows easy one-hand adjustment of the sails. The Twins rig ranges in sizes from 20 to 40 square feet. The 30-footer would be a good compromise, giving adequate power to a double foldable but not overwhelming any single you might want to switch it to.

You'll find several sails on the market that resemble the basics of the Twins rig, including one sold by Folbot. Or you could make a primitive version that will work in fundamentally the same way. Here are the driving lessons for using this type of downwind rig.

Setting-up While Underway

This is a maneuver you'll want to get handy at performing. The Twins and its look-alikes are meant to be used whenever wind opportunity knocks, for example, when a good following wind blows up or when you're 60 degrees or so off the wind's direction.

If you're in a double, the front paddler takes out the disassembled mast parts and feeds the hoops care-

Control board for a double.

Control board for a single.

Sailing with the Wind

When sailing relatively straight downwind, you use the Twins with its two halves opened up. When the two opened halves form a straight line, you get the maximum amount of downwind thrust.

The Twins sail doesn't have to be absolutely perpendicular to the line of travel of the boat. You can let its straight line come slightly to one side, which will work only for a few degrees off straight downwind.

You can slow down by simply letting loose on the bridle sheet. When you do, the two halves no longer form a straight line; instead they form an angle of about 150 degrees. This will slow you down. To depower completely, just let the sheet out all the way until the bridle strikes the mast. The two halves will have folded out in front of the mast where they will catch absolutely no wind.

Sailing Closer to the Wind

The Twins rig has a trick up its sleeve that allows you to sail with the wind on your beam. You simply fold one half over the other to form a single triangle. This cuts your sail area in half but starts giving you something that looks like a mainsail. In this position it resembles the Klepper M-1 drift sail.

To get the most out of the doubled-over Twins, a single boat should always use a leeboard, which helps it resist being pushed sideways by wind coming from the beam. You almost don't need a leeboard as long as you are short of a full beam reach, say, up to 60 degrees off straight downwind. Doubles can often get away without leeboards even when approaching a beam reach.

As in the case of the Batwing, finesse is needed for subtle rudder control and sheet control. Keep the rudder as straight as possible to keep from going into a stall or losing what you are gaining from the wind's force on your sail.

Don't oversheet, or pull the sheet too tight. Pulling tightly on the sheet works when going straight downwind with the Twins fully opened, but it doesn't give you more power when the sails are doubled over. Let the sheet out a bit, then pull in slightly. You shouldn't feel like you're holding the leash of a dog that wants to chase a rabbit.

All the time you're working with the sheet, keep fiddling with the rudder to get just the right angle to the wind. There are no hard-and-fast formulas. It's a feel that comes with time.

fully on to the lowest section of the mast. Practice this on dry land, so you know beforehand how it should look and how the pieces go on.

Meanwhile, the back person assembles the other two sections. These are then attached to the bottom section, which already has the sail hoops attached. The front paddler then crawls forward a bit to lift the mast and drop it through the mast partner and into the mast step on the kayak's floor. The front paddler hoists the sail with the halyard line and ties it off on a cleat, then pulls down on the downhaul line and ties it off.

If winds are gusty, don't hoist the sail to the very top of the mast. This will keep the largest part of the sail low and out of the way of gusts. However, the downhaul should be pulled down tightly, similar to how it is done with the Batwing.

Jib Sailing

While the chief purpose of a jib is to work with a mainsail to improve its aerodynamic efficiency, you can sail quite well with the jib alone. There are some provisos, though.

Jib sailing appears to work better with double boats than with singles, because anything more than the smallest of jibs tends to overpower singles. For example, the Klepper jib can be scary under certain circumstances in a single. The bow will want to dive under, and the wind whipping around so far in front of you may give you the feeling that you lack control. Paddlers who like to jib sail often find some way to cut down the area of the Klepper jib or they replace it with a smaller custom-made jib. Doubles seem to thrive on the regular jib.

Jib sailing.

You need to use leeboards for reaching. With the wind's force ahead of the mast, there is a greater tendency for the boat to slide than when the wind is hitting directly at or at an angle to the side of the boat.

To switch to jib sailing while underway, you pretty much have to have most of it already in place. You must have some way to get the jib in position, something like the setup mentioned above for the S-4. And you'll want to keep the mast in place. You can install the leeboards when you need them.

You can reach impressive speeds with a jib, especially in broad to beam reaches when you are operating 45 to 90 degrees off straight downwind. Going straight downwind requires a trick or two. Here are some pointers on sailing these ranges.

Downwind with a Jib

The Twins rig has sprit booms that can hold the sails wide open. On a jib you don't have such a device. To expose the greatest amount of sail surface to the wind, you need to extend the clew, the back corner of the jib, out to one side. If you push on it with the end of a paddle, you'll get some extra extension. Push out with the paddle's blade end, not a shaft end, which might slip and tear at the sail cloth. Make certain to hold the sheet out to that side too, as far as you can comfortably extend your arm.

Reaching

Broad and beam reaching requires a delicate balance of rudder and sheet. Let the sheet out until the back of the jib flutters. At that point, sheet in a bit. Just as in other light-craft sailing, you'll need to play with the rudder's angle to get it just right, that is, producing the most power from the wind while still heading the boat where you want to go.

CHAPTER 13

Camping

One of the most pleasant features of a folding kayak is how well it adapts to camping. Not only can you take a foldable half way around the globe, but once you arrive, you can enjoy kayaking for more than just day trips.

Folding kayaks are voluminous enough to carry a payload that could see you through a month's journey. Their payload weights generally run higher than those of comparable rigid kayaks, and loading up a foldable doesn't compromise its seaworthiness. Even the mini-foldables can carry a week's worth of gear safely. You can stretch this to several weeks if you know how to pack small and light.

You can load large items through the cockpit area so you don't get stuck working through the small hatches as in some rigid boats. The crossrib structure in the cockpit area provides perfect tie-on points for placing plenty of gear around you that you may want to grab in a hurry. The long rods and keel boards along the inside bottom offer convenient nooks for keeping round objects from rolling around. It's almost as if the frame concept was created with camping gear in mind.

How to Load a Foldable

Just because you *can* carry everything but the proverbial kitchen sink doesn't mean you *should*. And, as easy as it may be to shove items anywhere, you should also be thinking of proper trim, access to the rest of your gear, and other considerations. In the long run, you'll find more loading space if you put some thought into what you're doing. Your boat will also perform better under changing sea and wind conditions.

Optimizing Available Space

The beauty of packing a folding kayak is that you can get a sneak preview of how everything will fit in. How? Simply make the frame of your boat without its skin covering. That's the size and shape of the loading space you have available. See what can fit where and how you can get certain items into particular spots. Here's the step-by-step approach to use after you have the fully assembled frame in front of you.

1. Measure the opening at each rib and the space between them.

These extremely valuable measurements will tell you if, for example, a certain bag can be slipped past a particular rib opening and down into that end of the boat or not. Knowing the space between ribs will tell you if a certain dry bag can be secured lengthwise in that area.

Getting ready for a camping trip.

125

You could make a sketch of the frame with these measurements, or simply use the sales literature or assembly instructions from the manufacturer. One or the other should have a picture of the full frame. Just write in the dimensions.

2. Pack your gear bags and place them into the naked frame.

Start with any waterproof bags you may already have. Don't rush out to buy new bags until you determine what you might need. Sea trim will be discussed later in this chapter, but for now, place items where they best fit. Make certain that bags that you locate in an end section can actually be shoved there from the cockpit area.

Don't forget the storage area that is available around you inside the cockpit. For now, use cord to tie items into this area. Sit in the boat to make sure you have enough room for yourself. Check that the rudder cables won't snag on anything.

3. Mark the bags and sketch where they belong.

When you mark bags, indicate not only the area in which they fit but also their relative weight. H, M, and L, for heavy, medium, and light, will suffice. This is valuable information for trim. Make certain that your H bags can fit immediately in front and behind the cockpit section. If an H bag can't, plan to reduce its size until it will.

4. Establish how you might load bags into the ends of the boat.

You may want to pre-pack the ends when you make the frame, before inserting the frame halves into the skin. Such difficult-to-reach end space should be reserved for emergency items that you won't need in a hurry or on a regular basis, such as the hull patch kit. Feathercraft owners have hatches they can reach through to position awkward items. Otherwise, use a half paddle to shove items in toward the bow or stern.

5. Think about how you will unload the ends.

You may want to create a pulley and cord system for retrieving bags placed deeper in under the deck. Again, Feathercraft hatches help, but in other foldables, attach a cord or strap to the bags stowed in the ends. Secure the strap or cord on a nearby rib and use it to haul the bags out when unloading.

Loading for Best Trim and Stability

Never load any kayak by just throwing things in. You must consider such things as the boat's stability, its best trim for certain conditions, and protection from water damage. Here are some of the more important points.

Pack light.

This is the first commandment of sea-kayak camping. When looking at all that empty space in a foldable, it's awfully tempting to load it up to the brim. Avoid the temptation. When you think about loading in extra items, consider the effect of the added weight. A heavy boat requires more energy to paddle, because it rides deeper in the water and creates more wetted surface. A heavier boat will be more difficult to turn and maneuver. Also, a heavily laden boat is harder to deal with while launching and landing.

A good philosophy about any camping trip is to

Taking out gear.
(Walther/Klepper)

pretend that you're going to have to backpack the weight of everything. Make believe that all your gear must fit in a 6,000-cubic-inch backpack. Obviously, kayak campers don't really have to carry it all on their backs, nor are they limited to the size of a conventional backpack. But that imaginary backpack is a good place to start. Build up from there with essential gear, rather than starting with the double's potential 700-pound payload and the copious volumes its interior can absorb. You'll be happier in the long run.

Load for anticipated sea conditions.

Generally, you load a kayak with about 50 percent of the load on either side of the boat's center to balance the boat. Some boats behave better with a slightly heavier rear, say 55 percent of the load. But sea conditions often get in the way of such ideal weight-distribution schemes.

If your weather radio tells you that the wind and seas are likely to be coming from behind you on the course you're taking that day, place more of the weight behind you than you normally would. This will counteract the bow's tendency to dive when swells and wind propel you forward.

If you anticipate that wind and current will be coming at you throughout a good portion of the day, put a greater proportion of the weight in front. This will keep the bow down and prevent it from catching wind and slowing you down.

Wise placement of your heavy bags may be your best and easiest way to achieve the appropriate trim. But you don't want them too far forward or back. They should be placed immediately in front of or behind you. The very ends of the boat should contain the lighter gear.

Use the space around you as much as possible.

You have plenty of space to load gear in the cockpit area, the center of the boat. Keeping gear weight in the center is the ultimate trimming method for many reasons. Your steering is least affected when your boat is center-loaded, especially in beam winds. Neither end is likely to resist turning or, conversely, be prone to swinging around when you don't want it to. Center-loading also contributes to stability, and, in a capsize, will make it easier to right the boat. A folding kayak allows center loads whereas a rigid boat doesn't, and this feature helps make foldables such good pack horses.

Consider using bags as seats and seat backs to make double use of their space.

One bag that works well for this is the Voyageur Caboose Bag. It's about the size of a pillow and has a small tube for deflating or inflating the bag. Fill it with soft items such as clothes and you'll have a comfortable seat; another one tied behind your back can form a back rest. You can even adjust the firmness by blowing in or expelling air. The Caboose Bag conforms to various shapes, so it can fit into other parts of the boat, for example, tied to the ribs alongside you.

Avoid deck loads.

Consider yourself fortunate if you don't have D-rings with which to attach loads on top of your deck. If you do, avoid the temptation to use them for excess gear that you cannot fit inside the boat. Follow the rule: "If not inside, leave aside."

Deck loads are dangerous because they can catch beam winds. They raise your effective center of gravity, which reduces the inherent stability of any boat. In a capsize, they make it almost impossible to get the boat upright again, and they can get in the way of your reentry. If you have D-rings, use them only to secure something light, like a paddle float and hand pump.

Keep heavy items low in the boat.

For example, the floor of your foldable is the place to locate your water supply, which weighs a lot. Consider storing water in flat bags, sometimes called water sacks or desert bags. One of these will hold three gallons of water in a space only about six inches high. Water sacks not only keep your center of gravity low but also act as ballast.

When you're tying items inside the cockpit area, don't locate heavy items too high up the sides. If you have a tent in this area, keep it on or close to the bottom of the cockpit, alongside you or your legs. Reserve higher tie-ins for the lighter items, such as sleeping mats.

Protect everything in waterproof bags.

Some people make the mistake of protecting only clothing and sleeping bags. They think that tent poles and nylon-covered sleeping mats can survive getting wet. They can't. Aluminum tent poles, for example, are not made of the same marine-grade alloys as folding-kayak aluminum frames, which resist saltwater corrosion. The same goes for stoves. And, while a nylon-coated mat might not absorb much water, its surface will stay wet and be annoying in a tent.

Try to use small and medium-sized water-proof bags.

Larger bags are harder to slide in past the ribs closest to the cockpit. Some won't fit at all. Smaller bags can easily be placed in the underdeck areas, and when they're loaded around you in the cockpit, they won't take up the room you'll need to sit comfortably. Smaller bags are also a good insurance policy for your gear. If you have three small bags in place of one, and a bag tears, you have water penetration in only a third of that gear, not all of it.

Tie and lash everything.

You don't want loose items that could float free in a capsize or get in your way as you climb back into your seat. To keep gear contained in the front and back underdeck sections, try running webbing straps in an X-pattern across the ribs leading to these sections. Bungee cord will also do.

Provide yourself with easy access to everything.

An earlier section suggested pulleys and tie-on cords to retrieve items that are farther under deck. Another method for easier access is to use the long carrying bag that comes with some of the foldables. For example, the Klepper long bag is narrow enough to fit well into the underdeck area in front of you. While it is not waterproof, you can load it a third full with smaller items in Ziploc bags, then shove the long bag into the bowels of your boat as far as it will go. Push it in with a paddle. Then load some larger, heavier items into the rest of the long bag. When you land, pull these one or two bulkier or heavier items out first, then yank on the whole bag to retrieve the rest of the load.

Camping Considerations

Camping from a kayak lets you extend the adventure over days and weeks on the water. But, assuming you know how to load your boat correctly for prevailing conditions, what other points should you consider?

There are many. Three key considerations are where to camp, what equipment to have, and how to move your loaded boat and gear around on land when you have to.

If you're lucky you'll have a series of legal camp sites strung along your route at the right distance from each other to provide you with a good paddle each day. If not, you'll have to try another approach for your nightly encampment.

For kayak-camping equipment, backpacking gear will do, but you may want to add some special items made for camping out of your kayak. Moving your boat and gear on land can be made easier if you follow certain pointers.

Commando Camping

Camping these days has some new realities. A half century ago, you could pull up just about anywhere and find a spot to camp. With the advance of civilization, you now must be sensitive to the rights of property owners and to local laws. You don't want to ruffle anyone's feathers.

You can still find attractive touring areas where camping is permitted. In other areas, several designated scenic sites might work into your paddling mileage schedule. Be thankful that such places exist. You can help keep them open by practicing low-impact camping techniques that preserve their pristine beauty and reduce maintenance costs.

Many wonderful paddling areas just don't have such camping available. To enjoy them for more than just a day trip, you'll have to engage in a shadowy procedure few of us who are responsible citizens ever wish to do—commando camp. It's not legal, so you're not setting up for the night as you would in an official campsite. Instead, you camp in the least obtrusive manner you can, so no one need know you were there. You're taking your chances. But for many stretches of shoreline that you're likely to paddle, if you don't take this chance, you're not going to sleep that night, and perhaps not for several nights thereafter. Here's how to commando camp with the least risk to you and least disturbance to others.

1. To ask or not to ask.

Asking permission seems to be the antithesis of commando camping, but it's really your first rule. Size up the situation.

If you're in a remote area but there's a home nearby, you should ask politely about camping possibilities. Chances are highly in your favor that, being so remote, the owner may welcome someone to talk to, especially someone in a folding kayak who probably has a tale to tell. Besides, if you don't ask or advise the remote home dweller of your presence, you probably would be spotted anyway; such individuals are acutely aware of what goes on around them.

If you're in a more populated area, you're probably better off not asking, especially near a private home.

Commando camping near the Big Apple. The boat was later moved out of sight.

Vacation-home owners usually don't want anyone around them to share the natural wealth of the spot, or might be concerned about liability. Year-round residents are a toss-up.

2. Likeliest spots.

Some areas offer better commando-camping prospects than others. Large state or provincial parks work out okay if you don't camp near the more heavily traveled walking trails. Avoid camping near a road where a passing ranger could spot you. Railroad rights-of-way along coastlines and rivers are also good choices. Railroad detectives no longer patrol that property or bash in the heads of wayward hoboes. Abandoned industrial sites are likely candidates, although not very glamorous.

Do avoid municipal parks, road sides, and village outskirts. Also avoid camping near navigational aids such as range markers and lights. The Coast Guard levies heavy fines for obstructing the working of these devices.

3. Set up late, leave early.

Whatever you do, don't set up camp in broad daylight if you are trying to commando camp. If you find a likely spot in late afternoon, hang out as if you are just taking a rest. Check the site out. If it's suitable, casually prep the site a bit by kicking away stones from where you'll place your tent. Paddle away for a while, circle back when it's getting dark, and then set up. Plan to leave at or before first light. Not only does this help you avoid being spotted, it's also a practical way to paddle on long trips. Getting off to an early start means you can get a lot of paddling in that day. If weather turns sour later in the day, you'll have gotten in at least some mileage before being forced to halt. You'll be surprised at how easy it is to get an early start without breakfast, then have breakfast maybe three hours later at your first stopping spot.

4. Hide your tent and boat.

If your tent is bright orange, meant to draw rescuers' attention after an avalanche, don't dismay. You can cover it with an olive drab tarp. Pull your whole boat away from the water's edge and into the brush or among the trees. If it has a bright colored deck, turn it over to reveal the black or gray hull, which will not draw as much attention.

5. Show little light, make less noise.

You should never carry a bright Coleman lantern on any kayak camping trip, and you're even less likely to carry it when you don't want to announce your presence. A bright light would attract curiosity, and then someone could object to your presence or cause you trouble. Keep your sounds low. You don't have to whisper, but commando campers don't yell out to one another to get something from the boat.

6. No fires.

This is the strictest no-no. Nothing will get you into more trouble than building a fire in an area in which you don't belong. The smoke is likely to attract the attention of any official or property owner, and then they'll raise hell and demand that you leave immediately—even if ordinarily they'd be disposed to letting you camp. Some paddlers think it's okay to make their fires below the high tide line, but it's not. A fire is a fire in the eyes of most onlookers, no matter where it's built.

Camping Equipment

Here's a list of camping gear that's practical for kayak touring. Chances are that much of what you already have can be adapted for camping from a kayak. Or you may decide to buy some gear made especially for kayak camping.

Tent.

You might want a larger tent than you'd ordinarily carry in a backpack. The larger size can be useful for drying gear. Also, in the paddlers' damp environment, that greater space helps disperse body vapor and preserves a sense of dryness. To do that, the tent should have adequate ventilation.

When buying a tent for kayak camping, consider this: It should fit nicely between the ribs in your foldable, so its poles won't get bent out of shape. As a rule, any tent will work if its poles break down to lengths of less than about 22 inches for a Klepper, 18 for a Nautiraid, and about 28 inches for the rest of the foldables. Otherwise you'll have to lay the tent poles on the rest of the gear. Opt for a tent with a full fly cover, because mist rising off fresh and salt water will wet the lower parts of the tent proper if its rain fly does not cover them well. Make sure the tent provides good ventilation, or too much moisture will build up inside. Lastly, consider color. If possible, get an unobtrusive gray or green, not a bright blue or bright orange.

Tarp.

You'll want a rain tarp. Not only can you get protection under it during rain, it will also keep lake mist and ocean spray from chilling you as you eat dinner. If you hole up in mid-day to wait out a change of tide or wind, a tarp can keep you from frying in the sun. A 10- by 10-foot tarp is quite versatile, and you can set it up to protect two people.

Sleeping bag.

You can usually get by with a much lighter bag than you might think. In warmer months, you'll be generating so much heat at night from having been in the sun all day at a high activity rate that you and your partner will be little furnaces inside a tent. If you get chilled, use warm clothing to increase the warmth rating of your sleeping bag.

Be careful with down. If a down bag does get wet, it becomes useless, so you'll always be worried about keeping it dry. Opt for a synthetic bag. Many new fillers are being developed that have almost the same compressibility, weight, and warmth as down, and the best part is that they retain their insulation properties even if they do get wet.

Stove.

Choose a stove that's easy to light and maintain. The fewer parts, the better. You might be camping in sand, which can work its way into mechanical parts and cause the whole stove to fail. Butane stoves perform extremely well. Some butane-mix canisters even work in air temperatures close to freezing. The cans present a disposal problem for backpacking, but in your foldable you have the room to carry them out.

Food.

You might want to think twice about planning gourmet meals. Some kayaking manuals devote many pages to foraging for food along the shore that you cook with pastas and grains. But foraging takes time at the end of the day when you're tired and daylight is fading. Such items require extensive cooking time, and that uses up fuel—which increases the amount you must plan to carry in the first place.

You're better off with nutritional one-pot food that only needs to be heated, not cooked. Freeze-dried camping food can taste wonderful at the end of the day. Hunger adds a very tasty sauce to any food that's put before a famished person.

Camping in the Bahamas.

Water.

You'll need a way to carry plenty of drinking water. Kayak touring differs sharply from backpacking in that you won't have trails with drinking-water sources every so many miles. If you plan on saltwater touring, you'll need to carry one gallon or more of drinking water per day per person. The cost of desalinators can be prohibitive for all but the most dedicated of expeditions.

For a freshwater environment, you can find a relatively inexpensive water-purification system that will relieve you from having to carry the weight of all your water. If you're paddling on large freshwater lakes, you could take your chances by drinking lake water, but be sure to lessen your risk of ingesting bad bacteria by collecting your water well offshore before you land.

You won't need to use your precious drinking water for cleaning up. Sand and gravel will work for cleaning plates and pots at the shoreline. When you're freshwater paddling, the water is safe enough for bathing. Even in salt water, you can take a good bath if you use one of those camping soaps designed for salt water. Dry yourself quickly after emerging from any salt water to keep the salt crystals from drying on your skin and irritating it later.

Extra line and paper.

Make certain that you tie off your boat well. Wind waves, boat wakes, and rising tides can snatch any loose boat from shore, even if it was originally left a few boat lengths up from the water's edge. Even though it's a lot of work, get your boat well onto high ground and tie it off as though it were still in the water—for total peace of mind.

Write your name and your itinerary on a piece of paper, and place it inside a Ziploc bag inside your kayak somewhere it can easily be seen. If your boat ever strays from a beach with a passing wake, you'll have a better chance of getting it back or of someone summoning help for you. In a worst-case scenario—a capsize in which you lose your boat and swim to shore—the itinerary notes may direct searchers to where you are likely to be. Leaving this note is a good idea not only for camping but also day trips, in case you are separated from your boat.

Uninvited guests.

You won't want to discover uninvited guests—like mice, snakes, scorpions, or spiders—when you're already a half mile off shore, so always cover your folding kayak. If it has a spraydeck, leave it on; attach the spray skirts and tie them closed. This should keep out any stowaways.

Be meticulous about removing any opened food and crumbs from your kayak. Such savory items attract rodents and other beasts that can make mincemeat out of your canvas deck.

Portaging and Other Land Movement

Every ship must come to shore and so must your kayak. How do you move a gear-laden kayak, an object that might weigh half as much as a compact car? If you're traveling from one lake to another lake, what do you do about portaging? You have several options—besides breaking your back.

Land Movement of Boat and Gear

A good boat cart is worth its weight in gold. Most of them can be rolled right into salt water, because they're made of corrosion-resistant materials. If you're planning to buy a cart, get one that has fat wheels that won't sink in soft sand under a heavy load. You can help your cart negotiate the more difficult terrain by partially emptying your boat until the cart is easier to manage.

Keep some bags handy to stuff gear into as you unload at the shoreline. This means fewer trips back and forth to your campsite. The bags that your foldable came in are ideal for this job, and you'll have them along anyway. Mesh bags also work well.

Boat fenders are another tool for moving your boat on shore. You'll need three tubular fenders that you can keep deflated in your boat, then inflate when you need them. Use them as the Egyptian pyramid builders used rollers to move stone blocks. Place one fender under the bow, one dead center, one toward the stern. As you roll the boat on the front two boat fenders, take the one from the rear and place it in front of the boat. Roll the boat onto it, and continue the process with the others in constant rotation. You might be able to get by with two rollers, but three are better and easier to work with.

PVC four-inch-diameter water pipes will also work well as rollers, but they weigh more than boat fenders and take up more space. If you can cap the ends, you might use the pipes to store small, loose items within the boat.

Portaging

It certainly makes good sense to have a handle on portaging. How else can you enjoy the many strings of fresh-water lakes and rivers that interlace North America and parts of Europe? You have several choices:

Wheel your foldable on a boat cart.

This is certainly one of the easiest and handiest approaches. Your boat can traverse quite rugged terrain on a boat cart. The wheels on the two best carts, Klepper's and Nautiraid's, are large, tough and give adequate ground clearance, though Nautiraid's has a slight height advantage. Take care with where you place the cart on the boat. You want to locate it at a point where you're not holding the entire weight of the kayak in your hands but not so far toward the center of the boat that you scrape the bow or stern on the ground.

When carting your boat up hills, you should be on the downhill side of the boat, holding it as low as possible. From this position you can foresee any ground rubbing and avoid it. You also get the best leverage and control. When going downhill, reverse the position so you're uphill of your boat. If you are downhill, you won't be aware of rubbing, and most hull damage from carting occurs going downhill with the person in front. However, the recommended position offers less control and braking; take care not to have a runaway boat! On the flats, pushing offers you more control and it's easier on your shoulders.

Balance is another issue when using a cart for portaging over rough terrain. Lashing the boat firmly to the cart frame will help. You can never get it too tight. Cinch several sets of straps around the boat, then snug up the straps some more. If possible, place all heavy objects just above the cart. This means you may have to do some quick repacking, but it's worth it. You won't feel the weight as much, and the heavy objects won't throw you off balance.

Be a beast of burden.

Even if you're used to portaging a canoe, portaging a folding kayak is much tougher. You don't have a handy place to put a yoke and shoulder. If you decide to lash on paddles the way you would with a canoe and place these on your shoulder, you're in for an uncomfortable portage. Because folding kayaks are flexible, they transmit more up and down force onto the paddle shafts, which will be jarring your back. Extra padding might help.

Another solution is to use a tampoline band. Here's how to make one. If you're portaging a Klepper single, cement back to back two bands of Hypalon repair material approximately three inches wide and 22½ inches long. Use either the repair cement meant for patches or Barge cement, which won't come apart. Before applying the cement, place a strip of ¼-inch nylon cord at each end so that it's encased by the Hypalon bands, creating a bead at each end.

To use this tampoline band, let a bit of air out of the sponsons, slip the band's ends under the coaming and into the underside groove, similar to the way the beaded hem of the expedition tuckunder spraydeck fits. Then reinflate the sponsons. What you have is a much softer, flexible shoulder harness that moves with the flexible boat. The band forms to your back, distributing not only the weight but also the pressure. You carry it very much the way you would portage a canoe.

If you're portaging a double, you can do it somewhat the same way as you would carry a tandem canoe. One paddler carries the boat upside down, with his or her head against the rear seat. Pad the rear seat by tying in place something like a floatable boat cushion. The other paddler guides the carrier from in front. Or both paddlers can put their heads into the boat to disperse the weight. The taller paddler should be in front, so he or she can see what lies ahead.

Use an alternate method. When you must move from lake to lake or around inhospitable parts of a river, why not take advantage of a folding kayak's foldability? It takes an average of 10 minutes to knock down a folding kayak and about 15 minutes to make it again. Even if it takes you twice as long, you're still looking at just 50 minutes of work. If two of you are paddling a double, one could be disassembling or assembling while the other portages gear.

Most carrying bags for folding kayaks have padded shoulder straps and other comfort devices. If you're not happy with the bags that came with your folding kayak, look around for an external-frame backpack that could carry your folding kayak bags reasonably well. When not in use, the frame can be lashed to the rear deck. Being so light and open, the frame will neither raise your center of gravity nor catch crosswinds.

CHAPTER 14

*M*ore Fun with Foldables

Folding kayaks are misnamed; they should really be called all-purpose kayaks. They offer many possibilities in a small package, like the many facets of a cut diamond. Foldables will accommodate your needs as they have for thousands of paddlers before you. And people still keep coming up with new ways of enjoying the built-in flexibility of these versatile vessels.

Why are folding kayaks so much more adaptable to a wide range of uses than other small craft? It's hard to say what accounts for their ability to do your bidding. But a number of possibilities come to mind.

For one, folding kayaks have been going strong for nearly a century with remarkably little change in their basic design. Hundreds of thousands of people have gotten their hands on these vessels and studied them. Under such scrutiny, folding kayaks have been used for activities that range from the broadly appealing to the bizarre.

But there's more behind the phenomenal breadth of service than just the exposure of time. Stability and seaworthiness also underline the folding kayak's adaptability. The stable platform allows you to attempt many activities you wouldn't dare try in other small craft. Its open-water performance lets you move quickly over great distances in rough conditions, thus broadening your ability to do the things you want. You're not confined to a small area.

Another reason may be the take-apart skin-and-frame construction of foldables. One proven principle of creativity is that the more you have to work with, the more you can innovate. There's something about having all those parts and pieces and the process of assembling them that gets the creative juices flowing.

Whatever the reasons behind the phenomenon, folding kayaks work for more than just paddling, sailing, and camping, as discussed earlier. Here's some more fun you can have in a foldable.

Fishing

People have been fishing from foldables since they first emerged from the factory floors of Bavaria. The combination of folding and fishing is a natural fit.

Folding kayaks adapt equally well to freshwater and saltwater fishing. You can carry one into remote areas on horseback or on a human's back, wherever sparsely fished waters beckon. Once there, your luck is likely to be better away from the shoreline, and you can roam from spot to spot quickly. In salt water, rugged conditions are less likely to affect the single angler alone at sea in a foldable than in any other type of small vessel.

You can fish from just about any of the foldables, but the open-cockpit doubles seem to be ideal. These give you the most room to deal with the paraphernalia of the sport.

You can catch all kinds of gamefish. Weight? As much as you can handle. Large catches in a foldable have included a 100-pound halibut, which is about as much as any one person can deal with. But you can also go for smaller lake gamefish with light tackle and flies. You can cast fairly easily from one of these boats.

Trolling works well in a folding kayak. The average paddling speed is considered by many fishermen as ideal for this type of sport. What seems to work best is about 50 feet of line out and with varying trolling weights, depending on whether or not you're after bottom feeders.

Some tips on fishing in a foldable:

Be careful with sharp knives and hooks that can do damage to your boat—and yourself.

Be particularly cautious with a gaff, and keep a cork on the sharp parts until you're ready to bring a catch aboard. You may be better off with a net, depending on the size of fish you're after.

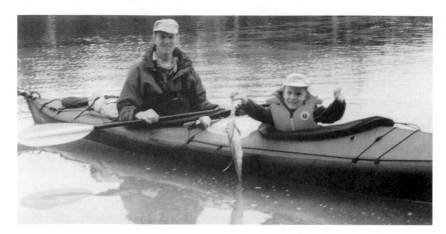

Fishing from a foldable.
(Feathercraft)

Secure tackle boxes and other objects.

One easy method is to place self-adhering Velcro strips on your boat and gear. You can also use webbing straps. Fishing poles can be put into paddle pockets or pushed under the deck either in front or behind your seat. Some folding kayaks have built-in mast partners that make a good place to park your rods. The mast partner also functions well to hold a trolling line high, as is done on larger vessels. The pole top being high in the mast partner makes the troll more lively, more likely to attract fish than one being towed behind from a low position.

Avoid soiling.

To protect your boat from fish blood and entrails, carry along large plastic sheets or garbage bags. Line the area in front of you with the plastic, because this is where you're likely to toss fish, and where you may have to deal with them. To secure the loose sides of the sheet, run bungee cord or line from the front of the coaming to the back. Water bottles and other heavy objects can keep the bottom of the sheet down and in place.

Keep all your work within the confines of the cockpit.

You can keep a bait bucket between your legs, and anything you catch can go into a basket in front of you. Don't put such baskets on the front or back decks; deck loads are risky business and can capsize you faster than anything else around.

Nature Watching

Folding kayaks live up to their ancestral Eskimo legends of stealth in tracking wildlife. Because they're extremely quiet modern foldables can move you up close to wary birds and animals. Their flexible sides absorb and silence any ripples and small waves. Their bow wakes are equally smooth and silent. The accidental slap of a paddle against the side of a foldable makes far less sound than it would against a rigid surface.

Stability and portability help for observing nature. The latter, as in the case of fishing, allows you to pack into remote waters where you find nature at its best. Stability is critical in getting close to what you want to observe. As you draw near, you can put down your paddle and drift without having to keep your paddle ready for a brace stroke. You can even lower your body profile by dropping down partially into your cockpit, and you can keep your arms inside.

Preparing yourself and your boat is fairly simple. Make certain you have nothing shiny showing that could reflect or transmit light. To further silence your boat, you can cover the coaming of an open-cockpit boat with rubber hose. To do this, simply slit the hose and place it along the length of the coaming in any spot where your paddle shaft might hit. Then, to get your body farther down inside the cockpit, remove your seat temporarily and sit on light padding.

Get yourself good binoculars if you don't have a pair already. In rigid kayaks, you probably wouldn't want to use anything more than 6X or 7X power, since the shaking of the boat blurs the image. But in a more stable foldable you can make use of 10X power. To help you see in low light, get 8X50 or 10X50 binoculars.

Photography

All the advantages that foldables offer for nature watching carry over into good photography. And you can get better shots in a folding kayak than you can in a rigid kayak, because you can put down your paddle and focus your attention entirely on the shot.

Some photographers use tripods in open-cockpit foldables, being careful with the leg points and the inside of the hull. Most people find that doubles are the best setup for photography; one person does the shooting while the other paddles and positions the boat for the shot.

You can use your ordinary camera equipment in a foldable, but take precautions not to get it wet. Several types of waterproof storage containers are made just for cameras. The hardshell boxes from Pelican and other manufacturers are probably your best bet, better than the soft storage bags. The boxes are quicker to open when a good photo opportunity presents itself, and they can be closed fast if water starts to slap into the boat. Soft storage bags have to be rolled and unrolled, an operation that can take a few valuable extra seconds to perform. The hardshell boxes also will do a better job of protecting the camera equipment from hard blows. Always tie the box or bag to a rib in your foldable with some webbing strap. Also have a dry cloth handy to wipe camera surfaces that accidentally get splashed.

Varying levels of water-resistant and waterproof cameras flood the market. Before you buy one, read the instructions to be sure it will do what you want. Watch out especially for the zoom lens of a water-resistant camera, because a bit of salt on the extended zoom can gum up its operation. Immediately after using any camera, wipe it clean and dry with a cloth. Even if a camera is weather-resistant, treat it as you would an ordinary camera. Consider the feature a fall back, not a fail-safe parameter.

Waterproof cameras generally live up to their billing, but even so, be careful with them. Wipe off salt periodically using a clean cloth dampened with fresh water. Be especially careful with your lenses. You're likely to keep the camera ready inside your boat without a case, but any water splashed on the lens will dull the sharpness of your photos. And saltwater crystals can permanently etch the lens. Make sure it can float when it's loaded with film and the batteries are installed. If you already own the camera, you could test how well it floats in your bathtub. If it sinks, get a flotation collar or neck strap.

Snorkeling and Scuba Diving

Snorkeling and scuba diving are great water adventures that lend themselves to the use of folding kayaks, particularly the open-cockpit doubles. Foldables offer the snorkeler or scuba diver a good diving platform, they're easy to exit on the water, and they're easy to reenter.

Many militaries use folding doubles for their covert diving activities. One partner is designated the paddler, the other the swimmer/diver. Both people have mountains of military hardware packed around them in addition to the diving gear needed by the swimmer/diver. In civilian use, most double paddlers take turns diving. And of course you could also go solo.

To get started snorkeling or scuba diving, put on your fins (and weight belt, if needed) while you're still inside your folding kayak. You'll have enough clearance for this. Roll out and drop over the side as you would from a rubber raft. But watch that your fins clear the cockpit's opposite coaming.

For scuba diving, you may find it easier to get into the harness and air tank once you're in the water and alongside the boat. Even though you have enough room to put on a scuba tank in the boat your center of gravity would rise and as you go over the side your boat would be less stable.

Smaller scuba tanks may be your first choice, because they'll fit easily between the ribs alongside your legs in the open cockpit area. Larger tanks are better reserved for solo diving from a double, when the tank occupies the seat of the other paddler. Measure the space between ribs on your foldable to check the size of the space. Placing a foam mat on the floor of your foldable will protect the scuba tank's regulator if the tank gets dropped into the boat.

Rowing a Klepper double in Bavaria. *(Walther/Klepper)*

After diving, get yourself back inside the foldable by starting from a horizontal position in the water alongside the boat. Kick with your fins to propel your body into the boat, similar to self-rescue reentry explained in Chapter 10. Don't try to come in from a vertical position, with your legs down deep in the water, or from a position directly perpendicular to the boat.

Spear fishing goes hand in hand with snorkeling and scuba diving, so if you're using a spear gun or sling spear, be careful of the fabric and hull of the boat. Follow the fishing guidelines covered above for other ways to protect your boat and gear.

Rowing

Yes, you can row or scull a folding kayak, but it must be a double with an open cockpit. The preferred rower is the Klepper because of its solid keel board. Don't fool yourself into thinking that a folding kayak when rowed will be as speedy as a racing scull. The latter is made just for the sport of rowing, while a folding kayak is an all-around vessel that can be adapted to be good at it.

If rowing is your preferred mode of moving through the water, you'll be able to cover a lot of it in a foldable. A Klepper has even been rowed around Cape Horn.

Several oar setups are available but the best seems to be the Oarmaster from Martin Marine. It has a sliding seat unit and outriggers that support the oars without any modification of the boat's coaming. The

Oarmaster by Martin Marine. *(Michael Skott)*

whole unit weighs 26 pounds and will work with a nine foot, nine inch set of oars. To fit the apparatus into the Klepper, you'll need to add a 14½-inch × 52-inch baseplate; ⅜-inch marine-grade plywood will do, but ½-inch would be better. You'll also need special track sliders from Klepper. The whole unit lifts in and out quickly.

Motoring

You can attach a motor to any open-cockpit double foldable. And you have your choice of either a quiet electric motor or an efficient gasoline-powered one.

Why have a motor? If you have some physical

Motoring to find wind.

problem that prevents you from sustained paddling, you could still enjoy the advantages of a folding kayak. Or if your adventure calls for going upstream for a long distance against a heavy current, you might opt to use a motor. Or you might just want a backup for your paddling.

Sailing kayakers are also starting to add motors to their large array of on-deck equipment. The kayaking schooner rigs have two sails, two masts, leeboards, outriggers, hiking seats, and more. All this extra gear makes it difficult to get a paddle in the water. A motor allows the sailor to move along without wind until conditions improve. If winds become too strong to tack against effectively, kayak sailors can switch to their motors to get back home.

An electric motor is ideal for fishing, because it makes very little noise. The electric motor of choice appears to be the Minn-Kota 35Na, which is powerful enough to move you steadily for a good part of a day. This particular model weighs only about 12 pounds, but then you have to add the weight of the motor mount plus the marine battery to furnish power to your motor. Electric batteries need occasional recharge.

If you're interested in a gasoline motor, you have plenty of choices among what are considered dinghy or trolling motors. Choose one that weighs no more than about 15 pounds so it won't destabilize the boat when used on a counterweighted motor mount or in conjunction with sailing outriggers. At that weight, you find several motors on the market that are between about 1 and 1½ horsepower. A gasoline motor will give you greater range than an electric motor, due to its need for recharging, and you can bring enough gasoline for hundreds of miles of travel without overloading your boat.

Either motor will work well as long as you know its limitations. You probably are not going to move faster than a normal, healthy crew paddling a double. Motors are failure-prone, like anything electrical or mechanical in a marine environment. Such motors work well for their intended use on the back of a dinghy or small row boat, where they're protected from splash by the boat itself. On a foldable, the motor is mounted about a foot and a half off to the side of the boat, where it gets exposed to all the waves, including your own boat's wake. Constant splashing can foul the air intake and exhaust, and even the most insulated motor can short out and drown.

CHAPTER 15

M*odifying Your Foldable*

Folding-kayak owners always seem to be on the alert for modifications to improve what they got from the factory. Whenever two Folbot or Klepper owners meet, one of the first things they do is compare what they've done with their boats. They poke their heads in, look over the deck layouts, comment on specialized equipment and the like. It's almost a ritual dance.

Whether you have two left thumbs or can barely get a stamp to stay stuck on an envelope, sooner or later, you'll be bitten by the modification bug. Folding kayaks will bring out the resourcefulness in you. Each time you assemble or knock one down, you'll probably get a thought or two about changes you might make.

One reason for such thinking is money. Some modifications that you can do yourself can save you the cost of buying an item from the manufacturer. Anything you can do for yourself will reduce the effective cost to you of enjoying your kayak.

For another, no one manufacturer has the answer to everything. You may like a feature on some other company's boat, and in many instances, you can adapt it to your own boat with make-do materials or by buying the components from the other company.

But most importantly, kayaking is a very personalized sport. No boat, no model, no matter how well thought out and designed, can meet the demands of every individual. Fortunately, folding kayaks, with their skin-and-frame design, lend themselves to tinkering and customizing to suit particular needs.

Below are some modifications that have been tried by other paddlers. These ideas come from the pages of *Folding Kayaker*, the bimonthly newsletter that offers tips and insights on using and enjoying folding kayaks. Some of the modifications are from readers of the newsletter who, like you, see a need and figure out a way of meeting it.

As you read through the modifications, keep your own mind open. The kinds of approaches used to come up with the particular solutions may suggest new ways you might look at any special situation you are facing. Remember that while necessity may be the mother of invention, it is simplicity that often fathers it. During the industrial revolution, some of the best developments were simple, not complex, answers to a need.

Here is a story attributed to Thomas Edison that you might want to keep in mind. During the development of the light bulb, there was a point at which some of his associates were trying to calculate the volume of gas needed to fill their odd-shaped glass bulb. They worked with their formulas for the volumes of spheres and cylinders but were stymied by the bulb's tapered shape. Edison happened to walk in on his vexed associates and asked what the problem was. He then simply picked up the glass bulb, walked over to a sink, filled the bulb with water, poured the water into a measuring beaker and said, "Here is your volume, gentlemen!"

Rudder Lifter for Older Kleppers

If you have a pre–1991 Klepper, you know it lacks a means of raising the rudder out of the water. The company had long argued that there was no need to lift the rudder, that it would swing up out of the way if any object were struck while the boat was moving forward. Nevertheless, dozens of approaches have been rigged up by Klepper owners to have some form of rudder lifter, including sewing a cleat to their canvas deck similar to the approach taken by Klepper competitors.

However, many owners shy away from sewing anything on their decks, particularly a rudder lifter.

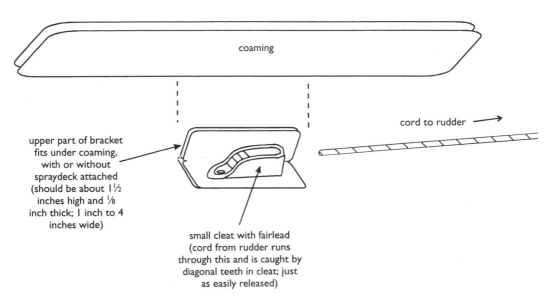

coaming

cord to rudder ⟶

upper part of bracket fits under coaming, with or without spraydeck attached (should be about 1½ inches high and ⅛ inch thick; 1 inch to 4 inches wide)

small cleat with fairlead (cord from rudder runs through this and is caught by diagonal teeth in cleat; just as easily released)

Simple, easy-to-use rudder lifter for pre–1991 Klepper.

And with reason—the Klepper rudder is the biggest in the business and could place a lot of stress on anything to which it was attached. Some people tie off a line from the rudder to a nearby rib or to a cleat screwed into the coaming. But that won't work when you use a spraydeck and skirt.

Here's a better way that requires no alteration of your boat in any way: create a device that will tuck under the coaming at a right angle. In that position the device will be held in place by the tension of the coaming and skin. The concept is not novel. Klepper's tuckunder spraydecks work on the same principle as do the J-bolts used to attach compass boards and leeboards to the boats. All you have to do is attach a clam cleat to the device and you're set.

One way to make such a device begins by looking around in a hardware store for a window sash lock that will work. It's basically a piece of metal plating set at right angles in which one part attaches to the top of the lower sash window and the other presses against the upper window to lock in place. The lock should have rounded edges that won't tear at the coaming or canvas when slipped between the two. You can place on it a junior cleat used in sailing, which you can get at a marine supply shop. You may have to drill in a new hole or two if the ones in the cleat and the window

sash lock don't match. To prevent rust, you'll have to apply coats of rust preventative to the sash lock, which isn't meant for use in a marine environment.

Another approach is to use a small piece of polyethylene as a base for the cleat. Use a heat gun to soften the material while you bend it over the edge of a work table. You can also use part of a plastic junction box used to hold electric outlets. Cut out the right angle you need from the box.

Here are some pointers for working out your own. First, find the cleat you want to use. The size of cleat will determine how large an L-shaped bracket you need. Clam cleats can be found at any marine shop. Make certain yours has a fairlead, the closed eye through which the line will run back to the rudder. The fairlead will prevent the line from being pulled out accidentally, provided you tie a large stopper knot in the open end of the line.

Next, attach the clam cleat using marine-quality fasteners, also found in any marine shop. Or you can use the soft rivets that Klepper sells for attaching replacement fittings.

The only critical measurements involve the portion of the bracket intended to slip under the coaming. You really don't want anything that is more than around an ⅛ of an inch thick, and it should be between one and 1½ inches high. The horizontal dimension can be anywhere from one inch to around four inches, whatever is required to attach the cleat.

Use your imagination when it comes to finding an angled plate that will work. Anything that follows the basic shape is fine. Just make certain it has no sharp edges that will scratch the coaming or chafe the canvas skin where this meets the coaming.

Don't forget to drill a hole in the rudder to attach the line. Such a hole is usually recommended by Klepper anyway. (Their suggestion is to have a hole for attaching a string to a rear deck bracket, to avoid accidentally losing the rudder were the rudder pin to slip loose.) The hole should be drilled along the top part of the rudder within an inch or so of where the rudder hinges.

D-Ring Patches

It doesn't take a genius to see that the hull of a folding kayak is a lot stronger than the deck. However, people who choose to make additions to their boats tend to see "deck," not "hull." So they sew things onto the deck, a tricky job requiring a good needle, proper thread, some backing material, and crossed fingers. Why crossed fingers? You hope the sewn-on patch or attachment won't tear out under stress and loads, leaving a compromising hole. Attach whatever you need to the hull, if at all feasible and convenient.

It's a simple process, as easy as attaching a patch on the hull after you've torn or gouged the material from rough use. The most common such attachments to the hull are D-ring patches. These have a variety of uses.

D-ring patches at the bow and stern on both sides of the boat are used to attach a handle for lifting the boat, pulling it ashore. Some folding kayaks like the Klepper Classic models don't come equipped with bow and stern handles, so the D-ring and strap arrangement takes care of this need. You'll find other uses for D-rings along the hull close to the seam with the deck. They can be used as tie-down points behind the rear seat for deck cargo, but remember to keep deck loads light for safety sake (see Chapter 13).

When you go for a D-ring, get the smallest patch size you can. They come as small as three inches in diameter. And the D-ring itself can be as small as ¾ of an inch. These often can be found in any marine store that has an inflatable-boat department. You're looking for a patch made of the same material as your hull, which in most cases is Hypalon (Achilles is one brand).

To attach the D-ring patch, follow the instructions in your repair sheet on patching the hull, using the contact cement recommended for that. The process is simple. Sand both the patch and the area on the hull where it will be attached. Be aggressive but not too aggressive. You want to get rid of the sheen on the hull. Apply the cement to *both* patch and hull area. Wait for the recommended period, usually 15 minutes or more, then apply more cement to the hull area. Wait another 15 minutes or so, and repeat again on the hull. After waiting the third 15 minutes, make certain it is still tacky. Now press the patch on, using a roller or dull putty knife to really press down and out toward the edges. It should be ready for use the next day.

Solo Seating for Double Kleppers

Unlike other double folding boats with open cockpits such as Nautiraid and Folbot, the Klepper requires a special seat for optimum solo paddling. Klepper offers one as an accessory, but it has problems. First, it's expensive. Although the Klepper solo seat gives better lower-back support than does the regular Klepper seating, some people still report that it doesn't give enough overall support, because its backrest is not particularly large. Then, too, the Klepper solo seat doesn't fold compactly, so it's a bulky item that adds to your load.

A Cheaper Version

So, what to do? Make your own solo seat along the same lines as the one sold by Klepper. A basic plan designed by Rodolfo Wazlawik of New York has been used by some people. The hardware runs less than $40. You'll need a piece of marine- or exterior-grade plywood. If you have to buy a full sheet, it adds to the cost. You can tailor the backrest to suit your breadth and height, naturally, within the confines of the cockpit area. The resulting solo seat is compact and folds down nicely. It also uses one of the regulation seat bottoms, which readily slip in and out. (The commercially available Klepper solo seat has a permanently attached cushioned bottom, which makes it difficult to fold up.)

Solo seating.

You'll need to use some hardware available from Klepper. The most important is the keel-board bracket that Klepper has for attaching the rudder pedals to the keel board as well as its solo seat. In addition, use a tongue fitting to mate the solo seat with the regular Klepper seat bottom.

Additional hardware can be found in hardware or cabinetmaker stores. You'll need brass, not brass-plated, hinges for connecting the back board to the seat board. You will also need webbing and Fastex buckles, which you can buy at any camping supplier. The webbing fits through slotted holes that you make near the edge of the back board for that purpose. It saves money, is unbreakable, and is ultimately a lot simpler. A seat cushion serves as padding for the back rest.

The woodwork does take time. You have to cut the various pieces to size, then sand them and apply varnish or urethane. Then there is the precise location of holes and brackets. You also have to have a piece of wood to accommodate the keel-board bracket. And you should glue some rubber or carpeting on the bottom edge, so it doesn't slide on the floorboard where it

rests. (Klepper's solo seat is raised slightly from the floorboard, and some people have had a problem with breakage in this area. Resting the seat directly on the floor spreads the load of the paddler more evenly.)

Another Approach to Solo Seating

The Klepper solo seat and home-crafted duplicates have some limitations. For one thing, they're all based on using the pedal/keel-board bracket. It raises whatever you have above the floorboard and, to accommodate the bracket, pitches any seat at an angle so that the front is higher than the back.

Here's a far simpler approach that will cost next to nothing. It requires half an hour of work, at most, and costs about $15 for a pair of T-fittings and an extra fitting tongue to place on the keel board. To make this modification, you first have to determine the seat's best trim position for solo paddling a double. Sit on a boat cushion and paddle around from a seated position a bit forward of the normal rear seat. If the boat feels balanced, mark the seat spot. Then mark a spot on the coaming for the T-fittings that will hold the seat back. The best way is to measure the relative positions of the seat back and seat cushion in the normal rear-paddler location and duplicate this relationship at the solo-seat location.

At this point, cut a hole in the keel board for the under-seat clamp that fits into the keel board. Attach the new tongue fitting so it will mate with the snap fitting at the front of the seat.

Now comes a harder part, emotionally. Cut slits into the canvas where you have marked the coaming for the seat back T-fittings. Make a small hole, just enough for the T-fitting to hold the seat back. The canvas in that area has little or no stress on it, so your hole isn't likely to tear further. For safe measure, however, add some fabric tape or duct tape around the edges of your cuts.

Now, anytime you wish to paddle your double solo, just move up both the seat back and the seat to the new position. Depending on where you place your solo setup, you may also have to adjust your rudder controls. To extend the cables, attach non-stretch sailing line to the end of the rudder cables to bridge over to the new foot-pedal position. If your foot pedals come too far forward on the keel board where it narrows, you may not be able to secure the foot pedals properly. A piece of plywood attached to the floor-

board with screws and wing nuts will remedy this. Then attach the foot pedals to the plywood with the clamps ordinarily used.

Feathercraft Hatches for Other Foldables

Feathercraft's deck hatches are the envy of owners of other folding kayaks. The hatches aid in loading and unloading gear into both ends of the boat. They also help you make more efficient use of all that space, since they allow you to reach in to arrange items into the areas between remote ribs. You can retrofit one to your boat as Richard Spener of Missouri did to his Nautiraid double and as several other paddlers have done to their Klepper Aerius IIs. To do so, use the basic materials available from Feathercraft—hatch cloth with bead, hatch coaming, and the hatch cover.

If you are considering doing this retrofit, remember that your biggest challenge is the risk you take in making the holes in your deck. Approach this with care, because you will ruin your boat if you don't. Once you've made the holes, your best bet is to have a professional sailmaker or shoemaker do the sewing. It's a fairly simple process for a professional to sew in the chimney-type base of the Feathercraft hatch system.

hatch cover with shockcorded rim that fits over lower flap piece when coaming is in place

coaming piece

chimney piece—folds down like a dry bag closure to keep water out

Velcro strip

2-inch-high flap piece—has shockcorded top rim that folds down over coaming piece to hold it snugly in place and which then accepts hatch cover when inner chimney is folded down

deck of folding kayak

This hatch assembly is standard on Feathercraft's latest models. The company will make these available to owners of other foldables who wish to add them at their own risk.

Feathercraft hatches for other foldables.

The rigid coaming rim and the hatch cover are designed to come on and off in the normal assembly process.

Be careful where you place the holes. You want them in an area where ribs and top bars won't interfere with access. In modifying his Nautiraid double, Spener decided to have the hatches in a location that could provide double security against heavy wave action caving in the hatch. The holes straddle the top bars of the fore and aft decks. If something were to come crashing down hard, the bar would give some support to the hatch. Please note, however, that Feathercraft has had no such problem in either its testing of the hatches or under surf conditions.

Cheap Spraydeck for Kleppers

Next to a sail rig, the Klepper spraydeck is the most expensive item you can buy for your boat. The tuckunder spraydeck with two spray skirts costs almost $400. The clip-on, three-piece version sports the same price tag.

Matt Woodford of New Jersey found a way around the cost dilemma by making his own. The least expensive approach is to try to replicate the tuckunder version and the way its hem fits under the coaming. Going for a replica of the clip-on version would require buying costly clips from Klepper, thus reducing the advantage of making your own. You could also use Velcro strips or snaps that fasten to both the coaming and spraydeck. But all these device-driven alternatives add to the cost. Besides, the tuckunder spraydeck has proved to stay on through all kinds of situations.

The factory version of the tuckunder seems to incorporate a cord sewed and glued into the hem of the deck for fitting into the groove on the inside surface of the wooden coaming. This cord hem could easily be replicated with some small-diameter nylon or polypropylene rope.

Another problem to solve is the hoop to which the spray skirt will be attached to the spraydeck. In the Klepper factory-built deck, the hoop is made of a flexible plastic material somewhat like a rubber hose but with articulated, curved grooves that do a pretty good job of securing the spray-skirt hem. It would be hard to find similar material already contoured for snugging on a spray skirt.

Other folding kayaks use a different form of hoop, and, like Matt Woodford, you may want to turn to their approach. Nautiraid has what seems to be a lightweight metal hoop sewn into the deck onto which you attach the spray skirt. It seems to be an uncomplicated approach. You might find a tough plastic hoop that will do the same. It's critical to get the hoops exactly in the right spot. For that you'll need a template or true measurements of the factory deck.

The replica spraydeck requires considerable sewing, and for that you'll need a good sewing machine capable of stitching through several thicknesses of the material you'll use for the deck. That material should be fairly waterproof. A nylon pack cloth would be good as long as it's not too light. Consider material that weighs at least 8.5 ounces per square yard or a Cordura nylon that weighs 11 ounces per square yard. The pack cloth comes in 60-inch widths, costs $10 per yard, and is available from Campmor. This company's toll-free number for mail-order service is (800) 526-4784.

Use an elastic cord at the front of the spraydeck so that it will fit snugly around the mast partner, the metal bracket with a hole in it. At the back of the coaming, sew in some grommets and shock cord to attach around the boomerang-shaped piece that closes off the back of the wooden coaming. To achieve a bead around the hem of the spraydeck, sew in some nylon cord. The hem then tucks under into the groove in the wooden coaming. This should work just as well as the factory version.

Use commercially available spray skirts. It would be hard to duplicate one for less than about $35, about what the standard spray skirt sells for.

Rudder Modifications

The most frequent complaint among folding-kayak paddlers concerns that little ol' thing at the back of their boat and how to operate it from the cockpit. "My rudder is causing too much drag." "Why am I always replacing yokes and rudder pins?" It's little wonder there's a rebellion among folding kayakers to take matters into their own hands and come up with a better system. Here are several:

The Balanced Rudder

This idea was created by Mark Balogh of Balogh Sail Designs and David Valverde of New York, and

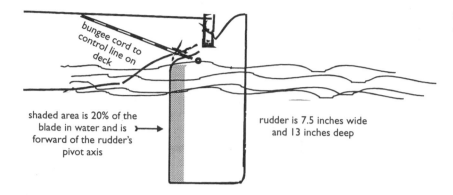

bungee cord to control line on deck

Balanced rudder for sailing, designed by Mark Balogh.

shaded area is 20% of the blade in water and is forward of the rudder's pivot axis

rudder is 7.5 inches wide and 13 inches deep

it's primarily aimed at achieving a better rudder for sailing. A balanced rudder prevents stalling a kayak under sail, and it does so by putting 20 percent of the rudder's surface ahead of the pivoting point. Sailing enthusiasts who have used one say, "It's like changing from manual to power steering in a car." When paddling a double, it also has practical application for use in turning. This is especially true when using larger rudders like those on the Klepper and Folbot. The balanced rudder is deeper in the water, so in waves it's less likely to be riding in the air and more likely to be biting into the water.

The balanced rudder pictured here can be fiddled with for Kleppers and similar foldables. The idea is that you need to get up to, but no more than, 20 percent of the swept area of the blade forward of its vertical pivot axis. This balanced area uses the water pressure generated by the boat's movement to help turn the blade.

With this setup, you can use a larger blade without needing to exert excessive steering pressure, particularly at high speeds. The 20-percent limit is critical; any more and you would lose rudder feel at your feet. More importantly, the blade will swing quickly to one side and slow down or stall the boat. Another advantage of the balanced rudder is that you can use the rudder as part of the lateral plane of the boat without inducing too much pressure into the steering system. This allows you greater flexibility in where the center of effort of the sail rig is in relation to the leeboard. If the sail plane is substantially aft of the leeboard, then such a balanced rudder becomes a beneficial part of the lateral plane of the rig without adversely affecting steering.

It's important to hold the rudder down at higher sailing speeds. If a balanced rudder kicks partway up because of speed pressure, it loses its balanced area and, because of its large overall size, becomes difficult to turn. To keep the rudder down, use a bungee-cord arrangement. A bungee or shock cord is knotted into a hole in the rudder, then run back about half way to the cockpit, where it's tied to a piece of line that leads to a cam cleat within easy reach of the cockpit. You can then adjust the pressure tighter for heavy winds, looser for light winds.

Hand Tiller and Secondary Steering

David Valverde has come up with an interesting hand tiller, as seen in the accompanying photo. It rides on the mast for the second sail on his schooner setup and uses the same basic tubing incorporated into Balogh's B.O.S.S. outrigger system. It gives him a good, reliable tiller that won't hang up and is easier on the hand than the one from Klepper. Valverde also has fitted a similar tube at the bottom of his front mast to act as a foot control bar, in case he needs to steer from the front seat.

Feathercraft Rudders for Other Craft

Feathercraft's rudder system is highly regarded in the kayaking industry. It costs about $90, works well on Feathercrafts, and is the rudder of choice as original equipment for a number of manufacturers of hardshells.

The Feathercraft rudder has some distinct advantages. It is long and narrow and drops deeply into the water to give you steering purchase in rough seas,

Hand tiller on a schooner rig.

when a shallower rudder would often be airborne. It can be lifted completely out of the water and fitted into a special holder on the back of the deck. In this position, the Feathercraft rudder offers a low profile to wind and wave. Other rudders can be lifted out of the water, but then they can't be fitted onto the deck.

You can retrofit this rudder onto a Klepper single or double. To do so, you have to file only a thin layer of metal from the Klepper built-in rudder holder. You can also fit the Feathercraft rudder on Nautiraids.

Feathercraft also makes a retractable skeg that fits on like a rudder. It would be ideal for the Nautiraid Mini-Raid which has no provision for a rudder.

Fitting the Feathercraft rudder or skeg to other boats requires gluing some strips of material to the hull and over the very stern. This is the way Feathercraft attaches rudders to its own boats. It's a fairly easy and fail-proof process.

Extra Protection for Hulls

This idea comes from several sources—including a look at the Ally Canoe, a folding canoe made by Pakboats. These frame-and-skin canoes are worthy cousins to folding kayaks, and as folding craft they're well suited to paddling on lakes and shallow rivers.

Ally Canoes are tough and rugged. What makes the Ally Canoe able to withstand abrasion and contact with rocks in shallow water is the foam liner mounted between its vinyl skin and aluminum frame. It's made of closed-cell foam that not only cushions impact but also provides flotation for this open boat.

Most damage done to the hull of any skin-and-frame boat comes from the hull being caught between the proverbial rock and hard place. The rock is, well, any rock in any shallow water, and the hard place is the frame member against which the hull is getting caught, or rather, pressed.

If you find yourself using a folding kayak in shallow waters, you might want to place some closed-cell foam between the bottom of the frame and the hull. Run this foam up along the sides to the level of the first set of long pieces. Go for ¼-inch foam, because anything thicker may interfere with inserting the frame halves during the assembly process. Placing anything under the frame of your folding kayak, be it a Feathercraft, Folbot, Klepper, or Nautiraid, can radically change the lines and chines of the hull. And if you change them, you change how the boat reacts and balances, because, in effect, you are rounding out the bottom. This is neither good nor bad, just something that will make boat handling different from what is normal.

The idea of adding some protective layer for special applications is not new. Klepper has long made a similar suggestion for paddlers using its boats in shallow rocky water. The company advises placing an inflatable sleeping pad under the keel portion of the frame, then partially inflating it.

The Ultimate Modification

If you think you've heard of everything, here's the story of the fellow who was unhappy with the length of his double Klepper. Don Barch of California wanted a longer one, longer than the 17-foot regulation boat. So he added more than two feet in length to his existing boat to get the boat of his dreams. Indeed, it sounds like a crazy idea. What do you do to the frame to extend it? How do you get the skin apart to lengthen it? And with what?

Barch thought that the cockpit area was too small. Paddlers were too close and their paddles clanked. He thought there wasn't enough storage room between the paddlers. Barch was also unhappy with the bow of the Aerius II; he believed it tended to dive too much into waves, slowing down the boat and splashing water up on the foredeck. In his eyes the bow was too blunt.

To get to his dream vessel, Barch decided that two areas needed work, the frame and the skin. In addi-

tion, any work on either of these areas would generate more work in other areas to compensate for new stresses, loads, and other fall-out effects.

Frame Changes

Attacking the wooden frame was the easiest part of the job and probably the area in which Barch felt most satisfied with the results. He did all of his major frame customizing at the bow half. He got rid of the standard bow piece and replaced it with a new, hand-crafted bow piece made of oak for good strength features. It had the upsweep he wanted to see for riding over waves. The way he configured it, the gunwales no longer came quite as close together in front as on the standard setup, but rather had a broader curve toward the bow. The stringers attached in somewhat the same way, mimicking the gunwales' new positioning.

The net effect of the new bow piece and the repositioning of the side pieces going to it was the addition of 34 inches to the overall length of the bow half of the boat. The stern half was fundamentally unaffected, except for some minor changes described below. With the greater length of boat, Barch added a second #4 rib in the cockpit area, which elongated the cockpit just as he desired.

Barch realized that greater length would put new stresses on the frame. To bolster things all around, he

blue canvas deck as in original boat

cockpit coaming, about 2 feet longer than original

original seam on deck that was lined up with front of coaming in original Aerius II

gray Hypalon bottom as in standard boat

new nose section made of blue wraparound Hypalon

Features:
• 34 inches longer than standard Aerius II
• greater bow upsweep
• 2 feet longer in cockpit

Frame changes:
• new wooden bow piece
• fore gunwales attach farther back on bow piece
• extra #4 rib, coaming pieces, stringers

Nineteen-foot Klepper designed by Don Barch.

did two things to both the bow and stern keel boards. One, he fiberglassed the top of the boards that you see when you step into the Klepper. Second, he Kevlared the entire bottom of the keel boards. He felt that the combination beefed up the bottom of the boat for somewhat greater stiffness and strength. To finish up the reconstruction of the frame, Barch added extra stringers to span the greater length of the boat. He used wooden dowels that mate with the existing stringers via standard PVC plumbing pipe sections.

He made some frame changes after experience on the water revealed some added stress points. The principal adjustment was at the stern where the stern piece mates with the rear gunwales. The mating brackets on either side were breaking free, so Barch put a metal plate on the stern piece and rescrewed the mating brackets to that. The new arrangement seems to be taking new stresses well.

Extending the Skin

Flush with his success redesigning the Klepper frame to suit his needs, Barch attacked the skin. It involved incredible labor and attention to detail, and it's the area where he's not totally satisfied with the results.

Here's how Barch proceeded. First, he worked on the hull. He removed the bow cap, a piece of Hypalon rubber reinforcement that fits over the front of the boat to act as a bumper. Underneath the bow cap is a seam joining the hull with the two sides. So the boat was opened at its nose.

Next was the deck. Barch opened a seam on the top of the deck along its entire length back toward the cockpit, leaving the boat open at the top in front.

Barch had a very simple answer to material needed at both the hull and deck. He got blue Hypalon rubber material from a raft company and used it for the entire front of the boat, both hull and deck. The blue matched the color of the canvas deck extraordinarily well. The bow of Barch's boat had a distinct, almost three-foot-long, blue nose that then flowed into the standard blue deck and grey hull.

The job was easy in theory, tough to execute. Barch used a sailor's awl to do the sewing by hand. Try as carefully as he could to gather the material evenly as he sewed along, he got a few wrinkles and what he termed a perceptible lopsidedness of port and starboard sides. The seams where the new piece met the regulation deck and hull were covered with the 2 ¼-inch kellstripping material available from Klepper. Potentially this created some drag, but not as much as might be expected.

Lengthening the Cockpit

With the top of the bow deck open, Barch was able to extend the cockpit to the length he wanted, and have its front apex sewn together farther along the original foredeck. It was fairly easy to extend the wooden coaming. His vintage of Klepper had a coaming that came in three pieces, the front V and two extensions toward the rear, so he just made longer replacements for the two extensions. Some of the lopsidedness resulting from how the 34-inch bow piece was attached is visible in the cockpit area, and one side is looser here than the other.

What about the sponsons? Barch did nothing with them, so now they don't come up to the bow and stern ends as they would in a standard boat. But this is similar to the setup in earlier Folbot Greenland II's, in which air sponsons didn't run the full length either.

CHAPTER 16

Repair and Maintenance

If you're like most paddlers, chances are that you will never need to make any repair on your folding kayak, even patching. Turn over a dozen foldables that have been used regularly for five years, and only one or two are likely to show even one patch. The rest will have clean bottoms.

And if you're like most folding-kayak owners, you won't do much maintenance beyond washing the skin and frame members occasionally to remove mud and saltwater residue. Your boat won't look any more worn than that of the paddler who polishes and varnishes every surface in sight.

Nevertheless, you should know how to patch and repair your boat in the event that something does happen when you're far from home. It's a jungle out there. You'll encounter hidden wrecks, sunken tree trunks, barnacle-crusted rocks, and broken-bottle beaches. And the power of the sea is enough to trash even large ships when it's riled up. Surf landings are rough on any vessel.

And if you want to get the longest service out of your folding kayak and enjoy hassle-free assembly and disassembly, a regular maintenance schedule may very well help it make a century mark, at least the frame anyway. This need not be a boot camp regimen; fairly simple attention will work wonders. It will also help you spot potential problems before they find you, out on a trip somewhere.

Repair

Repairs can be thought of as two types. The first are the emergency repairs done in the field. The second can be completed leisurely at home or during a break in a multi-week trek. Surprisingly few things can go wrong with a folding kayak that demand your immediate attention while you're out paddling. Even then, you can make a quick fix that will hold until you can correct the problem more permanently.

Field repairs are not very elaborate, nor need they be pretty. What you want to know is how to do something fast that will allow you to keep going. Some permanent repairs can take time. But with a foldable, you may be able to replace, not repair, an errant item, which takes very little time.

Field Repairs on the Run

You probably got a repair kit with your foldable. It most likely consists of some of the following items: large pieces of deck material that can be used to make a patch in a torn deck; a large piece of hull material, possibly including some keelstrips; cement to attach the hull-repair patch to a tear; sandpaper for roughing up the hull surface to accept the patch; clear vinyl solvent that will seal pin holes in the air sponsons; duct tape; and a spare part or two.

Take that kit and put it away at home someplace where you can find it if it's ever needed. You won't need all those items on most trips. So many paddlers dutifully carry the kit with them without asking some very real questions of themselves. "How likely am I to sew on a patch during a day trip or weekend camping outing?" "How willing am I to go through the ritual of roughing up hull surfaces and cementing and re-cementing patches with 15- to 20-minute waiting periods between coatings while sand is blowing over everything and the mosquitoes are biting?"

You need very few items from that kit for emergency field repairs. The duct tape is one, and it's fundamentally all you need for most emergency repair situations. In fact, you should purchase extra duct tape so you'll have enough for some emergencies you

Klepper repair items. *(Walther/Klepper)*

may run into. Be careful about duct tape. The shiny aluminum-faced kind isn't up to marine-environment repairs. It certainly will not hold tenaciously to parts and boat skins. Get the good stuff from your boat dealer or in the aftermarket. You could find a good version in photography shops where it's known as gaffer's tape. The best duct tape comes from the folding-boat manufacturers.

You also will want to retrieve any specialized item from the factory-supplied repair kit and take it with you when paddling. For example, if the kit has a spare air stopper for the sponsons, that's a good item to have in case you lose one.

If you have a foldable with an aluminum frame, your repair kit in all likelihood contains a repair sleeve of aluminum tubing sized slightly larger than the thickest long aluminum frame member. Bring that along. It takes a lot to bend or crimp an aluminum long piece tube. But if it does happen, the only quick repair is to slip that emergency sleeve over the broken or bent part and secure the sleeve in place.

Look at the Essentials list in Chapter 5 for other items to have with you. Chief among these is an all-around tool like the Leatherman Tool. You'll also want to carry some spares for parts that can break down and would be easier to replace than to try to jury-rig. The most likely weak points are the rudder pin and yoke. The pin can get lost, and the yoke can snap or bend.

Here are some emergency repair principles.

Duct tape is the solution to nearly any problem on a foldable.

Duct tape will adhere to the smooth surface of your hull for months and months. It will hold on to the canvas for weeks and weeks. It will keep cracked ribs and long pieces together for years.

Much depends on how you apply it. It will stick on the hull only if the surface is truly dry. Take the time to make it so. Then apply duct tape to the damaged hull with an inch or so of overlap. Place duct tape on both the outside and inside surfaces, if you can reach the inside easily. Round off the ends of the tape so you leave no right-angle corners that can catch and lift the patch. Press down on the tape and out from the center to expel air.

The tape should be applied to the deck in a similar way. Since most deck surfaces have a grainy texture, not smooth like the hull, it's important to apply pressure until you can see the grain bumps through the tape surface. Apply duct tape more generously with more overlap than on the hull. You may want to apply several layers.

Duct tape needs help when applied to frame members.

If you have a broken or splintered long piece, you should apply not only duct tape but also some form of splint to bridge the break. You can get quite a long-lasting repair of a broken long piece if you do the following. Put some duct tape at the break, enough to smooth out burrs and jagged edges. Then find a piece of wood, maybe part of a tree branch or a stick of driftwood. Attach this as a splint by first wrapping it in place with light cord or dental floss. If you don't have cord or floss, long strands of cloth from a T-shirt or bandanna will do. Then wrap the repair with plenty of duct tape in overlapping layers.

Don't fret over broken or loose fittings.

Folding kayaks have built-in redundancy. No one, two, or three broken fittings are going to affect the boat's ability to keep going. Other fittings will take the load. Also, the tension of the skin over the frame will help keep the frame snug and solid. You can wait until you get home to fix fittings. If it does bother you, use some cord to tie the long piece and rib together temporarily at the point of the errant fitting.

The fretting seems to be more of a problem in the minds of Klepper owners. If a fitting won't stay locked, they worry about the boat holding together. They fail to see that each rib is connected to the long parts in as many as seven places, more than in any of the other foldables. Even if three fittings aren't holding on a rib, the rest are enough to do the job.

Keep your mind open to indirect solutions.

Don't get caught up in linear thinking. You can repair a broken aluminum part with a wood splint. You can use a metal splint such as a tent peg to span a broken wooden part.

Speaking of tent pegs, not only are they good splints, they also come in handy for other repairs. The metal pegs that come with most tents, for example, can be used to temporarily replace a lost rudder pin on a Klepper.

The tent-peg idea should alert you to see if you can use any other items in ways they weren't intended. If you don't have what you need, rummage around in your things. As mentioned above, a torn up T-shirt makes a good wrap for a repair. So will a belt. A quick walk along almost any beach or shoreline is bound to turn up some flotsam that could be put to use.

Permanent Repairs

You usually will want to wait until you get home to make a permanent repair of any damage you incur. But if you have enough time, you can do almost any permanent repair of a folding kayak in the field under all conditions, including extreme cold. Foldables are the only sea kayaks that can make this claim, and it's one reason they're the first choice for long-range expeditions, especially in northern climates. You cannot permanently repair a holed or cracked hull of a rigid plastic or fiberglass sea kayak in such locales, because their repair materials will not work reliably in temperatures lower than about 45°F. Hypalon hulls, on the other hand, will accept a permanent patch at temperatures below freezing.

Here are some guidelines for permanent repairs.

You may want to exercise your replace-not-repair option.

With a folding kayak, you have that unique choice, at least when you get back home. With a rigid boat, you don't. Say your loaded double foldable gets bashed against huge boulders by a mean surf and you break the coaming. You can make an emergency repair and continue your trip. When you're back home, you may want to buy a new coaming or a part of one, since you can get just one side.

Consider the cost of that item versus messing with repair materials and their costs. Much depends on the nature of the part. If it's truly a minor component in the boat's structure, say a stringer, you can just leave it taped and never permanently repair it or bother with a replacement. Some major pieces, such as the main connectors holding the two frames halves together, would merit replacement, certainly at least a permanent repair.

Always opt for using the materials furnished by the manufacturer.

Be wary of substitutes from the outside world. Not all Hypalon-type materials are the same. A Hypalon strip purchased from a rubber-raft catalog may not have the same composition, adhesives, and core material as the original manufactured equipment. Some materials may only seem to work better than what the manufacturer provides. For example, Barge cement adheres permanently when the contact cement from Klepper won't. You may regret permanence, however, if in the future you need to lift that Barge-cemented patch to put on keelstrips.

Get the latest advice from the manufacturer and follow it.

Your boat may be a dozen years old and finally bend an aluminum rod. Call the company. The written instructions you received with your boat may be out-of-date. The company may have found better or easier solutions. It's even possible that the company might be willing to replace a piece that broke, if it suspects that the piece may have been part of a bad batch.

Be thorough when making a hull repair.

Generally you repair Hypalon the way that was described for attaching D-rings to the hull, discussed as a modification in Chapter 15. Take your time, have all the materials at hand before you start the job. It's critical that you really work on preparing the surface. That's the secret behind a lasting repair.

Use sandpaper to rough the surface really well. If you don't get the surface sufficiently scratched up, the contact cement and the patch will not hold well. On the other hand, you don't want to sand through the surface down to the core material underneath. That's why it's important to take your time; scratch the surface some, blow away the dust, scratch some more.

Apply the contact cement in several stages as instructed earlier. And be patient. Wait for the surface to get just a bit tacky. If you're going to err, it is better to wait longer than to rush the job. Five minutes too soon is bad, five minutes too long is okay.

Remember to round off the edges, as you would with any patch. If you leave the right-angle corners, your patch will most certainly lift off over time.

Other hull materials, such as vinyl or urethane-coated nylon, have their own set of repair instructions. You should follow the company's direction.

Aquaseal can work wonders.

This product, which had its origin as a repair glue for neoprene wet suits, has wide application for permanently repairing folding kayaks. Aquaseal can be used in a number of ways, but always use the accelerator material known as COTOL 40 that you buy separately.

You can use Aquaseal to attach a patch to the deck instead of sewing it on. Here's how. Get the deck material out of your repair kit. Cut it to a size that gives you at least a 1½-inch overlap beyond the damaged section. Round off the corners. Apply Aquaseal to both the patch and deck. Press the patch down hard. Then apply a bead of Aquaseal around the perimeter of the patch.

Aquaseal can be used directly on nicks in the hull that are too minor or small to warrant a patch. It will also repair ripped spray skirts and clothing.

Frame members will respond to a number of commercially available repair materials.

Many repair materials will work with aluminum, polycarbonate, polyethylene, and wood frame members. Again, see what the manufacturer recommends. If you're unsure, go to a marine supply shop and look through the repair section. Power boats and sailboats use much the same materials that go into the frame of your foldable. By buying your repair stuff from a marine shop, you assure yourself of getting something that will be waterproof and hold up in a saltwater environment.

One product you might want to look into is 3M's 3532 Urethane Structural Adhesive, which has a high viscosity, is putty-like in consistency, and can be used either for bonding broken pieces together or in conjunction with cloth as you'd use resins. It takes about 10 minutes to harden, but you should wait 24 hours before putting full stress on the repair. The adhesive is expensive, about $20 for a four-ounce kit.

You may also want to take a look at cold epoxy, which comes under a variety of brand names. It generally will work for marine applications.

Maintenance

You don't have to go overboard on maintenance. As stated earlier, many paddlers never varnish the wooden frames of their Kleppers, Nautiraids, and older Folbots, yet they get away with it. For example, the German-language copy of maintenance instructions for Kleppers tells you to varnish yearly, but that advice is absent from the English instructions. Yet there is no evidence that Kleppers last longer in German-speaking countries than in English-speaking ones.

Your most important maintenance material is not varnish, lubrication, wax, or anything exotic. It's water. Fresh water. Wash your boat regularly. If you can, wash it after each use. If you can't, then plan to wash it at least once or twice during the paddling season and before you put the boat away, assuming you're not a year-round boater.

Wash everything: the hull, inside and outside; the deck, topside and underside; and the frame members. Use a mild soap on the deck to get out salt crystals and the oiliness that salt water tends to have. Aluminum frame pieces need special attention. Wash the tubes inside and out. Dropping the pieces into a bathtub is an easy way to remove grit from the insides. If you don't, that grit will wear away at shock cord and gum up the male/female connection points.

Your boat can get by without washing. Some city apartment dwellers never get a chance to do anything with the hull. But your foldable will be happier if it does get washed every so often.

Here are two other maintenance steps to take with your boat during the season. One, wax the hull with whatever the manufacturer sells or recommends. A well waxed hull is better protected against damage from sun and salt. Wax will keep Hypalon and other hull materials from drying out prematurely. A waxed hull slides off sharp rocks and other abrasive surfaces better than an unwaxed one.

Two, if you have an aluminum frame boat, lubricate the joining ends regularly. A good preventative schedule calls for lubrication every two months, especially if the boat is being left assembled and getting wet on the inside all the time, particularly in salt water. Of course, wash the frame just about as often, too.

Getting Ready for the Season

The "boating season" may not open in your local waters until last winter's ice disappears. In the western-rivers region, the paddling season has more to do with rainfall amounts than temperatures. If you live where water sports are possible year-round, your local boating season may revolve around an annual profusion of flowers, migrations of wildlife, or around your family's vacation schedule. If you prefer to travel elsewhere to do your boating, your season could begin and end at any time. But no matter where you live or what your lifestyle, you can think of the boating season as whenever you most frequently get to enjoy adventuring on the water.

Every boater, from rafter to yachtsman, knows that you have to get your craft ready for the season. Problems may have developed unnoticed while the boat was in storage. Annual maintenance duties might never get done later, when you're just too busy having fun with your boat, so you'd better see to them now. Although folding kayaks are no more delicate than other boats, they do need some specialized attention. Here is a checklist of things to do before the upcoming season and tips to making it a happy one.

The Skin

Examine your hull for signs of aging.

How has it held up while in storage? Can you see any cracks or evidence of dryness? With older hulls, it may be time to apply some of the coatings to drastically rejuvenate the material (see What to Do with An Old Hull later in this chapter). Or is it time to consider a replacement? Otherwise, plan to wax the bottom after completing the rest of the items below.

Look for any holes or significant wear patterns.

Rather than just patch, this may be the time to keelstrip whole areas.

Study any old patches.

Are any ends coming loose? Very few patches will respond well if you just shove some rubber cement under the loose corners. You may be better off removing the entire patch and starting from scratch. Or you could try using some Aquaseal on that loose end.

Check your keelstripping closely.

You may find that edges have raised at various points. You will not want to remove entire keelstrips to remedy this. Try to hold those loose portions with toothpicks and apply rubber cement or Aquaseal from your repair kit.

Attend to the deck.

If you have a foldable with zippers, such as a Folbot or an older Feathercraft, lubricate these closures and check for stressed stitches. Tug hard on deck D-rings. It's better to find out now whether they'll hold up under pressure or not. The same with grab handles. If you have a Klepper and the stitches on the handles are puckering, cut them off and make a substitute with D-rings on the hull, using straps or cord as handles (see Chapter 15). In general, look for any loose stitching and then patch according to instructions from the company. Also on Kleppers and Nautiraids, wax the cockpit bead (usually colored black) that fits into the coaming groove.

The Frame

Kleppers, Nautiraids, and older wooden-framed Folbots.

Check for any signs of wood rot, blackened spots, especially around screws and rivets that hold vital parts together. You won't want these to pop loose out on the water. If varnished surfaces are rubbed bare, you ordinarily need not revarnish except in the area of major fittings. Unless it's a fetish of yours.

Feathercraft and aluminum-framed Folbots.

Take a careful look at the shock cords holding segments together and make any replacements now. Wash frame parts in fresh water, something you should do regularly anyway. Clean the ends of tubes to remove any grime, and spray them with whichever lubricant is recommended. Be careful with WD-40 because it's not so kind to rubber surfaces. You may want to try Tri-flow Teflon spray or Boeshield T-9.

Check fittings on all makes.

With Klepper fittings, ensure that tongues and locks will not come free. Tap gently on the locks and bend tongues gently so you don't snap them off. On

Feathercrafts, see if the pins that pop through holes when levering are still springy. Lubricate to make certain they work well.

What to Do with An Old Hull

What do you do with a tired old hull that has already seen 25 years of service? The issue comes up, for instance, when someone has found an uncle's old Folbot Super in the attic. Or it could be a hard decision you're facing with a 30-year-old Klepper for which a replacement hull costs considerably more than what you originally paid for your double when it was new, including sail rig, rudder, spray deck, et al.

Here are your options.

The Economies of a New Hull

When you think about it, a new hull is a bargain. What other kind of vessel can so easily be brought back to like-new condition so simply, although it does take a stroke of your pen to a check or credit card form. Rigid kayaks don't offer that option. When their hulls go at around 10 to 15 years, depending on their hull material and your usage, you chuck them.

A foldable can have any part replaced, including the hull. So, if you've had a kayak for 25 to 30 years, you can replace the skin, place it on your existing frame—good for probably half a century or more—and be on your way for another 25 or 30 years of fun.

The cost and availability of a new hull depend on the manufacturer. They run from fairly inexpensive to costly. Folbot can replace the hulls on most of its models. The exception is the models with wooden "longerons," for which the company no longer has the patterns. You can get a Hypalon skin (hull and deck) for your old Folbot for around $450. You can get the cost down even more if you opt for a skin with a vinyl hull that costs just $280. The Greenland II, Folbot's four-year-old model, can get a replacement skin for $580, but you'd have to have done something drastic with your relatively new kayak.

A Klepper hull is costly, but it's certainly worth the price. A gray-bottomed Classic hull replacement for a Klepper double costs $1,400. You'll get a good 25 to 30 years out of it, and it will have the latest fittings and improved deck webbing. The Expedition hull is more expensive at $2,150. It's lots of money, but your boat will be able to take unbelievable punishment on the roughest of surfaces, and you'll have paddle pockets and some other nice deck goodies.

Traditional Revitalizing Methods

Follow Occam's razor rule: don't go for a complex theory or solution when a simple one can answer the problem. Your problem may respond to some liberal use of keelstrips without going to the complexity of cold cash. These strips can buy years and years of happy paddling. The cost is much less than a new hull.

Another traditional method was to use Klepper's Hypalon rubber hull paint, Gummilack. But it may no longer be available. Gummilack was a quick fix of the last resort.

If you're tempted to slap on plain old paint or some other such covering liquid, think twice. Unless it's a specialized product like Gummilack or the Gacoflex described below, it may not work well. Ordinary paint-type products won't hold onto a surface intended to be folded and flexed or take the abuse of sun and salt water.

Gacoflex

Gacoflex H-22 is a specialized Hypalon coating meant for all sorts of applications, from roofing and decks to coating rubber rafts and folding kayaks. It will work on Hypalon, neoprene, and polyurethane but not vinyl. It coats the hull completely, filling in scaling areas and pinholes.

To use it correctly, you must first scrape off any loose hull material. Then wipe the hull with a special thinner called N-450-1. Then brush in the Gacoflex, applying several coats. The first coat should be well brushed into the hull's surface. Additional coats should be applied one right after the other to assure good adhesion between layers.

The hull should be on the boat frame when you apply the coating, and you should plan to leave the folding kayak assembled for a week or so. If you take it apart too soon, you risk having the hull stick to itself. This product is toxic to breathe, so plan to have adequate ventilation. Gacoflex H-22 costs about $32 a gallon.

It's tricky stuff to work with. Some paddlers have

Putting on a keelstrip.

had problems in applying Gacoflex. The product remained tacky for them and tended, at times, to stick to itself in the bag. Others find it simple to apply and are happy with the results.

Attach a New Surface

You may be able to cover the existing skin with a new covering layer. The benefit of attaching a new surface is that you don't have to be all that precise, since you're covering an already formed material with another. This idea comes from *Folding Kayaker* reader Robert Grant of Indiana.

EPDM is a rubberized fabric used by building contractors for roofing and other jobs. Feathercraft uses EPDM in small sections to protect the nose and stern of its kayaks. The EPDM fabric is .045-inch thick and costs 32 cents a square foot. It comes in 20-foot-wide sheets in long rolls. You get it cut to the overall size you need. A four- by 20-foot sheet costs around $25. The adhesive needed for EPDM costs around $15 a gallon. A gallon is more than you'll need, so try to buy it in a smaller can. You'll also need a special cleaner that helps prepare the surface. Be warned: EPDM is heavy and will add to the weight of your kayak. That's why Feathercraft doesn't use it for its full keelstrips.

Before going through all the expense and work,

first see if EPDM will hold on your boat and bond to it properly. Try it first on a piece of hull material from your repair kit. Then, to be doubly certain that your actual hull is not too chalky to bond with the EPDM, place a small patch of the fabric on some spot. If EPDM passes both tests, then proceed as follows.

Clean the existing hull with the special cleaner for EPDM. Then cut the material into three long strips. Make chalk marks on the hull for lining up the EPDM strips. Work from the center of the boat to one end and then to the other. To make the material easier to handle, you can double it over itself while working on it.

When you're sure of the position of the EPDM in relation to the hull, apply the EPDM adhesive cement to one strip of the EPDM fabric at a time and to the area of the hull where it will be placed. Wait for the adhesive to dry to a slightly tacky state. The contact-adhesive surface sticks only to another adhesive surface. Therefore, you can place layers of newspaper in between to allow you to get the strip into position without sticking it prematurely to unintended areas of the hull. Then, pulling out the newspaper, press the EPDM fabric into contact with the hull. To finish the job, apply EPDM caulking to the area around the ends. This caulking comes in a tube.

Appendix

SUGGESTED READING

Other than the book you're holding and the newsletter, *Folding Kayaker* (see Periodicals), few direct sources of information concentrate on hands-on advice about folding kayaks. That's one of the reasons this book was written.

Still, there are a number of books and periodicals that you will find worthwhile reading. Some are inspirational, with a strong folding-kayak theme. Others offer specific information vital to any sea kayaker.

Books

The following reading list is eclectic rather than a broad survey of what's available. For example, it lists just one book on navigation, *Fundamentals of Kayak Navigation*, which is the best and probably only such book you'll ever need.

The listing is divided into three sections: books in English; books in German; and guidebooks to paddling in several choice areas.

In English

Alone At Sea by **Dr. Hannes Lindemann.** (Pollner Verlag, 1993.) A "must read" for any folding kayaker, for any sea kayaker for that matter. Dr. Lindemann's account of his transatlantic journey in a stock Klepper folding kayak will inspire you and should convince anyone of the underlying toughness of these boats. The book had been out of print. This new edition contains an important chapter that was previously missing in the English version.

Baidarka by **George Dyson.** (Alaska Northwest Books, 1986.) An unbelievably beautiful book to read and look at. It traces the origins of skin-and-frame boats, which folding kayakers can closely identify with. Dyson details the vivid history of European encounters with the Northern cultures along the West Coast of North America. And he runs you through how to make your own skin-and-frame kayak. If you're contemplating making your own foldable kayak, this is a good place to start.

The Boater's Weather Guide by **Margaret Williams.** (Cornell Maritime Press, 1990.) A short book with leagues of information about weather for the small boater. Read it and you are never likely to be caught off guard by changing weather conditions.

Cockleshell Heroes by **C.E. Lucas Phillips.** (Weyman & Sons, 1957.) It's out of print but you can find it in many libraries. A true account of the 1942 British commando raid on Axis shipping in the French port of Bordeaux, 62 miles up the Gironde estuary from the sea. They got there by folding kayak. Also look for the movie of the same name that stars José Ferrer and appears on TBS every once in a while.

The Essential Sea Kayaker by **David Seidman.** (Ragged Mountain Press, 1992.) Though directed to hardshell kayakers, this comprehensive guide offers much to both beginning and experienced sea kaykers.

Folbot Holidays by **Jack Kissner.** (Creative Holiday Guides, 1945.) A quaint book compiled and partly written by Kissner, the founder of Folbot. Whimsically organized, it consists mainly of first-person accounts from early Folbot users, with some ad hype thrown in. You won't find it in bookstores but Folbot has boxes and boxes of the book for the asking.

Fundamentals of Kayak Navigation by **David Burch.** (Pacific Search Press, 1987.) A classic from the day it went to press. You will find yourself returning over and over again to read sections as you encounter new problems of moving about on open water. It may be the only navigation guide you'll ever need.

Gathering Paradise: Alaska Wilderness Journeys by **Larry Rice.** (Fulcrum Publishing, 1990.) Rice takes you on a number of kayaking journeys you will find both memorable and instructive.

The Happy Isles of Oceania: Paddling the Pacific by **Paul Theroux.** (Putnam, 1992.) Theroux's travels by folding kayak allow him to get a different, up-close perspective on this corner of the ocean sea. Excellent reading, as are all of this author's books on offbeat conveyances to reach unusual destinations.

The Hidden Coast by **Joel Rogers.** (Alaska Northwest Books, 1991.) Rogers writes about more than a dozen trips of personal discovery along the Pacific Coast from Alaska to Baja. Beautifully photographed. It'll make you want to drop everything and go paddling.

Kayak Touring by **William Sanders.** (Stackpole Books, 1984.) A good general book on kayak touring that does not deride folding kayaks as do some other sea-kayaking books. Good information on camping and gear.

Movin' Out by **Harry Roberts.** (Stone Wall Press, 1979.) This book and a companion piece on winter camping, *Movin' On*, offer some of the best and most practical advice ever written about camping. Written in a very personal style by Roberts, a well-known canoeist who edited a number of leading paddling publications.

Qajaq by **David Zimmerly.** (Alaska State Museum, 1986.) This is another skin-and-frame book, but from a scholarly perspective. It makes fascinating reading for folding kayakers. As you look at the many drawings of the different types of kayaks, you'll appreciate more and more the lineage of foldables.

A Scientist at the Seashore by **James Trefil.** (Collier Books, 1984.) A scientific look at the ocean and beach and the transitional zone between them. You'll learn why salt water is salty, how sandy beaches were formed, and you'll gain a deeper understanding of tides. The discussions are sometimes quite complex, but if you stay the course, you'll be a more savvy paddler because of the knowledge you'll gain.

Sea Kayaking, A Manual for Long Distance Touring by **John Dowd.** (University of Washington Press, 1983.) This is the seminal sea kayaking manual. It is written with a respect for folding kayaks that befits a man who has done some epic voyages in one. A good all-around book.

Seekers of the Horizon by **Will Nordby.** (Globe Pequot Press, 1989.) An anthology of sea-kayaking adventures including an abridged account of Dr. Lindemann's classic voyage and other pieces by folding kayakers such as Larry Rice and Dr. Paul Kaufmann.

The Starship and the Canoe by **Kenneth Brower.** (Harper & Row, 1978.) The narrative parallels two men of vision: Freeman Dyson, noted physicist, and his son, George Dyson. One seeks to build a space ship, the other a kayak. A thought-provoking book that you will find hard to put down.

Waves and Beaches by **Willard Bascom.** (Doubleday, 1980.) This book will help you fathom the dynamic environment on which our vulnerable-looking craft venture forth. It's lots of reading but will pay off in practical understanding of beaches and waves.

In German

As in physics and some other sciences, a good deal of the written work on folding kayaks is in German. Here are some key titles you may want to pick up even if your command of German is limited. One in particular should be on the bookcase shelves of every folding kayak owner, *Der Handernkahn.*

Alleingang im Kayak by **Dieter Kreutzkemp.** (Pietsch Verlag, 1990.) Narrates a 3,000-kilometer trip down the Yukon River in a Pouch single-seater.

Das Baldverlorene Paradies by **Herbert Rittlinger.** (Pollner Verlag, 1993.) A new edition of Rittlinger's classic account of traveling through Europe by folding kayak, written in the 1930s. Rittlinger did a lot to popularize the sport of kayak wandering.

Das Faltboot by **Klaus Bovers.** (H.S. Walther GmbH, 1984.) Published by Klepper, but it is more than a promotion piece for the company's products. Nicely done with concise discussions of history and some of what goes into making a folding kayak, and broad information on using one.

Der Handernkahn by **Ursula and Christian Altenhofer.** (Pollner Verlag, 1989.) Get this book even if you don't understand a word of German. It traces the history of folding kayaks from before Heurich and Klepper to just after World War II. The photos and illustrations are priceless. English-German cognates will help any open-minded reader comprehend the valuable information the book provides.

Ganz Allein zum Amazones by Herbert Rittlinger. (Brockhaus Verlag, 1973.) Extensive travel through South America in a Klepper by the folding-kayak wanderer, Rittlinger, who was the first person to paddle the entire length of the Amazon River.

Im Banne der Arktis by Konrad Gallei and Gaby Hermsdorf. (Pietsch Verlag, 1981.) Kayaking the west coast of Spitzbergen.

Im Faltboot um Kap Hoorn by Arved Fuchs. (Pietsch Verlag, 1991.) An account of the first successful winter circumnavigation of Cape Horn that was done in a single Klepper. A true adventure story.

Nile und Niger by Achill Moser. (Pietsch Verlag, 1989.) Adventurous river journeys through Africa in a Pouch two-seater. It includes a section on adventure-travel tips.

Ost-Gronland by Konrad Gallei and Axel Thorer. (Badena Verlag, 1987.) A kayak adventure in East Greenland in a Klepper.

Guidebooks

Any number of information sources can tell you about places you may want to paddle. Cruising and sailing guides are good sources. The sailing industry has given birth to a number of such books. Even though they're aimed at boats larger than yours, you'll find them useful.

Another good source are guidebooks devoted to canoeing and kayaking. The book shelves of local paddling shops usually have a number of titles covering nearby areas. If you plan to kayak in a particular spot, find a local shop, then call to ask that some books be mailed to you.

As a starter kit, below are listed just a few such books. Some of the publishers have other titles you may want to get.

The Alaska River Guide by Karen Jettmar. (Alaska Northwest Books, 1993.) Many of the rivers covered in this book are doable in folding kayaks. Jettmar gives some good advice on camping and paddling in this last frontier.

The Coastal Kayaker: Kayak Camping on the Alaska and B.C. Coast by Randel Washburne. (Globe Pequot Press, 1983.) Washburne's book is a practical guide to extended trips in these areas and contains some good general information as well. Washburne also authored another guide you might want to check out, *Kayak Trips in Puget Sound and the San Juan Islands* (The Mountaineers, 1986).

Sea Kayaking Along the New England Coast by Tamsin Venn. (Appalachian Mountain Club, 1991.) A terrific book that guides you to great paddling that is just a few hours' drive away for many people. Her description of each spot is quite complete with historical and practical information to help you understand what you're looking at and keep out of danger. Venn also has a similar book on the Middle Atlantic states that is due to be published in 1994.

Sea Kayaking Canada's West Coast by John Ince and Hedi Kottner. (Raxas Books, 1982.) An excellent guide by two folding-kayak paddlers. Good explanations on how to get to put-ins and what you will find along your paddling route.

Periodicals

Even though general paddling magazines offer little direct information on folding kayaks, they are worth receiving on a regular basis. They provide features on gear and techniques as well as safety advice that applies to all sea kayakers. Many of the adventures covered have been done in folding kayaks, although little mention is made of this, nor are any specific tips offered on how these boats were used.

For direct information on folding kayaks, you may want to get my newsletter, *Folding Kayaker*. It is devoted entirely to folding kayaks, with boat reviews, advice on gear, techniques specific to folding kayaks, tips on modifications, and just about anything you'd ever want to know about foldables. Part of this book is based on articles that first appeared there. For information, write to *Folding Kayaker*, P.O. Box 0754, New York, NY 10024 or phone (212) 724-5069. You can e-mail me through the Internet at 73531.1221@compuserve.com.

Below are some general paddling publications that you'll find useful.

ANorAK, 34 East Queens Way, Hampton, VA 23669. A newsletter entirely written by readers. Between the quirky contributions, you will find some good information.

Atlantic Coastal Kayaker, 29 Burley St., Wenham, MA 01984. An excellent publication with insightful articles on a wide range of sea-kayaking subjects. The editor is Tamsin Venn who has written two guidebooks mentioned above. Published by Bob

Hicks, who also puts out *Messing About In Boats*. While the latter has a much broader coverage than *ACK*, you'll find its pages very useful if you're looking for sailing information. Its general modification ideas and ads can also trigger some applications to foldables.

Canoe, Box 3146, Kirkland, WA 98083. The oldest and widest circulated of the paddling magazines. Good information in each issue on gear and techniques. Also has an annual issue about kayak touring.

Paddler, 4061 Oceanside Blvd, Suite M, Oceanside, CA 92056. Another good general magazine with articles on travel, gear, and techniques.

Sea Kayaker, 6327 Seaview Ave. NW, Seattle, WA 98107. A magazine entirely devoted to sea kayaking. Little coverage of foldables, except for the many trips that are taken in them. Excellent general articles on technique and gear that you'll find useful.

VIDEOS

Several of the manufacturers offer video tapes, either free or for a nominal charge. They generally are aimed at giving assembly instructions or to promote their products, but they do so much more.

Klepper has two videotapes. One is strictly on assembly/disassembly, but it's a good video to show to friends who ask about that pile of duffels in the corner of your closet. The other video has some assembly instruction but is artistically filmed. The camera angles of the wooden frame are almost poetic. The outdoor filming in the Pacific Northwest and the Bahamas is stunning and will get you itching to pack your foldable and get out there.

Feathercraft has at least three videos. One is mainly promotional, showing people paddling both singles and doubles in different settings. It's so well done that you're likely to pop it into your VCR any time you feel a bout of cabin fever coming on. The others are assembly videos that teach you the intricacies and an appreciation for how well designed these boats are.

KAYAKS AND ACCESSORIES

Below is the list of folding-kayak manufacturers and makers of accessories mentioned in this book.

Folding Kayaks

Feathercraft, 1244 Cartwright St., Granville Island, Vancouver, BC, Canada V6H 3R8. Phone (604) 681-8437. Besides kayaks, the company offers accessories including PFDs, paddle floats, pogies, etc. The company will make some accessories to order such as spray skirts with hand warmers and pouch pockets. You can buy direct from Feathercraft or from dealers spread throughout Canada, the U.S., and Europe. There is no discount for buying at the factory.

Folbot, P.O. Box 70877, Charleston, SC 29415. Phone (800) 744-3483. Sells several models of boats plus some accessories such as boat carts, sails, etc. Mainly sold direct although there are some dealers around. Sales in Canada are through Folbot Canada, Inc. P.O. Box 518, Montague, PEI, C0A 1R0. Phone (902) 838-3860.

Klepper. Sells boats and accessories such as sails and boat carts. The U.S. now has several regional importer/distributor operations. Hans Klepper Corp, 168 Kinderkamack Rd, Park Ridge, NJ 07656. Phone (201) 476-0700. Services the East Coast and states not covered by the other distribution points.

Klepper West, 6155 Mt. Aukum Rd, Somerset, CA 95684. Phone (916) 626-8647. Handles California, Oregon, Washington, Idaho, Nevada and Arizona. Klepper West has a good selection of books including the new version of *Alone At Sea* by Dr. Lindemann and *Der Handernkahn.*

Klepper has an official repair and modification center, the Klepper Service Center, 2526 S. Adams St, Denver, CO 80210. Phone (303) 782-9743. For other distributors in the U.S. and Canada, contact one of these locations.

Nautiraid has a North American distributor just outside New Orleans, in St. Rose, Louisiana. It has a full array of spare parts, plus a repair service for fixing up hulls and frames. Call for dealers in your area. Nautiraid USA, P.O. Box 1065, St. Rose, LA 70087. Phone 800-KAYAK-99.

Pouch boats are being imported into the U.S. by Pouch USA, which also happens to be the Klepper West distributor. For more information, contact Peter Schwierzke at Klepper West, above.

Accessories

Baidarka Boats sells Nautiraids and several other makes of folding kayaks. It stocks good repair materials such as marine-grade plywood, as well as special folding-kayak accessories including Kaipaks, the sidebags that strap onto nearby cross pieces in a folding kayak. Box 6001-CM, Sitka, AK 99835. Phone (907) 747-8996.

Balogh Sail Designs, or BSD, is the maker of several sailing rigs that will fit most folding kayaks. Its line of products include the Batwing, B.O.S.S. outrigger system, and Twins sail. Star Route Box 79, Cedar Island, NC 28520. Phone (919) 225-6631.

Boulter of Earth offers several items you may want. It manufacturers the Drift-Stopper sea anchor and a cable locking system, the Surelock, that can be used to secure an assembled kayak to a roof rack or tree. Its other items of interest, such as a rechargeable air horn, can often be found in paddling shops. If you can't find them, contact Boulter of Earth, 21 Dartmouth Crescent, Toronto, Ontario M8V-1W9. Phone (416) 252-9747.

Colorado Kayak Supply is the maker of Stohlquist dry suits, paddling jackets and pants, as well as CKS kayak dry bags. You generally can find these at paddling shops or you can order direct from CKS, P.O. Box 3059, Buena Vista, CO 81211. Phone (800) 535-3565.

Extrasport is the maker of the Seaker PFD. You should find it at regular outlets or you can order direct by contacting Extrasport, 5305 NW 35th Court, Miami, FL 33242. Phone (305) 633-2945.

Kokotat makes dry suits and paddling apparel. Available in many stores or you can contact Kokotat, 5350 Ericson Way, Arcata, CA 95521. Phone (800) 225-9749.

Voyageur makes exceptionally good dry bags of all sizes and applications such as the Caboose bag, also flotation bags. For more information, contact Voyageur, P.O. Box 207, Waitsfield, VT 05673. Phone (800) 843-8985.

Werner Paddle makes some of the best models of kayak paddles around, including the popular Camano. You should be able to find them at most paddling outlets. For more information or special orders, contact Northwest Design Works, Inc., 12322 Highway 99 South, Bay #100, Everett, WA 98204. Phone (800) 275-3311.

Index

A

Accessories, 49–62
    cost of, 29–30
    essential, 58–59
    sailing, 119–20
    sources of, 158–59
Ally canoes, 145
Amundsen, Roald, 15
Anchors, 57–58
Aquaseal, 151
Aquaterra, 55
Assembly-disassembly, 12–13, 24, 33
    speed of, 25, 114
Atlantic Kayak Tours, 118

B

Bailers, 56, 59, 105–06
Balogh
    Batwing, 116, 119–22
    B.O.S.S., 119–21, 144
    Mark, vii, 143–44
    Sail Design, 51, 58–59, 116, 159
    Twins, 122–24
Beam, 5, 11
Books on foldables, 155–57
Box, packing, 13
Bracing, 74–77, 89–90
    practicing, 76–77
    sculling, 76, 90
    slap, 75, 89–90
    sweep low, 75–76, 90
    telemark, 76, 89
Buoys, 95
Buying a foldable, 29–31
Byrd, Admiral Richard, 15

C

Camping, 10, 125–32
    commando, 128–29
    equipment, 129–31
Capsizing, 98–107
Cartopping, 7, 112–14
Carts, 52, 132
Charts
    marine, 94
    tide, 94–95
    using, 96, 97
Chine, 145
Choosing a model, how to, 23–31
Cleat board (for sailing), 118–19
Clothes
    extra, 58–59
    winter, 60–62
Coaming, 15, 146–47
Coastal paddling, 94
Cockpit, 79, 134, 140–42, 146–47
Colorado Kayak Supply, 57, 159
Compasses, 57, 95
Confidence drills, 98–100
Cost. *See* Price
Cotton canvas, for decks, 28
Cotton, Phil, vii, 21
Courtney, Roger, 18
Currents, 94
Customs agencies, 112

D

Deck lines, 60
Decks, 28–29
Deeprose, Donna, vii
Delphin, 14–15
Distances, judging, 97
D-rings, 140, 150, 152
Dry suits, 60–61
Duct tape, 149
Durability, of foldables, 6–7, 24–26,
    33, 78
Dyson, George, 5

E

Eldridge Tide and Pilot Book, 94
EPDM hull fabric, 154
Equipment, for foldables, 49–62
    essential, 58–59
Eskimo kayaks, 3, 109
Eskimo roll, 11, 17, 64, 74, 100
Evaluations of kayak models, 32–48
    doubles, 32–39
    eight key factors, 33
    min-foldable singles, 43–48
    singles, 39–43
    summary chart, 40

F

Feathercraft, 19, 21, 28–29, 30,
    49–50, 66, 105, 111, 142–43,
    152, 154, 158
    Elite, 60
    K-1, ix, 41, 80
    K-2, 33–34, 87
    K-Light 1, 43, 44–45
    Short Touring (ST), 43–44
    Skeg, 51
Feathering, 65
Fiberglass, in kayaks, viii, 7, 10
Fishing, 10, 133–34
Flexibility, in foldables, 4, 5
Flotation bags, 54–56, 98, 104
Folbot, 17, 18, 21, 29–30, 50, 111,
    116, 122, 144, 152, 158
    Aleut I, 8, 45–46, 55
    Greenland Series, 21
    Greenland II, 34–35, 153
Folding Kayaker, vii, xi, 138, 154, 155,
    157
Food, 59, 130
Foot pedals, 66
Frame, 7

maintenance, 151, 152–53
wood vs. aluminum, 27–28
Fundamentals of Kayak Navigation, 93, 155

G
Gacoflex coating, 153–54
Gloves, 62
Gore-Tex, 61
Grant, Robert, 154
Gummilack paint, 153
Guyot, Philippe, vii

H
Happy Isles Of Oceania, The, 3
Hatches, 142–43
Heath, John, 5
Henderson scuba suits, 61
Heurich, Alfred, 14–15
Hull, 6–7, 15
    attaching new surface, 154
    maintenance, 152
    materials, 28–29, 154
    old, 153
    prices, 153
    punctures, 7, 149, 150
    revitalizing, 153
    used boat, 31
Hypalon hulls, 28–29, 110, 132, 150, 153
Hypothermia, 60, 101

K
Kaipak bag, 56
Kayak manufacturers, 158
Kayaks, hardshell, xii, xiv, 2, 19
    vs. foldables, 3–11
Kayaks, northern, 3–4, 5
Kayaking, sea. *See* Sea kayaking
Kayaking, whitewater, xiii
Kissner, Jack, 21, 155
Klepper, 15, 16, 17, 18, 19–21, 28, 29–30, 50–51, 57, 111, 130, 132, 138, 140–42, 143, 145, 151, 152, 153, 158
    Aerius I, 6, 11, 41, 42, 120
    Aerius II, 17, 36–37, 121, 140–42, 146–47
    Arctic Tuckunder spray cover, 50–51
    Expedition, ix
    Expedition Clip-on cover, 50
    Johann, 14, 15

M-1, 51, 123
Quattro, 37, 60
S–4, 6, 51, 116–19
Touring Spray Cover, 50
2000, 46–47

L
Landing, 78–79. *See also* Launching
    through surf, 81–83, 91–92
Launching, 78–92
    doubles, 90–91
    from beaches/shores, 78–79, 91
    from docks, 79, 91
    low-high brace, 82
    paddle use for, 78–79
    through surf, 80–83, 91
Learning curve, 6
Lindemann, Dr. Hannes, 17–19, 36
Ljungstrom sailing rig, 122
Loading a foldable, 125–28
Locking a kayak, 10, 115
Longerons, 153
Lozano, Bill and Janice, vii, 118

M
Magazines, 157–58
Maintenance, 12, 151–54
Maneuverability, 33
Manufacturing of a foldable, 20–21
Materials (kayak construction), 27–29
Meyer, Fridel, 15–16
Military kayaks, xiv, 7, 18
Misconceptions, 11–13
Modifying foldables, 138–47
Motoring, 136–37

N
Nature watching, 134–35
Nautiraid, 18, 21, 29, 30, 51, 111, 130, 132, 152
    Mini-Raid, 25, 47–48, 145
    Raid 1, 42–43
    Raid 2 Expedition, 37–38, 120, 142–43, 158
Northwest River Supplies, 57
Nylon, for decks, 28

O
Oarmaster, 136

P
Packing a foldable, 110–12

Paddle brace, 11
Paddle float, 59–60
Paddles, 29, 52–53, 68–69. *See also* Strokes
    Camano, 53
    Eddyline, 53
    extra, 59
    feathered, 65
    length of, 52–53
Paddling techniques, 64–77. *See also* Launching and Strokes
    for a double, 86–92
    in waves, 84–85
    low–high brace, 82
    open water, 83–85
    signaling change, 87–88
    surf, 80–83, 91–92
Pakboats, 145
Parts, 31, 150–51, 153, 158–59
Pawlata, Edi Hans, 17
Performance, 11–12
Personal flotation device (PFD), 53–54, 58–59, 96, 100
Photography, 135
Pogies, 62
Polartek 100, 61
Polyester, for decks, 28
Pope John Paul II, 17
Portability, 33
Portaging, 131–32
Pouch, 116, 158
    Eureka 2, 38, 39
Price, 12, 23, 29–31, 33
    depreciation, 12, 33
    of shipping, 13
Pumps, 56, 59, 105–06

R
Racing, kayak, 11
Radio, NOAA weather, 93–94
Repairs, 59, 148–51
    ease of, 10
    field, 148–50
    kits, 148–49
    permanent, 150–51
Rescue skills, 100–07
    group, 106–07
Rice, Howard, 7
Righting a kayak, 100–02
Right of way, 95
Rob Roy, 14
Romer, Captain Franz, 16

Rowing, 136
Rudder, 26, 29–30, 51
    balanced, 143–44
    Feathercraft, 144–45
    lifter, 138–40

S
Safety, xiv, 11, 53–55, 58–59, 93–97
Sailing, with foldables, 10, 24, 26,
    116–24
    jib, 124
    techniques, 119–24
Sails, 51–52, 58–59, 116–24
    downwind, 122
Schott, Karl, 15
Schweria, Carl Borro, 15
Schwierzke, Peter, vii
Scuba diving, 10, 135–36
    suits, 61
Sculling, 11, 74, 90, 136
Sea kayaking, xiii, 12, 64
    history, 14–22
Seaker PFD, 54, 159
SeaLine bags, 56–57
Sea savvy, 93–97
Sea socks, 29, 34, 105
Seating, solo modifications for double,
    140–42
Seaworthiness, xiii, xiv, 1, 5–6, 12, 33,
    125
Shipping, 13, 112
    price, 13
Shopping for a kayak, 23
Side bags, 56–57
Simpson, Doug, vii
Single vs. Double, 23–24, 26
Size, 23–24
Skeg, 51

Snorkeling, 135–36
Solo paddling, 24
Special Boat Section (SBS), 18
Speed (efficiency), 11, 33, 125–26
Spener, Richard, 142–43
Sponge, 59
Sponsons, 6, 17
Spray covering, 29, 30, 49–51, 143
SSA scuba suits, 61
Stability, xiv, 1, 5–6, 26, 33, 98,
    126–28
Stiller, Dieter and Eric, vii
Storage bags, dry, 57
Strokes
    backing up, 73
    blade placement angle, 68–69
    body parts, 66–67
    bracing, 74–77
    forward, 64–71, 86–88
    low-high brace, 82
    maneuvering, 73
    push-pull, 67–68
    sideways, 74–75
    stern-rudder, 89
    telemark turn, 89
    turning, 71–73, 88–89
    zone of power, 68
Surf, paddling through, 80–83, 91–92

T
Theft, 10, 115
Theroux, Paul, ix–x, 2–3
Tides, 94–95
Tiller, hand, 144, 145
Tracking, 33
Traffic, 95, 96
Traveling, 10, 109–15
    by bicycle, 110

    by bus, 115
    by car, 112–15
    by plane, 109–12
    by train, 115

U
Ultraviolet light damage, 28
UPS shipping, 13
U.S. Coast Guard, 54, 93
Used kayaks, 30–31

V
Valverde, David, 144
Varnishing, 151
Versatility, of foldables, 7–10, 33
Videos, 158
Vinyl, for hulls, 29
Voyageur, caboose bag, 127
    floating bag, 55–56, 57, 159

W
Walther, Carl, vii
    Herman, vii, 19–21
Washing foldables, 151
Water, drinking, 131
Water feel, 6
Waves, dealing with, 84–85
Waxing hulls, 151
Wazlawik, Rodolfo, 140
Weather forecasts, 93–94
Wet suits, 60–62
Wind
    effect on paddling, 83–84
    effect on course, 96–97
Woodford, Matt, 143

Z
Ziploc bags, 128, 131